TONGUES OF MEN AND ANGELS

TONGUES OF MEN AND ANGELS

The Religious Language
of Pentecostalism

BY

William J. Samarin

The Macmillan Company, NEW YORK, NEW YORK
Collier-Macmillan Limited, LONDON

ACKNOWLEDGMENTS

The author wishes to thank the following:

The Oxford and Cambridge University Presses, for permission to quote from the *New English Bible,* second edition © 1970.

The National Council of Churches of Christ in the U.S.A. for permission to quote from the *Revised Standard Version of the Bible,* copyrighted 1946 and 1952.

The Full Gospel Business Men's Fellowship International for permission to quote from *Voice* magazine the material in Appendix A.

Doubleday & Company Inc. for permission to quote from *Lost in the Fun House* by John Barth.

Copyright © 1972 by William J. Samarin

The Macmillan Company
866 Third Avenue, New York, N.Y. 10022
Collier-Macmillan Canada Ltd., Toronto, Ontario

Library of Congress Catalog Card Number: 70–162335

First Printing

Printed in the United States of America

Though I speak
with the tongues of men
and of angels . . .

St. Paul
(1 Corinthians 13:1)

CONTENTS

INTRODUCTION   xi

1. Glossolalia in Christianity   1

2. Explained Psychologically   18

3. Acquired "Supernaturally"   44

4. Described Linguistically   73

5. Contrasted With Language   103

6. Compared With Other Forms   129

7. Prayed, Prophesied, and Interpreted   150

8. Sung and Written   174

9. Use and Disuse   188

10. Pleasing and Symbolic   197

11. Participation and Politics   212

12. Sacred and Profane   227

APPENDIXES   237

BIBLIOGRAPHY   257

INDEX   269

INTRODUCTION

THIS IS A BOOK about religious language. Like Freud's study of the human psyche, it starts with aberrant behavior. It deals with *glossolalia* in the Christian religion.

Glossolalia is "speaking in tongues," long familiar in our society because of its use by Pentecostals, but it goes back at least to the very beginning of Christianity. It is what St. Paul referred to as "tongues of angels."

There are hundreds of thousands of tongue speakers today. Not all of them are in the traditional Pentecostal churches. Presbyterians, Episcopalians, and other main-line Protestants—as well as Catholics—have got into the news because of the glossolalist "charismatic movement." Because of their large numbers and because they are often educated and well-established members of our society, their use of "nonsense speech" has demanded an explanation.

This book therefore seeks to answer the question, "Why do people speak in tongues?"

Most answers to this question have been psychological, based on the assumption that since glossolalia is not normal, there must also be something abnormal about the speakers—at least when they are producing tongues.

The approach in this book is linguistic. You can't explain why people engage in unintelligible speech before you understand exactly what it is they produce. This should be a perfectly obvious point of view, but it seems to have escaped most people. The linguistic description is based on a large sample of glossolalia. This was not difficult to obtain. Many people consented to have their glossolalic prayers recorded in one context or another, privately or in group meetings. Large public meetings were also recorded. The clearest recordings were then phonetically transcribed and analyzed.

Explaining why people speak in tongues also requires knowing who the speakers are and how they use tongues. My approach is therefore sociological as well as linguistic. In fact, it is *sociolinguistic*, to use a current term. Religion has to be observed and participated in to be understood. Over a period of five years I have taken part in meetings in Italy, Holland, Jamaica, Canada, and the United States. I have observed old-fashioned Pentecostals and neo-Pentecostals; I have been in small meetings at private homes as well as in mammoth public meetings; I have seen such different cultural settings as are found among the Puerto Ricans of the Bronx, the snake handlers of the Appalachians, Russian Molokans in Los Angeles, and *pocomania* sectarians in Jamaica. This "participant observation" was supplemented by interviews and the use of a questionnaire (described in Appendix A).

This is therefore not a book about "Holy Roller" or Episcopalian or Catholic glossolalia, but of any form and use of glossolalia in religion. As a consequence, many glossolalists will think that they are in some ways misrepresented in this book. An Episcopalian may reject the notion of public messages in glossolalia, and he might decry the use of tongues in exorcism. Such objections do not invalidate my observations. They only confirm the diversity I have observed—a diversity that has too long been unknown. In fact, glossolalists will learn much from this book, although the experience may be an embarrassing one at times.

Finally, my approach is "secular." This is implied by the way the question was put. Instead of "Why do people speak in tongues?" many Christians would ask, "Is this of God?" They can pose their questions as they will, but they can never answer them without an objective understanding of what people actually do. I have probably not raised all the questions they might want to raise, but I answer some of them (and perhaps raise others they never thought of).

My audience is the general public—most of all, people who are curious about glossolalia and would like a serious treatment of the topic. In writing this book, I tried to remember that most of them are not specialists in linguistics or the social sciences. This meant defining technical terms and explaining the implications of some of my discoveries and analyses. It also meant simplifying bibliographical citations (described in the Bibliography). But I also had to keep in mind the relevance of this book for specialist readers like psychologists, linguists, sociologists, and anthropologists.

I must mention objections that might be raised by two kinds of readers. Glossolalists will say that my secular stance distorts my understanding of the phenomenon, because it is a spiritual (or divine) one. They will insist that without sharing their experience I cannot understand it. What they really mean is their total religious experience, not just the verbal part of it. But I am not evaluating the validity or nature of religious commitment and belief. I am, above all, looking at the behavioral manifestations of this faith, and it's all there to be heard and seen.

Social scientists, on the other hand, might express disappointment over the absence of an explicit theory of human behavior and the infrequency of statistical analyses. The one was intentional and the other unavoidable. Although I fully appreciate the importance of theory in scientific research, the general public—for whom this book is intended—has far less patience with it. I did not set out to apply a particular sociological or psychological theory but to answer all kinds of questions that are summarized in only one: "What in the world is glossolalia?" Nevertheless, all kinds of social-scientific notions are implied in the answer which makes up this book. The answer is based on inferences drawn from the information that was carefully collected. I have also tried to be cautious and reasonable in its interpretation. Sometimes I speculate —not fancifully I hope—in the belief that it is better to make some inferences than to ignore the facts altogether. But statistics do not verify all of my conclusions. I cannot, for example, show precisely what percent of my recorded sample from English speakers has non-English sounds or what percent of the people studied believe that glossolalic prayers are more efficacious than natural-language prayers. For some matters I can only give my considered judgment. A statisticated study would have been narrower in scope or vaster than I dared to undertake. This is an overview, more detailed in some instances than in others, but always, I hope, responsible and trustworthy.

Although this is a book specifically about glossolalia, it is, as I have already said, a book about religious language. In other words, it illustrates how man uses language when he practices religion. Other such studies have dealt with theological language (currently being called "God-talk"), liturgy, and special types of discourse like prayers and sermons. Unintelligible or anomalous speech has been ignored. In some respects, therefore, this work is a pioneering effort. An objective study of this behavior turns out, as the final chapter shows, to be a sympathetic one.

Finally, this is a book about anomalous speech in any of its forms and in all of its uses. "Religious" glossolalia is shown not to be an isolated phenomenon. It is only the full development of a tendency revealed in various modes of speech throughout the world. If glossolalia is the speech of angels, then we all, to some extent, speak both "the tongues of men and of angels."

I owe a real debt to two groups of people. Without the help of glossolalists this study would have been impossible. I congratulate them, first, on their willingness to cooperate in the study of this speech that, although poorly understood, figures so importantly in their religious life. I refer to those who were interviewed, those who filled out my questionnaire, and those who consented to have their speech tape-recorded. Their cooperation takes on special significance in the light of the conclusions that I have had to come to. I hope that they will not take these as a violation of trust. After all, I had to be honest with all the information at my disposal. This honesty, I can assure them, is accompanied by my sincerest good will. They might be happy to know that our intimate "dialogue," even in the privacy of my study, where I tried to understand them, has been a rich and rewarding experience.

I am also in debt to a conscientious, careful, and quite critical group of readers to whom I subjected an earlier version of this book. They include Christians and non-Christians, Protestants and

Catholics, non-Pentecostals and former Pentecostals, laymen and clergy. Among them are a psychologist, a social worker, and a theologian, in addition to several anthropologists, linguists, and sociologists. It is a pleasure to mention them by name: Werner Cohn, Patrick Doran, James Fernandez, Nathan Gerrard, Henry A. Gleason, Jr., Donald Harding, Virginia H. Hine, Bart Jones, Peter Richardson, Stan Skarsten, Frank Smith, and Walter Wolfram. The book is now different from the version they read and, I am sure, much better.

Dr. Ian Stevenson, Director of the Division of Parapsychology of the Department of Psychiatry at the University of Virginia School of Medicine, lent me two tape recordings of nonreligious glossolalia. A sample from one of them is included in Appendix C. His helpfulness is appreciated.

glos • sa / 'gläsə/ N. -s. : a single continuous act of glossolalia

glos • so • la • lia /gläsə'lālēə/ N. [gloss- 'tongue' + -lal- 'speak']
1 : a vocal act believed by the speaker to be language and showing rudimentary language-like structure but no consistent word-meaning correspondences recognizable by either speaker or hearers; (in Christianity) speech attributed to the Holy Spirit in languages unknown to the speaker and incomprehensible without divinely inspired interpretation—*several in the congregation broke out in glossolalia; bits of glossolalia were interspersed in the sermon; she never experienced fully developed glossolalia and gave it up in later years* [cf. 1 Cor. 12:30—*Have all the gifts of healing? do all speak with tongues? do all interpret?*]; syn. tongues, cf. xenoglossia. 2: (loosely) unintelligible speech, gibberish—*glossolalia couldn't have been less comprehensible than what he uttered*

glos • so • la • lic A. : pertaining to glossolalia—*the preacher interpreted the meaning of the glossolalic pronouncement*

glo • so • la • list N. -s : a person who makes use of glossolalia

TONGUES OF MEN AND ANGELS

GLOSSOLALIA IN
CHRISTIANITY

GLOSSOLALIA IS NOT the name of a language but of a phenomenon. The word is based on the Greek roots for "tongue" or
"language" and "to speak." It therefore simply means "to
talk languages," but the term is a technical one in English, and it
had a special meaning even at the beginning of the Christian era.
Glossolalia was known, for example, among the first-century Christians in the Greek city of Corinth, and when Paul wrote his pastoral
letter to them he referred to it simply as "speaking in languages."
(Some of the Biblical record will be examined at the end of this
chapter, for glossolalia cannot be understood without it.) The so-
called "King James Bible" or "Authorized Version" of 1611, however, added "unknown" to the expression, probably because the
translators were in doubt or in disagreement as to what kind of
speech was actually described.

There is no doubt today, however, about the nature of glossolalia. When people "speak in tongues," they are producing utterances
of short or long duration that sound like languages to them even
though they may have only the faintest idea what the "grammar"
or "vocabulary" might be; it is enough for them that the production
of this speech is religiously significant.

That is hardly a definition of glossolalia, of course. A better one might be something like the following: *A meaningless but phonologically structured human utterance believed by the speaker to be a real language but bearing no systematic resemblance to any natural language, living or dead.* There are, however, other definitions. That is, the term glossolalia has been used in several different ways, a situation that has led to much confusion and misunderstanding. The following chapters will, it is hoped, make it clear what Christians, at least, do when they talk in tongues.

Christian Use Today

There are untold thousands of glossolalists in the world today. Some estimates would make it several million.[1] What these people have in common, regardless of their nationality, social class, or position in the Christian religion, is not simply that they talk in tongues. In fact, most of them would say that this skill, or "gift" as they would put it, is less important than the experience that produces it. The name that this experience is most widely known by is "the baptism in" or "the filling with the Holy Spirit." The ways in which it is conceived and described vary greatly, depending in large part on the person's knowledge or use of the Bible, his own religious tradition, his personality, and so forth. What this experience means to glossolalists is a richer or more complete religious life. To many it is not just a step forward on a journey already taken but an entirely new kind of experience. For all, it means a new sense of the immediacy of God. It seems perfectly natural to them that one of the manifestations of this "new dimension to life," as they put it, should be the use of a "spiritual tongue."

That is all too brief and too clinical a description of a way of life that these people consider more meaningful than anything else they know. No description is really fair unless it attempts to describe

[1] The total number of Pentecostals is indeed very high—Nichol estimates eight million (p. 1) and Damboriena twelve to fourteen million (p. 142)—but we cannot assume that all of these are real glossolalists. These are what we shall call traditional Pentecostals who are affiliated with churches (or sects, as sociologists call them) that proclaim themselves as such. Neo-Pentecostals, as is seen below, share some of the doctrine but remain within their own religious traditions. The term Pentecostal will be used in a general way for all types.

the ethical, psychological, and social aspects—for most people, in fact, benefits—of this movement. But a fair description would have to be a lengthy one. Here is only one first-person testimonial, selected by chance from the hundreds that are available. See Appendix B for another.

Although I was a Christian before my experience in the Spirit, I had never seen God's power in my own life, in my Church, in the world. However, I had read of others who knew this power . . . and I wanted to know God in this way.

For some time I had been praying with a friend that God would give us what we knew we were lacking in our lives. At this time my friend shared with an Anglican priest who told her of his experience of the Baptism in the Spirit, and she asked God to fill her in this way. I was very antagonistic particularly on the subject of speaking in tongues. However, when I met this priest and others that shared his experience, I recognized a quality in their Christian lives that I lacked and I wanted. However, I was disgusted at the way they claimed you went about getting it. I was emotionally very tight and controlled. I had learned to protect my feelings by keeping them hidden, and I was most reluctant to expose them in any way. Therefore a tremendous inner struggle ensued as I wrestled with the priorities.

I eventually decided I wanted more of God enough to risk my emotions to Him, and alone with Him asked to be filled with His Spirit. Gradually but very specifically changes occurred in me. I had never been able to cry freely, even alone, and I began to cry openly with myself and with friends. I asked my friend, the Anglican priest, to pray with me and he prayed for the healing of my emotions, asking Jesus to go back to the moment of my conception and then through each stage of my life, touching, healing, and opening my emotions. Within three months, a non-Christian friend of mine who had been away from [the city] the past few months and who came to visit me, noticed such a dramatic change in my personality that she demanded an explanation. Many people who knew me commented on my greater freedom. I recognize that at that point in a very dramatic way I received tremendous emotional freedom. I feel this process has continued in a much more gradual way since that time. This has affected me particularly in my role as a teacher. The emotional and spiritual strain of teaching was almost overwhelming me before my experience, and since [then] I have felt I have more resources to cope with the strain and more means of release.

For me personally, speaking in tongues has been a tremendous blessing. In my "tongue" I am able to express myself to God more freely than in any other way. My tongue always reflects my true emotion, and I cannot camouflage my true feelings in it, nor do I have any desire to. I also feel it helps me to pray more effectively for others, and I have witnessed deep healings in people's lives when I have felt led by God to pray for them in my "tongue." Since my experience in the Spirit I have come to know what "joy" is in a much deeper way and I know the reality of God's presence in me and with me. Witnessing becomes a natural outcome of my excitement and gratitude.

However, the most important aspect of this experience for me is that now I know that God can and will use me for others and that there are answers for those who sincerely seek. I feel that one needs the infilling of the Spirit for power for others. My great frustration as a Christian before my experience was that I was unable to help those in need and I didn't understand how to lay hold of God's power. I tried so hard myself to be of help and constantly fell flat on my face. Since that time I have glimpsed how God's Spirit works through my weakness, and I can believe He can meet any need. I see answers to my prayers and I hear His Voice so much more clearly, and I know what He has done and is doing in me. There have been many rough spots and many failures, but I know a deeper confidence in what He is and what He has made me.

This religious experience, apart from the place that glossolalia plays in it, is not foreign to orthodox Christianity. The similarities are greatest when personal religion is emphasized. This experience, however, is the distinguishing characteristic of a contemporary movement. This is commonly called the "charismatic movement," because of its rather clearly expressed values and goals and an organization whose function is the realization of the goals. The movement is further characterized by a conceptual framework in which the beliefs are organized and by which they are legitimized: namely, the kind of relationship to God whereby the person is possessed, guided, surrounded, or empowered by God (the metaphors are numerous). God is existentially and palpably immanent: He reveals himself in a way you can feel. To this immanental emphasis is linked the concern with the charisma, the gifts that are granted by the Holy Spirit. Some charismatists enumerate nine such gifts,[2]

[2] In this book the terms charismatist and charismatic refer to the beliefs and the believers associated with these charisma. They therefore comprehend, and are sometimes used synonymously with, the terms glossolalist and glossolalic; the latter are obviously more restricted in meaning.

each baptized believer not necessarily having more than one of them, but glossolalia is—at least to many people—the indispensable minimum, and to all in the movement, the most frequent of the gifts.

As a movement cutting across institutional lines, neo-Pentecostalism, as it is sometimes called, is a remarkable phenomenon. People who have had "the experience," as they sometimes call the Spirit baptism, are found in a great variety of Christian churches. The membership of those who responded to my questionnaire (described in Appendix A) is indicative of the variety, but it is undoubtedly far from complete: for example, Congregational, several kinds of Baptist, Lutheran, Episcopal/Anglican, Disciples of Christ, Methodist and Wesleyan Methodist, Church of God, United Church of Canada, Netherlands Reformed Church, and the marginally-Christian sect of Christian Israel; not to mention the churches that have been charismatic since their beginning, such as the Assemblies of God, Foursquare, Full Gospel, and the Apostolic Church; finally, even Catholic. Catholic charismatic groups are important enough to deserve separate consideration.[3]

The economic level of two neo-Pentecostal groups totalling 272 individuals studied in southern California by S. C. Plog shows a median income of something over $621 per month; the salaries ranged from $100 to over $1600 per month. For both groups, the most frequently represented occupational categories were "professional and technical" (34%), "housewives" (24%), and "clerical-secretarial" (17%). The populations were comparable in age (44 was average in one and 42 in the other) and sex (59% women and 41% men in one; 51% women and 49% men in the other). Tongue speaking was high in both groups (73% and 85%) as well as church attendance (95% and 100%). The ecumenicity of the group is also visible in the fact that forty different Protestant denominations were represented. Similar characteristics emerge from responses to my own questionnaire and the study by Gerlach and Hine (1970).

It no longer appears appropriate, therefore, to characterize

---

[3] By the word "group" I mean any number of individuals who recognize themselves as some kind of unit. It may be one with a history of several weeks or months. It may, on the other hand, be an entirely fortuitous one, such as an occasion when several people meet for prayer and sharing.

Pentecostalism as arising from or being nurtured by sociocultural disruption, low status, and dissatisfaction (repeated in connection with older Pentecostalism by, for example, A. Parsons, p. 258, and W. Wood, p. 110). These terms certainly do not apply to such charismatic groups as the one found in a large and comfortable metropolitan church of the United Church of Canada that "has gone Pentecostal," as people say. These people are the kind one sees at such middle-class places as artistic performances and good restaurants. They are therefore separated by a great distance economically and culturally from their store-front Pentecostal brethren, yet they belong in some sense to the same tradition. So Paul's words, addressed to the tongue-speaking believers in Corinth, seem somewhat less appropriate to the Pentecostal movement than they used to be: "Now remember what you were, brothers, when God called you. Few of you were wise, or powerful, or of high social status, from the human point of view. God purposely chose what the world considers nonsense in order to put wise men to shame, and what the world considers weak in order to put powerful men to shame" (1 Corinthians 1:26–27, TEV).[4]

Neo-Pentecostals are not always easily identified, because only some of them become members of charismatic organizations like the Full Gospel Business Men's Fellowship International (abbreviated FGBMFI, following its own practice), the most important and most ecumenical one. Led by laymen and clergymen (not only business men), its loosely defined members subscribe to a statement of faith that is explicit about the place of Spirit baptism in the life of a Christian.[5] Its aim is the propagation of the "full Gospel" which includes the baptism as well as the traditional evangelical doctrine of conversion.[6] The organization seeks to achieve

[4] Unless specified, quotations from the Bible are in the AV (so-called Authorized Version). Other versions used are: NEB (New English Bible, Oxford University Press), RSV (Revised Standard Version), and TEV (Today's English Version, American Bible Society).

[5] Information about the membership of the organization could not be obtained, but in August of 1969 there were 300,000 regular subscribers to its organ, *Voice*.

[6] The expression "full Gospel" has long been used by Protestant groups to indicate their difference from the established churches which did not teach or emphasize doctrines such as the "second blessing" (another name for this special work of the Holy Spirit after conversion), miraculous healing, speaking in tongues, and the like.

its goals by the publication of various kinds of literature but primarily in public meetings sponsored by local chapters and regional bodies. These meetings are open to everyone since their purpose is to reach the greatest number of people with the "full Gospel." At the 1966 regional meeting in New York City, for example, Roman Catholic clergymen and laymen played a prominent role in the mass meetings.

But the Fellowship is only one of unnumbered organizations and groups, some seasonal (like summer camp meetings), others regional or local (like groups of like-minded students at a university, within a single denomination, church, or area). The first *Directory of Charismatic Groups* listed 488 such groups in existence by the end of 1970 in the United States alone. The Omega Fellowship is one of the smaller movements. Affiliated with no specific church, it is supported by charismatists from many different churches and even by people who have no church membership at all. With a "minister at large," the organization serves primarily to provide encouragement and guidance to a loose confederation of groups throughout the United States. Unlike the FGBMFI meetings that are large and public in nature, Omega meetings are small, like group-therapy sessions. The dominant themes are sharing and helping. Ecclesiology, and to a large degree even traditional theology, have relatively little importance.

Finally, there are the countless secret charismatists who have confessed their experience to no one or to only a few like-minded friends. They may fear the consequences of disclosing their views (since the consequences might be embarrassment for others or rejection of themselves), or they may simply want to keep the experience an exclusively private matter. Several of my respondents were secret charismatists, like the member of the United Church of Canada who sought the baptism after reading a newspaper article about it, and who, at the time she wrote me, had contact with only one other charismatist by mail.

When charismatic members of noncharismatic churches are vocal or organized, they sometimes create difficulties for the establishment, partly because their views are at variance with the established ones and partly because strong beliefs often lead people to align themselves and challenge each other. Inevitably there are investigations and studies at various levels of ecclesiastical hierarchy. In some cases there have been purges, in others withdrawals of individuals or groups, and in still others accommodations which have maintained the outward unity but seldom done more than diminish the tension within.

Historical Antecedents[7]

Given the magnitude of the contemporary charismatic movement, it is of considerable significance that it is being contained, with some exceptions, within the established religious structures.[8] This is evidence, on the one hand, of change or adaptation in charismatic ideology and, on the other hand, of change in western culture that makes people more hospitable to variety in religious experience and practice. This evolution deserves serious study on the part of historians. We will touch upon it in this book only insofar as it has linguistic manifestations.

What must be seen here, first, is that this coexistence is of very recent date. The year 1950 might be more or less arbitrarily assigned as the beginning of the modern charismatic movement. What preceded was a period in which charismatists—Pentecostals they were simply called—were considered very unrespectable, being almost exclusively lower-class members of our society. Pentecostalism was well known, although poorly understood, as a "lunatic fringe" of the Christian religion. It was also considered heterodox by large numbers of church bodies, even Protestant evangelical ones that to an outside observer are in some cases hardly distinguishable (except for the charismatic doctrines) from the Pentecostal groups.[9] The latter were, and to some extent still are, boycotted by some interdenominational organizations.

[7] The history of Pentecostalism has been treated in an academic but not social-scientific way by Bloch-Hoell (somewhat prejudiced against it) and Nichol, both writing from within the church. Hayes and Mackie attempt to expose its errors. Bartleman and Frodsham are, on the other hand, Pentecostalists: the first gives a first-person account of the early years and the second gives a survey.

[8] For further information about the neo-Pentecostal movement the reader should consult the work by social anthropologists Gerlach and Hine (1970). The present study concerns itself with this movement, as with traditional Pentecostalism, only when glossolalia is at issue.

[9] "Evangelical" is contrasted with "liberal" in one dimension and with "fundamentalist" in another. Some might say that there are no "main-line"

What must be understood, in the second place, is that this same despised Christian "third force," as Henry van Dusen (1958) called it, is the source of the present movement. While many contemporary charismatists might bristle at being identified with traditional Pentecostalists, their cultures—viewed ethnographically—are very similar. This is seen primarily in the emphasis on Spirit baptism with its accompanying glossolalia. But it is seen also in a characteristic religious rhetoric, in the use of certain gestures (like the raising of hands), and in certain ways that people behave toward each other. At an ecumenical charismatic meeting a Congregationalist is often almost indistinguishable from a Full Gospelist!

The Pentecostal movement may be said to have begun at the turn of the century, bursting forth at "revivals" in Los Angeles early in 1906. These were the Azusa Street meetings that spread their sparks throughout North America and very soon to Europe and other parts of the world. But the Pentecostal fires, for their part, were ignited by earlier ones, primarily in the American South, where the holiness movement had been vigorous since the Civil War.[10] For example, the Church of God (Cleveland, Tennessee, so as to be distinguished from other churches by the same name) dates its beginning at meetings held in Camp Creek, North Carolina, in 1896. It is not surprising, therefore, that these older Pentecostal groups look upon the present charismatic movement as a Johnny-come-lately. Thus Wade H. Horton of the Church of God writes with the arrogance of experience:

. . . if any voice has the right to be heard on glossolalia, it should be America's oldest Pentecostal church. . . . It is difficult to understand . . .

---

evangelical or fundamentalist denominations although there might be churches or local congregations of these types within the main-line denominations, like the Presbyterian or United Church of Christ. Further refinements are not necessary in this study.

[10] The holiness movement may have started in the Methodist denomination, but it soon became interdenominational. It encouraged Protestants to strive for personal piety, and in its stronger forms emphasized spiritual perfection, partly by avoiding worldliness and partly through various religious practices, such as faithful Bible study and prayer. Surrender to God was a crucial step, often made at revival meetings. As a movement (outside the charismatic one) it may be dead, but it persists in some fashion as a characteristic feature of evangelical and fundamentalist churches and theological schools.

why it is supposed that these newcomers to Pentecost, who have spent many years either avoiding or opposing the experience, can become such authorities overnight (pp. 14,15).

Similar views would probably be held by some other long-established members of, say, the Pentecostal Fellowship of North America. There is now a kind of Pentecostal "Establishment" which seems to have difficulty in assigning a place to the representatives of the present charismatic movement. The Roman Catholics, for example, could not be tolerated.

Pentecostalism is a daughter of the holiness movement, but an errant one, or so many have considered it. This is seen not only in its insistence on a certain quality of life but also on the need for a special kind of personal experience with the Holy Spirit that makes this life possible. One acquired this experience at camp and revival meetings (colorfully described for the first part of the nineteenth century by Buley, pp. 417–488), and it often produced visible effects like dissociative symptoms (for example, falling in a faint) and some kinds of anomalous verbal behavior. But traditional Pentecostalism has made a dogma of glossolalia as evidence of this baptism in or filling with the Holy Spirit. So what is now the fifth point of the creed ("Statement of Faith") of the Pentecostal Fellowship of North America reveals both the heritage and distinctiveness of Pentecostalism: "We believe that the full gospel includes holiness of heart and life, healing for the body and the baptism in the Holy Spirit with the initial evidence of speaking in other tongues as the Spirit gives utterance."

Some might hold (as does Warburton) that traditional Pentecostal and holiness churches must be distinguished, because the first believe in tongues, for example, and the second do not. But this distinction is difficult to maintain, since, in the first place, some traditional Pentecostals do not seem to insist on tongue speaking as necessary for validating the Spirit baptism in spite of the official doctrine. Thus, the Pentecostal Assemblies of Canada do not mention glossolalia in their *What we believe* (presented in tract form for general distribution), and one of their ministers explained this omission by saying that they did not want to give the impression that they were overemphasizing tongues. In the second place, many neo-Pentecostals, like Christenson, a Lutheran minister, do not believe at all in the validating or, as it is also called, the evidential function of tongues (p. 13). Further evidence for fluidity in the lines between the various sectors of the movement is the fact that although the FGBMFI maintains the "official" Pentecostal doctrine about tongues, public meetings include charismatists of every kind.

We cannot spend much time on Christian-influenced forms of glossolalic behavior, although it is interesting to observe cases when a society fails to adopt glossolalia, adopts it with significant alterations, or "goes out of its way" (taking the idea from an unlikely source) to adopt it. For example, it has been reported to me by knowledgeable people that in some parts of Africa where Pentecostal missions have established churches, glossolalia is unknown, and the only characteristically Pentecostal emphasis is that of healing. It would appear that the recipient societies, even if possession were part of traditional religion, could not attribute to glossolalia a function that was meaningful in terms of their culture. In other African groups, however, glossolalia—at least in name—has been adopted but modified to fit the existing pattern. These are the various Christian or Christo-pagan sects that have, for the most part, sprung from mission churches, Protestant or Catholic. One anthropologist specializing in their study estimates that about 50 per cent of them are tongue speaking. It is doubtful, however, that this is always glossolalia, as I use the term. In fact, when evidence is available, the speech often turns out to be hardly anything more than gibberish or meaningless collections of words. Personal observation, but in another part of the world, verifies this judgment.

In Jamaica, as in other parts of the Caribbean, there are religious sects (derisively called "pocomania" by outsiders) that are supposed to practice glossolalia at the height of emotion or possession. The joint meeting in Savanna-la-Mar of the local group with the congregation from Montego Bay was typical of such meetings, where a Christian "liturgy," hardly visible under an embroidery of dancing, singing, testimonies, drumming, possession, etc., could be perceived only by someone acquainted with the Christian tradition. One woman "spoke in tongues." This was after an unusually long and intense period of possession during which she careened about before a circle of worshippers, helped and guided by other whiterobed women. Finally, she collapsed on her knees, at the edge of the circle, facing away from the center, still physically supported by several others, and broke her silence. I was told that she was talking in tongues, but when I bent low to hear what she was saying, I heard only disconnected Jamaican English.

In these groups, anomalous verbal behavior, whatever its nature, is rationalized and given respectability by identifying it with the Christian phenomenon. Thus, according to Sundkler, Zulu Zionists have syncretized Christian with traditional beliefs and practices. In the traditional culture, persisting in many healing practices, a patient inhaled the smoke of specific concoctions that introduced certain spirits to replace the illness. Since the spirit could be an Englishman or a train, the patient so possessed would talk or make noises like one (pp. 248–250). In Zionism it is the Holy Spirit that is supposed to possess a person, but it "speaks" in the traditional way, sometimes only in snorts.

Glossolalia in the Early Modern Period[11]

Going farther and farther back into church history for the antecedents of contemporary glossolalia becomes increasingly difficult, because references to glossolalia become both scarcer and more vague. Overzealous apologists for glossolalia therefore err in trying to trace a direct line from the present to the Biblical period.

Going backwards in time from the nineteenth-century religious movements in the United States, one can document glossolalia, or what might have been glossolalic behavior, to the post-Reformation period. In the nineteenth century glossolalia occurred in London, where it seems to have been a common phenomenon in the Catholic Apostolic Church which, contrary to what its name might suggest, started with the Presbyterian congregation of Edward Irving in the 1830's. The Irvingites, as they were also called, became so disreputable in the eyes of the London presbytery that they were forced to leave their church. However, glossolalia was only one of several doctrinal "errors." About a hundred years earlier the followers of George Fox, who to this day are known as

---

[11] Most of the surveys of post-Biblical glossolalia are derivative and superficial. Lombard's is not only one of the earliest but the best. Cutten copies. Kelsey and the works in W. Horton (ed.) are, in the first case, sympathetic and, in the second, wholly partisan. Drummond and Warfield deal with the Irvingite (or Catholic Apostolic) Church.

Quakers, frequently experienced abnormal motor behavior and uttered incomprehensible speech.[12]

About earlier groups, the Camisards and Jansenists of seventeenth-century France and the Anabaptists and the Waldenses in the sixteenth century, all frequently cited as having been glossolalists, linguistic information becomes scarcer and very unreliable. We cannot be certain at all that their verbal behavior was like modern glossolalia.

To deal with the Roman Catholic church in all of its history is too complex a task for a survey as brief as this chapter is, but it does appear that the Roman church has been wary of incomprehensible utterances in religious life. In *The Roman Ritual,* for example, established in its present form around A.D. 1000, the symptoms of possession are said to include the "ability to speak with some facility in a strange tongue or to understand it when spoken by another" (Weller, Vol. 2, p. 169).

In fact, at least since the days of John of the Cross and Teresa of Avila, Roman Catholics have been rather distrustful of subjective religious experience with a strong emotional component, known by some theologians simply as "religious experience" (McDonnell 1970:37).[13] Ronald Knox, the noted author, theologian, and dignitary of the Roman church, was so disgusted by a nonrational and nonauthoritarian approach to religion that he wrote,[14] "To speak with tongues you had never learned was, and is, a recognized symptom in cases of alleged diabolical possession" (p. 551). But McDonnell, a Benedictine theologian, says, "Long before the beginnings of Pentecostalism as a movement within Catholicism

[12] In the light of English religious history, therefore, it is hardly justified that an Anglican cleric should observe that the birthplace of modern Pentecostalism is Los Angeles, "also the home of Hollywood" (Webster, p. 20).

[13] But Max Weber, the renowned sociologist, would go farther back into the church's history: "In [pagan] Rome the nobles . . . completely rejected ecstasy, like the dance, as utterly unseemly and unworthy of a nobleman's sense of honor. . . . Most Romans regarded dancing and music as unseemly. . . . The Christian community of Rome in particular adopted this attitude against ecstasy quite consciously and consistently. In no instance did this community accept on its own initiative any irrational element, from charismatic prophecy to the greatest innovations in church music, into the religion or the culture" (1963:180–181).

[14] For example: "All this confusion, this priggishness, this pedantry, this eccentricity and worse, follows directly from the rash step that takes you outside the fold of Peter" (p. v).

there had been individual Catholics who had had the Pentecostal experience" (1970:35n).

Today things are entirely different. There is indeed a veritable "Catholic Pentecostal Movement" which Kevin Ranaghan, one of its leaders, conservatively estimates at between twenty-five and thirty thousand people. Even if the figure is somewhat smaller, the movement's growth must be considered phenomenal, starting as it did late in 1966 and numbering only about five hundred, less than a year later. Its geographical center originally was the American Midwest, principally among students and young professors at Duquesne University (Pittsburgh), the University of Notre Dame (South Bend, Indiana), both Catholic, and several universities of the state of Michigan. It started in prayer meetings of a neo-Pentecostal nature in an Episcopalian parish.

There are now charismatic Catholics in every section of the United States, many of them in the clergy and the religious orders, about six hundred of whom met in 1969 for the third annual Catholic Pentecostal Convention at the University of Notre Dame. They see this movement as a fulfillment of Pope John's prayer that the Holy Spirit's wonders might be renewed "in our time" in all of Christendom. Some neo-Pentecostalist Catholics in responsible positions express guarded but sincere appreciation for the movement: for example, ". . . the Pentecostal spirituality, namely, the fullness of life in the Spirit and the exercise of the gifts (not just tongues), is of unassailable validity" (McDonnell 1970:49). Even Roman Catholic bishops in the United States, while cautious, say that "the movement should at this point not be inhibited but allowed to develop" (p. 54).[15]

Glossolalia occurred at the very beginning of the Christian era, a fact vigorously advertised by contemporary charismatists, explained away by anticharismatists, and generally minimized by church historians. The evidence is quite clear in the New Testament.

The fullest treatment of tongues is in the twelfth and fourteenth chapters of Paul's first pastoral letter to the believers in Corinth, a church that was divided in its loyalties, in disagreement over several matters of belief, and errant in the practice of certain reli-

[15] For further information, see Kevin and Dorothy Ranaghan's *Catholic Pentecostals* (1969) and McDonnell's more theological study (1970) which also has a bibliography of Catholic reports and discussions.

gious rites. Some of the Corinthian Christians spoke in tongues, but they prided themselves in possessing this spiritual (that is, Spirit-given) gift and they disrupted religious meetings with its misuse. Paul, personally acquainted with the congregation and fully aware of the problems it faced, gave some common-sense advice to both the glossolalist and nonglossolalist members of the congregation. Being himself a speaker in tongues, he was in an excellent position to mediate between the factions.

What Paul did was to scold the factions for the trouble they were causing and to show them what they really ought to be emphasizing. One thing was intelligibility. This is why prophecy was better than speaking in tongues and why utterances in tongues were to be interpreted. But even if understanding was better than not understanding, the paramount thing, Paul made clear, was how people treated each other. It is in the middle of this thoroughly practical —and in some sense political—discussion, therefore, that one finds the classic Christian praise of "charity" or love (1 Corinthians 13) that begins:

Though I speak with the tongues of men and of angels, and have not charity, I am become as sounding brass, or a tinkling cymbal. And though I have the gift of prophecy, and understand all mysteries, and all knowledge; and though I have all faith, so that I could remove mountains, and have not charity, I am nothing.

How widespread the practice of glossolalia was in the apostolic period is not easy to determine. What one says about its occurrence, use, and significance depends on how one interprets the Biblical documents. It is possible, and I think necessarily assumed, that some Christian groups were more charismatic than others, but we have no way of knowing for certain how these differences may have correlated with geographical and sociocultural factors. It is a mistake, however, to credit the Greek congregations with the introduction of glossolalia in the Christian religion, for there is ample evidence that glossolalia occurred among the Palestinian Christians. The most dramatic incident took place on the Jewish holy day of Pentecost, but the record describes it as a case of something we now know as xenoglossia (Acts 2:1–14). (The difference between xenoglossia and glossolalia is discussed in Chapter 5.)

Theological debate over these crucial passages has been violent.

The traditional Pentecostal view is that there is no difference between Acts and I Corinthians: Whether or not one can recognize a glossolalic utterance as being in some specific human language, it is nevertheless a real language. Christians who are opposed to Pentecostal doctrine insist that all glossolalic utterances in the first century were in languages recognized by the community although not known personally by the persons who used them miraculously. From this follows their condemnation of contemporary glossolalia since tongues are hardly ever identified as normal languages. A "higher critical" approach, treating the Bible as a collection of human texts (an approach that evangelicals and fundamentalists do not use, since it "tampers with" the Scripture), would make the Acts account some kind of reinterpretation of the original event, which consisted of real—that is, incomprehensible—glossolalia. In this view, the speech events reported in Acts and discussed in I Corinthians would be the same linguistically.

It is interesting to observe that although nonbelievers may have thought that tongue speakers were drunk or insane (Acts 2:13; I Corinthians 14:23), there is no record that people associated this phenomenon with "demons." In the Gospels, demons that possess an individual always seem to talk that person's native language.

Although Christians traditionally take the day of Pentecost just referred to as a turning point in the history of the church—specifically, the beginning of the era in which the third person of the Trinity was to be principal actor—there are some people who claim that glossolalia did not begin with this first outpouring of the Holy Spirit. They see glossolalia in Old Testament references to prophetic utterances, especially those when a person is under the inspiration of the Spirit of God. Speaking in trance seemed to have been common among the prophets. Here is one such case: The prophet Samuel anoints Saul with oil, tells him that he is prince over Israel, and then tells him what is going to happen shortly:

... as you come to the city, you will meet a band of prophets coming down from the high place with harp, tambourine, flute, and lyre before them, prophesying. Then the spirit of the Lord will come mightily upon you, and you shall prophesy with them and be turned into another man. Now when these signs meet you, do whatever your hands find to do, for God is with you (I Samuel 10: 5-7, RSV).

Again, we cannot be sure if patterned, improvised, and incomprehensible speech (what I call glossolalia) is what was uttered on such occasions.

It is better to be critical than to accept every kind of anomalous verbal behavior as examples of glossolalia. But even if it could be proved that ancient peoples—even those outside the Judaeo-Christian tradition—were acquainted with the kind of glossolalia about which we now have very good information, this would only substantiate one of the main points of this book: that glossolalia is a much more normal phenomenon than people take it to be. The whole of Chapter 6, in fact, is devoted to this topic.

The contrary is the usual belief. Whereas glossolalists believe that there is something supernatural or miraculous about tongues, others—Christians and non-Christians alike—are convinced that tongue speakers are different from others either in terms of personality or clinically, at the moment they speak. The next chapter examines some of these attempts to explain in psychological terms why anyone, Christian or not, would engage in glossolalia.

2

EXPLAINED
PSYCHOLOGICALLY

TALKING IS ONE of the most natural things people do. Children are expected to learn to talk, and adults are expected to talk a normal amount. It is only when a person's speech varies from some pattern that it is noticed: he talks too much or too little; he talks when he should be silent or he is silent when he should talk; he talks too loudly, too softly, or too shrilly. All of these—and many other—deviations from what a society considers "normal" suggest a poorly adapted individual: abnormal speech suggests an abnormal person.

What, therefore, leads people who have already acquired language that is accepted by their society to adopt what other people consider deviant forms of language? Why, in the case of glossolalia, should people in all seriousness indulge in meaningless verbalizations?[1]

Psychologists and psychiatrists, occupied as they are with abnormal human behavior, have tended to see glossolalia in terms of aberrations, ignoring or simply not knowing the "normal" base of

[1] In this book, meaningless is always used in a linguistic sense, discussed more fully in Chapter 4. Any speech act can, of course, have real psychological or religious significance.

glossolalia as a linguistic phenomenon. Their attitudes are seen in some typical definitions of glossolalia:

. . . a fabricated language or speech in an unknown tongue, occurring in religious ecstasy, in hypnosis, in mediumistic trances, and in certain pathological mental states (Drever).
. . . a dissociative phenomenon or the severance of associational bonds which have existed between words and ideas (Vivier, p. iii).
. . . the entranced submission to some obsessive gibberish under the illusion of being inspired by mystical "tongues," which are thought to come from heaven (Luchsinger, et al., p. 790).

The nature of these abnormalities that are believed to cause or lead to glossolalia are reviewed in this chapter under the headings of personality, physical causes, and psychopathology.

Personality

Strong assertions have been made about the kinds of temperament and personality one finds among tongue speakers, but few indeed have been based on adequate psychological investigations. It was not at the conclusion of any study, therefore, that G. B. Cutten announced that glossolalists are garrulous, credulous, unintelligent, with an underdeveloped capacity for rational thought (pp. 4, 6, 79, 121–122). And when Lombard, in his doctoral dissertation in theology, called Pentecostals impressionable (p. 146), we are not informed about the basis of his judgment. Even a psychologist who avers that they are more than normally submissive, suggestible, and dependent when in the presence of an authority figure, real or imagined, is only stating a hypothesis that is itself based on another hypothesis about the relationship between a hypnotist and his subject.[2]

[2] Pattison, Lapins, and Doerr's study of forty-three people from a number of churches (not specified) who had been "healed by faith" (thirty-nine of whom were glossolalist) claims that "these subjects present psychological characteristics indicative of a strong need for social acceptance and social affiliation." This need gives rise to the "extensive use of denial and repression as major coping mechanisms" (p. 10). There was, however, "no gross pathology" (p. 8). Although the Spitzer Mental Status Schedule, the Minnesota Multiphasic Personality Inventory, and the Cornell Medical Index were used as testing devices, the presentation of the study is so tendentious that it succeeds only in being unconvincing.

There are only two comprehensive investigations that deserve our attention. One is by a psychiatrist and has never been published (Vivier). The battery of tests included the Willoughby Test (for general level of neuroticism), the Rosenzweig Picture Frustration Test, the Cattell Personality Factor Test, the Thematic Apperception Test, in addition to tests for suggestibility and questionnaires of various sorts. The total number of people studied is sixty-four; this includes the test group of Pentecostal glossolalists, one control group of co-church members who had not yet spoken in tongues but who believed in it, and another control group of conservative Protestants who did not approve of glossolalia—all in South Africa. Vivier's summary characterization of the tongue-speaking group (p. 432) as compared with the control groups shows the following "tendencies," presented verbatim with the deletion of two unclear points:

1. There are fewer formalized thought processes;
2. There is less egotistic manipulation of the environment;
3. They show more preference for feeling than thought;
4. There is more projection of feeling and thought;
5. Direction of aggression following upon frustration is punitive;
6. The method of repression is used for purposes of adjustment, more than egotistic self-assertiveness;
7. They show an interest for the unusual and extraordinary;
8. They show themselves not to be bound by the traditional and the orthodox.

The other study is Wood's. It aimed to test the assumption that "intense, immediate, positive emotion in religion [what he calls enthusiasm] is particularly attractive to certain personality types" and that Pentecostalism provides this kind of experience (p. 10). Using Rorschach blots as a testing instrument, he finds differences between Pentecostal and non-Pentecostal perceptions; he concludes that there must be "differences in basic perceptual habits and, consequently, in personality types" (p. 97). He therefore predicts that people who produce records similar to those of the Pentecostal will be more attracted to Pentecostalism, admitting, however, that the Pentecostal Rorschach profile might be developed *after* participation in the group, a fact that would invalidate his hypothesis (p. 108).

Whatever these studies may be worth, they must be used with

caution, remembering that at least one other study of Pentecostal groups, which included scales to test alienation, dogmatism, and powerlessness, reveals the difficulty of using the concept of personality in accounting for Pentecostalism. This is the work under the supervision of anthropologist Luther P. Gerlach in connection with the study of movement growth (reported in Gerlach and Hine and further discussed below).

What accounts for the apparent differences of opinion—differences in subjects unrelated to Pentecostalism or differences in interpretation? For example, Vivier's glossolalists are "people who, psychologically speaking, have had a poor beginning in life. This has been reflected by the difficulty in adjustment to their home situation in infancy and later adulthood" (p. 432). Those observed by Gerlach and Hine generally are "normally adjusted and productive members of society" (Hine 1969:216).

Another negative conclusion about the correlation between personality types and glossolalic behavior results from the study of sociologist W. Cohn. On the basis of information obtained from tests and interviews about the personalities of college-age subjects (in terms of the Freudian concepts of oral and anal tendencies) he tried to determine if people of a certain type would react favorably to Pentecostalism: about fifty were taken to Pentecostal meetings and one hundred sixty were shown two films of a Pentecostal nature. There proved to be no significant correlations; "the relationship between psychological factors and membership in social groups," he feels, "is still a riddle" (1968:38).

One more study of sixty-two subjects drawn from three Pentecostal churches of a northwestern city in the United States comes to a similar conclusion: "When compared with other groups, such as college students and the normative samples of the CPI [California Psychological Inventory test], the open or non-dogmatic Pentecostal believers appear as well-adjusted and interpersonally skillful as do people in general" (Gilmore, p. 164).

There probably are some personality differences between Pentecostals and non-Pentecostals, say, within the same Anglican or Catholic parish, but at the moment we simply do not know enough to *explain* glossolalia—that is, account for it—in terms of personality types. Yet we continue trying to do so, and I share this failing in my undisciplined moments. On one occasion, observing a certain neo-Pentecostal at a public meeting keeping to himself except to make critical remarks, I said to myself, "He's just the type. He's the kind you would expect to use his tongues to overcome his inability to interact with others." I had learned previously that this man was a leader in his group, and that his glossolalic messages (to be discussed in Chapter 7) were used for guidance.

Physical

Glossolalia has also been explained as the manifestation or correlate of physical events experienced by a human. It is seen either as a kind of automatic behavior or as a feature of an altered state of consciousness.

Automatisms. When glossolalia is described as an automatism, it is said to be an "involuntary movement of the speech organs" (Coe, p. 114), "a stereotyped pattern of unconsciously controlled vocal behavior" or "psychomotor behavior" in which the "conscious centers of the psyche are bypassed." Typical also are the words of Cutten: "We have to do with a state of personal disintegration, in which the verbo-motive centers of the subject are obedient to subconscious impulses. . . . [In tongues the] subconsciousness concentrates its energy on one motor or sensory function" (p. 160). Elsewhere he characterizes a glossolalic utterance as "a mass of meaningless syllables gushing forth under the control of the excited lower centers" (p. 147).

It is, to be sure, not difficult to illustrate "unconscious" or "involuntary" glossolalia from reports by the speakers themselves, as I found through my questionnaire and in personal interviews: as when a person prays in tongues inaudibly and becomes aware of it after a while; or when a person bursts forth with "spontaneous utterances" (that is, without forethought) in a group; or when a person speaks in tongues when he intends to speak in English. The last happened to a Lutheran minister who was teaching a confirmation class just a half-hour after he had begun to speak in tongues for the first time. Some people even report using tongues while asleep: One person says that praying in tongues has become such a part of her life that she wakes up at night and her "mind is praying in the Spirit"; another says, "A few times I have prayed in tongues in a dream." Other people have claimed that on occasions they could not stop once they had begun. One charismatist leader reports, on the basis of his own observations, that this almost always happens at the initial experience of speaking in tongues. He heard of one case where a woman could utter nothing but glossolalia for about three days (but I have doubts about this and similar reports).

Even without these kinds of experiences, many glossolalists insist that they cannot speak in tongues "at will," that they always do it involuntarily. Statements to this effect have very often been taken to mean that "something comes over a person." For the glossolalist, of course, this is the power of the Holy Spirit. But we must be cautious about interpreting this so-called involuntary behavior. It is perfectly understandable that the person who believes that glossolalia is to be used only for private prayer would find it practically impossible to speak in tongues at will, for example, to let you hear what it sounds like. In other words, apart from a person's psychological make-up that determines, so to speak, what he "can" and "cannot" do, it is what he has learned to do that determines his behavior. So when a glossolalist is with a group of co-believers, and when everyone else has taken his turn at prayer, he prays not "involuntarily" but for very understandable reasons. (We are talking here, of course, about practiced glossolalia and not about the first experience, but others do not always specify the kinds of information on which their explanations are based.)

In any case, the psychological explanation that makes glossolalia involuntary or automatic behavior goes back, if we follow William James, to about 1886, when it was discovered that:

. . . in certain subjects at least, there is not only the consciousness of the ordinary field, with its usual centre and margin, but an addition thereto in the shape of a set of memories, thoughts, and feelings which are extramarginal and outside of the primary consciousness altogether, but yet must be classed as conscious facts of some sort, able to reveal their presence by unmistakable signs. . . . The most important consequence of having a strongly developed ultra-marginal life of this sort is that one's ordinary fields of consciousness are liable to incursions from it of which the subject does not guess the source, and which, therefore, take for him the form of unaccountable impulses to act, or inhibitions of action, of obsessive ideas, or even of hallucinations of sight or hearing. The impulses may take the direction of automatic speech or writing, the meaning of which the subject himself may not understand even while he utters it (pp. 188–189).

Even James, however, is borrowing, on his own admission, from a friend and senior psychologist, Frederic W. H. Myers. It was he who gave the name *automatism* "to the whole sphere of effects, due to 'uprushes' into the ordinary consciousness of energies originating in the subliminal [another one of Myers' terms] parts of the mind" (James, p. 189). Glossolalia was clearly comprehended by this term, as is seen by the comments made by both Myers and James on the case of Le Baron. (About him more will be said later.) However, James felt that Le Baron's glossolalia was only a "rudimentary form of motor automatism" (Le Baron, p. 278).

For James, the reason for glossolalia was simple enough: It was symptomatic of some illness or aberration. But others, while clinging to the notion of automaticity, have tried some explanations that did not depend on ultra-marginal or subliminal life.

Cutten's explanation is the most naive. It attributes glossolalia to a breakdown in thought:

. . . when a person stands up to speak [even in normal circumstances], it is not the utterance but the thinking, back of the utterance, which causes the strain. With those who find even rudimentary thought difficult, speech of an intelligent nature cannot long progress, the thinking process soon refusing to function; and when, owing to the ease of operation and the suggestion to action, speech continues after thought is exhausted, a series of meaningless syllables results (p. 5).[3]

Moreover, this automatic speech may tax the "phonetic apparatus" beyond what it is able or accustomed to do (Cutten, p. 171), and may lead to phonological anomalies. But these, as a careful study of glossolalic texts has demonstrated, are rare. Of course, speech can always be distorted by strong emotions or excessive speed, but these distortions do not explain the fundamental nature of glossolalia, which is to be described in chapters to follow.

Vivier's is a graphic explanation. According to him the explo-

[3] An entirely different function is attributed to automatisms by Lombard (here in translation): "In pseudo-verbal automatisms the rare expressions that the hearer recognizes or to which the speaker assigns a specific meaning are most often invocative. These words, emphatically uttered, signal the affective aspect of the situation" (p. 126).

sion in the discharge of intense feelings in the baptism experience is so great that it causes a dissociation of neural associations (like the concussion of a bomb breaking windows, one supposes). This takes place because the experience exceeds the "normal powers of thought and description" (pp. 433, 438). This is another specious description that assumes more than it accounts for. After all, all of man's environment—real or imagined, physical or psychological—"exceeds" him in being more than he is, but this does not prevent him from talking about any of it, in bits, spaced out in time; the marvel of human existence is that man can mediate so much of his experience in language. Besides, this explanation assumes that the Spirit-filled person *wants* to talk about his peak experience.

The glossolalist obviously has some reason for engaging in pseudolanguage, and for doing that rather than being silent or singing or jumping around, for example, but it is not necessarily or simply to relate an experience that exceeds the "normal powers of thought and description." And although there is an emotional component—sometimes even intense—associated with glossolalic speech, its *nature* cannot be assumed from the presence of glossolalia; that is something to be demonstrated in other ways. Besides, the baptism experience is not limited to a specific time (although it is not unusual for charismatists to remember the exact dates, and even hour, of their experience), for these people would insist that being filled with the Spirit is a way of life, something that one strives for all the time. But if there are peaks and troughs in this religious life subsequent to the initial one, it is certainly not the case that glossolalia occurs only with the peaks. Therefore, if glossolalia can be independent of highly charged psychological states, whatever that might mean for the responsible observer of human behavior, it is not merely the product of such states.

Similarly, music and dance—especially vith strong rhythm— are frequently cited as inducing factors in glossolalia. The reason given is the belief that "natural brain waves" are altered by external sound waves (as explained by Neher, Needham, and Sturtevant). But it is never made clear why the brain configurations should lead to meaningless utterances as patterned as those we commonly see in religious glossolalia. *Pakalamisa takatula* is a good sample, but I produced it myself at the typewriter as easily as I sing *trala lala*.

But these, according to another view, are only mediate causes. Thus, William Sargant assumes that when glossolalia is produced, the brain is in a peculiar state that could be described as a cortical inhibition, the kind of condition that is supposed to occur during electro-shock treatments. The state is temporary, but it permits a person to develop new patterns of speech. Whatever merit this hypothesis has in clinical or experimental psychology, it is superfluous for glossolalia, for tongues occur in a number of very normal situations.

Those who consider glossolalia to be a motor automatism might also imagine that some individuals are more susceptible to this kind of behavior than others. This possibility was looked into by Vivier, whose work has already been cited, but it was not strongly confirmed.

It would seem wise, therefore, to abandon the terms "automatic" and "involuntary" with respect to glossolalia until we know more about the many correlates of the acquisition and use of tongues, such as time, place, setting, number of participants in a speech event, belief of the function of glossolalia, and psychological state of the speaker. (Unfortunately, I failed to include a question in my questionnaire to deal specifically with this topic.) Certainly, cases like Sherrill's, when he sometimes has to "mouth nonsense syllables in an effort to start the flow" of glossolalia, which sometimes never comes (p. 146), are not to be explained automatically by the involuntariness of glossolalia.

Altered states of consciousness. If glossolalia is some kind of automatic motor activity, then it arises, people have said, in an abnormal state of consciousness. Like jerking, shaking, and crying out uncontrollably, or like fainting, lying stiff, and having no recollection of what has happened, glossolalia is supposed to be the result of a "disorganization of the ego," as Lombard called it (pp. 14, 142). But that is only one characterization. It goes by other names: dissociation, trance, hypnosis, altered mental state, and so forth.

Perhaps there are several different but related phenomena comprehended by Ludwig in the expression, "altered states of consciousness." These ASCs are "mental states . . . which can be recognized subjectively by the individual himself (or by an objective observer of the individual) as representing a sufficient deviation, in terms of subjective experiences or psychological functioning, from certain general norms as determined by the subjective experience and psychological functioning of that individual during alert, waking consciousness" (pp. 69–70).

What is comprehended by Ludwig's definition is considered to be an ASC, but understanding the condition itself is another problem. One explanation is that it is a state "in which the generalized reality-orientation has faded to relatively non-functional unawareness." This is Shor's (p. 591), who, although talking specifically about trance, in relation to hypnosis, is dealing with the same problem. What he means by the "generalized reality-orientation" is the following: "The usual state of consciousness is characterized by the mobilization of a structured frame of reference in the background of attention which supports, interprets, and gives meaning to all experiences" (p. 585). Losing this state, and thereby going into a trance, is illustrated by something as common or normal as being engrossed by what one reads. Shor tells of an experience when his wife had spoken to him without his knowing what was said or even what had happened. In his trance he knew only that he was aware of something, and it was not until after he had "come to" that he realized what had happened and what had been said to him. This state of being, he says, was induced by his having assumed a "specific referential schema" that was necessary for understanding the difficult book he was reading. He had momentarily been adrift, oblivious of his position with reference in time and space to everything around him.

Glossolalia has been considered one of the effects of an altered state of consciousness, because it seems to accompany some of the various kinds of behavior, like trance, that are comprehended by this term. Here is part of the account of how a young man first began to speak in tongues:

As I knelt there in front of the chair, with my hands flat on it, Father [the Episcopalian priest] and his wife placed their hands on my head and shoulders. As they prayed for me to receive the gift of the Holy Spirit . . . I was filled . . . every part of me, every bone, tissue, and muscle. So complete was Its electrifying presence that my hands became heavy and felt as though they were bursting with electricity. Then both hands began to rise and Father placed his hand on them and his other hand on my cheek and I burst out in an unknown tongue. My spirit, the inner man was completely in the control of the Holy Spirit. . . . My whole body tingled and was filled with [Christ's] warmth (Kelsey, p. 167).

The symptoms are seen in the feeling of weight, electricity, tingling, and warmth. (Perhaps the hands also rose "unconsciously," but since hand raising is as much a Pentecostal gesture as crossing oneself is a Catholic one, the candidate was probably performing a culturally expected action.)

These symptoms of heaviness, electricity, tingling, and warmth are reported by some of my own respondents. (There was no specific question to elicit information about ASC. Some of the statements occurred under the queries, "Relate any unusual or memorable experiences that you have had in connection with speaking in tongues" and "Have you ever felt unusual sensations in the vocal organs while speaking in tongues?" Others occurred at random in the questionnaire.) One person has a sensation like a "slight electrical charge" in her throat when she speaks in tongues. And a Presbyterian clergyman reports that when he spoke for the first time he felt "a marked touch" upon his throat and mouth, and that subsequently he often feels "a gentle electricity, a kind of warming" of his tongue and lips.

Feelings of warmth are also reported, but only in a few cases. A young Presbyterian minister writes: "Sometimes I try to avoid God and am upset. Tongues will restore things—even causing a cleansing, burning feeling in the stomach."

An uncritical view would accept all such reports of physical sensations as dealing with ASCs, but doing so would conceal some significant aspects of these experiences. They are not the same simply because, for example, the same rhetoric is used of them. A "pricking pain" may be reported by different people, but of different parts of the body and in connection with other subjective states. One person who reports such sensations at the back of her tongue says they occur especially when she tries to refrain from speaking in tongues and feels the prompting of the Holy Spirit. In other words, she seems to have psychosomaticized her inhibitions about glossolalia. Such an interpretation is plausible in view of her doubts about the experience. Doubting, for example, prevented her from using tongues the day after her initial experience. And even that was a very difficult one for her. She writes about it in these words:

[When I first began to speak], my tongue felt several times normal size and I could not control the movements of it. I briefly felt a desire to speak—almost to the bursting point and a weakness that caused me to think I would faint in front of those present. When I said, "O.K., Lord, if you want me to faint, I will," and yielded to the feeling, I immediately began speaking those strange sounds which continued for about five minutes. Then the wonderful presence of the Lord flooded my soul and for the remainder of the day I was "drunk" on the Spirit.

If anxiety can be localized in sensory experience, so can euphoria. We can therefore expect the emotions associated with glossolalia to be described in a rhetoric charged with positive terms. There is a general feeling of power: A seventeen-year-old boy says that he had no special difficulties the first time he began to speak in tongues, but "I came to a crucial point where I felt an enormous power within me and once I opened my mouth, the words just flowed out." An older man says that a welling up came with assurance of the authenticity of the experience. He had come home and was preparing to retire for the night, after having received the baptism, "seeking a confirmation of the whole matter, when something within, like a geyser, began bubbling, spouting then erupting in a tremendous outflow of praise and worship, almost an agonizing experience."[4]

Since it is common for human beings to localize their emotions in the abdomen, it is not unusual that glossolalists also do. Thus, one person says that her speech comes from the solar plexus: "It is as if there it is spoken softly, without sound." (She almost never speaks aloud in tongues.)

Another person localizes glossolalia in the chest, but for an interesting reason. He writes that he has not had unusual sensations in the vocal organs, "only subtle 'open' sensations in the throat. The deep welling up seems to be from farther in my chest and is in proportion to the willingness I have to concentrate on the wonderment of 'Christ in us.' " It is safe to speculate that he has per-

---

[4] Euphoria can be experienced even when a person is consciously pretending to talk in tongues. One of Carlson's subjects who imitated glossolalia (in a study discussed on page 76) said this of her experience: "I loved it! . . . It didn't 'turn me on,' but I liked it. What amazes me is how easy it is to just let all of this 'verbal garbage' run. . . . Just let language go away, and things just pour out. . . . You're detached and you're looking at it, and you really have nothing to do with it at the same time."

ceived both the physical state of his chest cavity and the paralinguistic characteristics of his speech, and has interpreted acoustic
"depth" and muscular state in psychological terms. (Of course,
the stimuli could have worked in both directions.) He appears to
have experienced nothing more than the kind of culturally-defined
"sound symbolism" one finds in the use of a bass voice in western
societies to represent God's pronouncements to man; a low, even
sepulchral, voice connotes remoteness and authority.

More convincing as evidence of altered states of consciousness
are reports of hallucinations, amnesia, "awayness," and acute sensory perception. Four of my respondents, all women between the
ages of thirty-four and forty-eight, and only one of them from a
Pentecostal background, recorded having had visions of some type
in connection with glossolalia: such as having seen Jesus or "seen
colors [and] worshipped God on a white stairway or green grass";
being "transported to the very gates of heaven and heard the rejoicing and praise." Although it is not clear that glossolalia was
actually concomitant with visions in these cases, in the following
there seems to be no doubt: "One morning while praying in tongues,
I saw the cross in a red glow—everything was red, but there were
two red beams coming down from the cross to two people. One
was a lady in the hospital who had fallen down one flight in an
elevator shaft and was in critical condition in the hospital. . . . The
other was a dear friend of mine. I was told [internally, by God] to
pray for these two people and did."

Auditory and olfactory hallucinations associated with glossolalia
appear to be rare—if written accounts can be trusted. (I failed
to elicit this kind of information in my questionnaire.) Only two
cases have been reported to me by other investigators, both occurring in neo-Pentecostal groups, both in connection with prayer
sessions, and both experienced by women. One of them perceived
Jesus through "smelling his presence." It was a beautiful smell, she
said. During the group's prayer time she would exclaim, "He's
here! I can smell him." In the other case, the experience took
place on three different occasions. Some of the members of the
group supported the woman's report but others remained skeptical.
An open and sympathetic discussion concerning the possibility
that this might be a "gift"—something given by God to an individual—served to maintain the unity of the group and tended to support the woman in her own religious experience.

The apparent scarcity of "symbolic smells" may be due to accident in research. Our work has been based on Protestant Pentecostals, and Protestants may know less about sacred smells than Catholics. When Catholics become charismatic, they bring with them their own cultural baggage (not a pejorative term), as the following testimony of a student at the University of Notre Dame (U.S.A.) illustrates. The quotation also illustrates the psychological preparation for the hallucination:

[At the end of the meeting to explain the charismatic experience, the Duquesne University professor] began to pray, and I was struck with the power and conviction of his prayer. I thought, "Here is a man who speaks with authority, who really knows what he is talking about. This must have been the kind of authority people saw in Christ." As he began to pray, I decided to make a real effort to pray with him. . . . He prayed for two things: first, that we would all be freed from any power of Satan, and second, that we would be filled with the Spirit. . . .

[The next night] nine of us gathered with the Duquesne professor for prayer, and we asked him to lay hands on us and pray for the baptism of the Spirit.

And so he went around to us one by one—I was the last. He would first command in the name of Jesus that Satan depart from us, to free us from his temptations, doubts, and obstacles, and leave us free to respond fully to God. Then he laid his hands upon us and prayed. . . . It was quiet—silent except for his voice. As each was prayed over he [the professor] seemed to sink into silent and deep prayer. . . .

The professor stood before me for a moment and then, in Christ's name, cast out Satan. As soon as he said the words I knew that a demon had left. I felt myself physically shaken and smelled clearly and distinctly the smell of burning sulphur, a smell I know well from chemistry lab. And immediately I knew what had happened. God was allowing me a sign that what had been oppressing me for two months, and before which I had felt helpless, was the power of Satan (*Vision,* Spring, 1968, p. 10).

It is also interesting that glossolalic aural hallucinations—hearing unintelligible speech from God or man—have not been reported, at least as far as I have been able to tell. This absence is curious, since glossolalia is supposed to be speech that comes from outside man. Some might see it as evidence of the egocentric orientation of the glossolalist: He is more the actor than the audience.

In some altered states of consciousness people report a clarifying of the thought processes and a greater, more sensitive awareness of their environment. Statements made by tongue speakers might be interpreted as indicating this kind of experience, as when respondents write that "speaking in tongues heightens my awareness" or that they have "an exceptionally clear thought pattern." It has even been reported that glossolalia is used to "clear the cobwebs" when one is frustrated with an intellectual problem. (We will come back to this topic in Chapter 10.) When this awareness takes an acute form, it results in what is known as nature mysticism, where one feels himself at one with certain physical objects or even the whole world. Here is an account of such an "unbelievable" experience "recalled frequently with joy" as my respondent described it:

One beautiful spring day, returning home from an errand by a country road, the frogs and crickets were in full chorus for the first time. I was rejoicing in God and His creation all around me in tongues and spiritual [that is, glossolalic] song, when suddenly, interspersed in this language, were replicas of the sounds of frogs and various types of grasshoppers, crickets, and other unseen creatures that I could hear. It was tremendous. I felt levitated, part of the Whole.

Amnesia—not remembering an experience one has gone through —appears primarily, if not exclusively, in the ethos of traditional Pentecostalism where it seems to validate a powerful experience. It is therefore perhaps not irrelevant that it is an Assembly of God evangelist of a rather flamboyant type who reports that "they said I spoke for three or four hours when I was filled with the Holy Spirit." (True amnesia, of course, can be verified; simply not remembering what had happened at a three-hour meeting is not necessarily amnesia.)

Loss of control or consciousness might seem to be indicated by the metaphorical language that is used of tongue speaking: not having "control" over one's vocal organs, having the language "just flow out," being "possessed" by the Holy Spirit, etc. If this is the only feeling that is reported, however, it is unlikely that an altered state of consciousness is involved. Practically every one of my respondents reports a perfectly normal state of consciousness (in response to my question, "How much are you conscious of what is happening around you while talking in tongues?"). They illustrate by saying that they can be engaged in several other activities at the same time—driving a car or airplane, washing dishes, reading or writing, listening to another person in a conversation—just as one is able to do these things while using normal language audibly or inaudibly. Glossolalists, in fact, are insistent, in spite of their rhetoric, that they are not automatons. Thus, Gasson, at one time a follower of spiritism, says that God "does not take away our powers of thinking or conscious action" (p. 44). The demonstration, therefore, of a casual experiment that simple writing tasks were grossly altered during glossolalia must be discounted until much more is known of it. There are other psychological explanations for poor motor behavior: after all, one may perform very badly at cutting and serving a cake if everybody at the table watches. This is why one respondent said that he was not conscious of his surroundings when he spoke out in a gathering but was fully conscious during glossolalia when he drove his car.

Because of the contrary view still held by people with limited information about glossolalia my own view must be stated explicitly. It is based on extensive first-hand observations of glossolalia in actual use in natural settings—not simply in clinical experimentation—and on scores of first-person accounts from personal interviews, answers to questionnaires, and testimonies in religious literature. It is, moreover, substantiated by the almost equally extensive research of Gerlach and Hine and a few others whose works have not been published. We have come to the same conclusions independently, but we would agree that the acquisition of charismatic or Pentecostal glossolalia is *sometimes* associated with *some* degree of altered state of consciousness, that this *occasionally* involves motor activity that is involuntary or, *rarely,* a complete loss of consciousness, and that in any case subsequent use of glossolalia (that is, after the initial experience) is *most often independent* of dissociative phenomena.

We are therefore in categorical disagreement with the position that glossolalia is "an event of vocalization uttered while the speaker is in a state of dissociation," that it is, in fact, "an artifact of trance" (Goodman 1969a:238). In this view, even intelligible words can constitute a total glossolalic utterance (p. 233).

Our disagreement is not an arbitrary one. It depends on the empirical basis of the conclusions and the ways in which the data are interpreted. Goodman's data are very limited. Moreover, in spite of the claim that the glossolalia samples come from "four cultural settings," it is admitted that for one set obtained from a television network there is no information about the religious background of the speakers (p. 233) and no independent corroboration that the speaker was indeed in trance. Finally, the interpretation completely overlooks the possibility that the intonation she attributes to trance is nothing more than a style of speaking that can be used in any religious discourse. If I am correct in my understanding of what she describes, then I have heard mild forms of this intonation in many sermons where there was not the slightest suggestion of trance and an extreme form of it in a testimony by a man from Arkansas at a Full Gospel Business Men's meeting. One will also find this style among the sectarians of the Appalachians. Because a certain speech style is widespread does not mean that it is produced by trance. It takes very little first-hand observation to notice that preaching and praying styles are shared like any cultural feature.

In short, to show that glossolalia is a trance phenomenon, one must first prove that trance occurs and then show that glossolalia does not occur without it. There will always be instances of trance-speech, but it will be impossible, I maintain, to demonstrate that glossolalia is always dependent on trance.

Psychopathology

When interpreted as the evidence or function of abnormal psychological conditions, glossolalia has been described in terms of repression, release, and regression.

Repression. With this function glossolalia is supposed to be hidden or empty communication. One suggestion, for example, is that it "serves to provide verbal form to a conflicted wish while at the same time hiding the wish by stripping the verbalization of communal meaning. Some degree of conscious expression is allowed to the conflicted wish, but the wish itself escapes conscious recognition." This is something like going through the ritual of gift-giving with an empty box. The idea is obviously borrowed from the interpretation given to the strange speech of schizophrenics whose meaning, even when normal words are used and the syntax is fairly grammatical, is often inscrutable without an interpretation from the patient. Laffal, who makes this hypothesis (1965, p. 88), heard his samples of glossolalia from the lips of a schizophrenic patient. Having myself heard the tape recording of it, I can attest that it is indeed glossolalia. Equating the same motivation for both forms of "nonsense," however, is another matter. One would have to show that among nonschizophrenic persons there in fact was a wish that had to be repressed. All of my experience with normal glossolalists convinces me that to find supporting evidence for this view is very unlikely.[5]

Calling both schizophrenic speech and glossolalia "nonsense," it should be added, is making too broad a generalization. In the first, some kind of message does get through. In the second, there are virtually no words whatsoever, as we shall see in Chapter 4. Besides, the speech of the schizophrenic is obviously determined by the grammar of some natural language known to him, so that what a German says will be significantly different from what a Russian says. In glossolalia, on the other hand, there is far less influence of another grammar. There is therefore no linguistic justification whatsoever to consider both kinds of speech as examples of a single phenomenon. Schizophrenic speech is *not* "structurally the same as glossolalia," as one psychologist claims. If schizophrenics can talk in tongues, it is only because they are in some sense normal enough to do so, for they are not non-persons.[6]

I would speculate, then, that only those with an abnormally low development of linguistic competence (in addition, naturally, to those with physiological defects) will be unable to produce pseudo-language.[7]

[5] This might seem like begging the question, because some people would like to insist that glossolalists are in fact *not* normal. But the contention of this whole chapter is that you cannot use glossolalia to *prove* that they are psychologically abnormal. Other clinical evidence must be used.

[6] It would be useful to make instrumental comparisons between schizophrenic speech and the glossolalic utterances of normal individuals, for Saxman (1965) claims that the former has definite acoustic characteristics that are instrumentally determined. There have been reports of instrumental studies of glossolalic speech, measuring fundamental frequencies and so on, but nothing has been published.

[7] But one study of a child with Down's syndrome reveals how common glossolalia-like speech is among humans. In addition to his everyday-speech, this mongoloid child used what the observer thought was a "hokus-pokus style" that was whispered and accompanied by hand-waving that reminded

There are, however, other reasons for not being able to make glossolalic utterances, just as there are reasons for some people being "unable to learn foreign languages," as they say. The language teacher is, nevertheless, committed to the belief that that student can indeed do exactly what he says he cannot do. The difference between language learning and acquiring the "gift of tongues" is that no charismatist ever says that everyone can talk in tongues; instead, he reinforces the proselyte's conviction that "I could never do that without the help of God." That is why, as we shall see in the next chapter, the acquisition of glossolalia is considered a miracle.

Emotional release. This is the function most commonly attributed to glossolalia, a cause one person says that has "very few exceptions" (Motley, p. 26). Perhaps the speakers themselves are partly responsible for this explanation because of the rhetoric used to describe their experience. One person called it an "emotional release," a "release from the bondage of human tensions into the freedom in the Spirit"; and a preacher in a store-front Pentecostal church urged the handful of people present to "cut off" and "get out in the deep."

Release is obviously a term that can comprehend a wide range of experiences, and these can have different causes. One of the simplest notions is that when tensions build up, as one writer put it, "action of any kind is a relief." Cutten describes the event as "the result of a mere excess of feeling" (p. 172). Similarly, Pattison, a psychologist, says: "Any of us could 'speak in tongues' if we adopted a passive attitude about controlling our body and speech and had an emotional tension pressing for expression. . . . Trying to talk while . . . laughing results in vocalizations which have all the characteristics of glossolalia" (1964:3). The last sentence is inaccurate, as this book demonstrates.

---

one of spell-casting, perhaps in imitation of something seen on television. This is a sample of the speech, here modified in orthography (for which see page 58): *tópi, tŏpa, tĕpă, chápi, pĭyapĭtá, pĭyĭpĭtĭpá.* What is interesting about this case is the use of anomalous speech with something experienced as beyond the ordinary, a correlation that occurs again and again in the world, as we shall see in Chapters 6 and 11. (The study is that of Ann Bodine, "The phonological system of a five-year-old mongoloid," an unpublished contribution to a summer workshop on "Language, Society, and the Child," University of California, Berkeley, 1968.)

Views like these were until recently largely based on observations of traditional Pentecostal meetings that are emotional to a rather high degree. The following is my own. The meeting was a "tarrying service" in a Canadian church affiliated with the Pentecostal Assemblies of Canada, a mostly white congregation that appeared to be lower middle-class.

The regular service had begun at 7 P.M. and the sermon was on the theme of the baptism in the Holy Spirit. At 8:30, when the service should have been over, the pastor announced a "tarrying service" for those who wanted "to get right with God" and to have "more power in their lives." Those with a special desire were to take the first row of seats and others were to sit behind them. Some people came directly to the platform at the front of the church. During this time there was prayer from the whole congregation, some weeping in great sincerity, others shouting their petitions to God. In the meantime, the organist and pianist kept up an uninterrupted musical accompaniment of Gospel hymns. From time to time the congregation, at someone's initiative, would sing the words. The totality of events seemed to crest and fall a number of times without any apparent management on the part of the pastor. Around 9:30, however, he was back on the platform, after having strolled among the congregation, and he suggested that everybody praise Jesus. There ensued a new crescendo of activity, the verbal part consisting of short phrases being repeated again and again. Then, for the first time, I saw the pastor, now in fuller control of himself, say something to the organist, whereupon the latter began to play a song with a little more beat. It was then, at 9:40 P.M., that a woman at the front of the church made a cry and, with lifted arms, began to careen backwards away from the platform, turn, then come forward again. With spine and arms thrown backward she vainly tried to keep her balance. Finally, she fell to the floor on her back and began to cry *Dadadadadadadada* . . . (although the consonant could have been "t" instead). Occasionally she would shriek *Eeek,* and later, when she had calmed down a bit, she uttered what sounded like *shikago.* (I could certainly be mistaken, of course, but it is interesting to note the similarity between this word and "Chicago," that the woman was a Negro, and that Chicago a few weeks previously had seen riots.)

It would not surprise me if this woman's utterances were considered glossolalic by the sympathetic people who witnessed her behavior. Certainly the pastor was visibly pleased when she began to stagger in her dissociative state; he smiled (for the first time since 8:30) and yelled out "Halleluiah!" Here was a physical demonstration of the working of the Spirit. No one, not even the pastor, I believe, could give an accurate account of the linguistic behavior of this seeker. I was surely the only critical observer, and in my opinion this was not glossolalia linguistically defined.[8]

This assumed cause for glossolalia has in turn been explained socio-economically. The widely held view is that emotionalism and motor phenomena often develop in social groups that are deprived (Worsley, p. 248). This was applied to traditional Pentecostalists because of their position in the social scale of industrialized societies. This, however, was an ad hoc explanation, because there are nonemotional movements, and the neo-Pentecostal movement includes followers who are far from deprived.[9]

Where there is no socio-economic deprivation, people trying to account for glossolalia assume an "emotional deprivation." Among middle-class westerners, therefore, there is supposed to be a "terrible isolation and loneliness," a definite repression of "religious feelings, aspirations, and ideas" which cannot find adequate expression in "words and wordiness" (Oates 1968:97,48,41). Glossolalia then is a "sudden chaotic breakthrough" of expression that goes "all the way back to the era of one's most elemental attempts to communicate with other people" (pp. 97,91); it is like "an infant crying without language," in fact, "a childlike, unguided, and unpatterned kind of speech . . . meaningful to the person . . . in much the same way that the first utterances of a small child are meaningful" (pp. 55,85).

This is all very difficult to prove, of course. One would have to show that glossolalists did in fact have repressed emotions. More-

[8] Here and at several other places I question or challenge reported instances of glossolalia. In most cases there is little problem in placing faith in a report. If, for example, a person prays or gives a message in glossolalia as the sole speaker with others in attendance, he will have to engage in sustained speech that is convincingly similar to natural language. On the other hand, where there is a great deal of noise and confusion, where vocalizations are not meant to have communicative function—that is, where one is simply giving evidence to the power of the Holy Spirit—we are justified in being more critical. In other words, once we agree on a definition of glossolalia, we can generally judge on the reliability of what is reported.

[9] Some supporting facts were given above; see also Gerlach and Hine 1970. Yet people continue to ignore contemporary developments. Pentecostalism is still defined as a "religion of oppressed, undereducated, and impoverished social strata, especially when they are socially dislocated during periods of rapid change" (Warburton 1969:138; also Wood 1965:109).

over, there is patent error in saying that glossolalia is like a child's speech; or if it has truth, then it is as true as saying that natural human language is like animal "language." There are *some* similarities; but it is the differences that are crucial, as we shall see in Chapter 5. Another error is to describe glossolalic expression as if it were the release of bottled-up gas. If this were so, then glossolalic speech would always be accompanied by a lot of fizzing and frothing; but it can also occur, as we see in this study, with great serenity.

Explaining glossolalia in terms of emotional deprivation also errs in not distinguishing social from individual psychology, for it is clear that the educative process often—but not always—leads to intense feelings of expectancy or anxiety (Chapter 3). This is why another explanation of glossolalia describes it simply as a feature of hysteria. Because of mental disintegration, there is linguistic disintegration; one is the effect of the other (Oman, p. 48). In other words, in certain intense emotional situations "people are given social sanction to participate in expressing their feelings *in action* rather than *in words,*" as one psychologist put it. But since the extreme symptoms of hysteria are only rarely associated with glossolalia today, he must define hysteria merely as an "intense, emotional, spiritual experience." In this way the emotion is inferred from the incidence of glossolalia and then glossolalia is explained by the inferred emotion.

In Jungian terms glossolalia is froth of a different kind. It is the manifestation of the invasion into one's consciousness of the "collective unconscious," a disorder that reveals a psychical disequilibrium because the contents of the invasion are not fully integrated; the new and old are not in complete focus (Jung, p. 163). But Jung appears to have had little first-hand experience (if any at all) with glossolalia. Kelsey, an Episcopalian rector well-acquainted with the phenomenon, uses Jungian terms to show that man has direct contact with God through this collective psyche, identified in Christian theology, he says, as the "Holy Spirit" (Kelsey, Chapter 7). And Lombard, writing under the influence of early developments in psychology, sees the switch to a new "language" as an effect of a change in personality (p. 149). It is more reasonable, however, to claim (as we will later in this book) that it is the *symbol* of such a change.

If for Kelsey glossolalia manifests a psychic reality, for Laffal, a psychologist, it manifests a psychic construct. Following Freud, who posits a psychic "energy" present in the individual at all times, Laffal suggests that glossalalia is "perhaps the clearest example of the discharge function of language," because it serves to discharge "the psychic energy associated with wishes and conflicts." In other words, glossolalia "brings close to consciousness what the individual cannot put into words" (1965:63). The tongue speaker, then, is giving expression (under hypnosis) to a "strangulated" emotion related to some traumatic experience. But there are differences that are significant. His patients described events in detail whereas glossolalists describe nothing at all; it is not even certain that they have any traumatic experiences which have been suppressed. Vivier, who studied glossolalists from a psychological point of view, would agree: "The factor of repression present in the glossolalics is not the cause of dissociation in the Freudian sense" (p. 435). It is significant that in the Gerlach and Hine investigation "only 16% reported that they were experiencing any sort of crisis just prior to their Spirit Baptism and glossolalic experience, with 84% describing their pre-conversion situation as one of gradual spiritual growth" (Hine 1969:219). If affect or feeling is simply the source of glossolalia, as it is for a vigorous "Bronx cheer," why is it encoded in this and not another way? The reason, I suggest, is that the individual has learned to use this means. However, a good example of "discharge glossolalia" is that of the child who vented his anger at a brother (see below, page 142).

Release is said to be a factor in socio-cultural patterns of behavior. It has been suggested, for example, that glossolalia cannot —or will with very little likelihood—occur in every kind of Christian group. This being so, one would expect to find significant differences between glossolalist and nonglossolalist Christians. This is probably true in some respects, but significant differences have yet to be demonstrated. The present characterizations are far from satisfactory. One of them, for example, sees all Pentecostal groups regardless of their origin and present associations as representative of fundamentalism in contemporary Christianity. This is considered to be a culture that is in open conflict with the established church. For neo-Pentecostalism this would mean a rejection of the "liberal" theology of the main-line churches. In this view glossolalia takes place in a "culture of conflict and struggle," and although the charismatists maintain their membership in the established churches they are, in fact, only nominal or estranged members of these churches. In this context, release would be seen in the opportunity that glossolalists had to express their hostility to Christian organizations or institutions that are uncongenial to these people.

This is an interesting attempt to account for glossolalia, but it too fails, and it fails because it does not square with all the facts. There is plenty of evidence to contradict the statement that conflict is a defining feature of the neo-Pentecostal movement. There is, for example, nothing in all of the hundreds of testimonies I have read or heard, some given in public and some addressed to me personally, that would suggest that people sought the experience because they needed a way to express their dissatisfactions with established religious institutions. This negative conclusion is confirmed by my study of one neo-Pentecostal group in a congregation of a "main-line" Canadian denomination. Fundamentalist is hardly an appropriate term for this particular denomination, congregation, and group of charismatists. It should be added that this "culture conflict" explanation fails also because it ignores the very important movement among Catholics in North America who, far from being fundamentalist or radical, appear to be more faithful to the culture of their church than some other Catholics who have been active in underground movements of one type or another (McDonnell 1970:50).

Regression. This is a psychological notion with verbal analogues —or so it appears to some people. One view would hold that glossolalia is regressive in the sense that it serves as a means of "restoring infantile megalomania" and of expressing feelings of omnipotence or egocentricity and also frustration over unfulfilled desires. It is shared by a clergyman, a seminary professor of psychology, and a social anthropologist (Oman, p. 49; Oates 1967:96; Worsley, p. 247). According to this explanation, what makes glossolalic behavior childish is not that it expresses simple emotions, but that it supposedly takes a childish form. In this view glossolalia is babbling, a return to or survival of childish language (Lombard, 123,126,231f), in fact, a "reverberation of very early days in the history of the race" (Cutten, p. 2)!

This is a linguistic characterization, but it really does not look at the facts. Although glossolalia must certainly have something in common with child language, since it is uttered by a human being who once was a child, it also is like adult language. Perhaps some glossolalic utterances are simpler than others, but all are significantly different from the pre-grammatical stage of child language. In fact, it is impossible for a person to talk as he did when he was six months or a year old. An adult, for one thing, knows that /p/ and /b/, /a/ and /o/ are functionally different: that, in other words, it makes a difference how one says the first sounds in English words like *pit* and *bit*. But when a child babbles, he says something like *pipi bipi bibibi,* rambling in a random way, sometimes using other labial sounds, roughly equivalent to /f/, /w/, and others that would require phonetic diacritics that would only complicate the discussion here. So when an adult "reverts" to a childish behavior, he can only caricature it in baby talk.[10]

If regression is to be used at all in describing glossolalia, one needs to be somewhat more disciplined than some people have been. For example, glossolalia can be called regressive because the most common sounds of any speaker appear to be the ones that are learned earliest by a child. Thus, although the sound represented by "th" in *the* is rather common in English, at least by frequency of occurrence, it is learned after /t/ and /d/. It is significant, therefore, that this fricative sound is not common in glossolalia of people for whom English is the first language. It is possible, of course, that there is some kind of avoidance of this sound precisely because it is characteristic of the English language. (More is said in Chapter 4 on this topic.)

Summary

Almost a century of psychological discussion of anomalous speech, like glossolalia, has been reviewed in the preceding pages. The attempt to explain glossolalia psychologically is not an impressive one. For one thing, prejudice has prevented many observ-

---

[10] A clear case of the association of baby talk with personality disturbances is that which is reported by anthropologists Henry and Henry about Pilagá Indians. Among these people, orphans are mistreated so badly that they either retreat to using baby talk or, in the most severe cases, to autism. One of the unusual features of this behavior is that baby talk may persist until the child's ninth year. Baby talk, it should be noted, is recognized by linguists as a more-or-less patterned deviation from adult speech and not just gibberish.

ers from seeing all that they should have seen. The bias is not entirely antireligious, because some of the harshest critics have been people within the Christian tradition. It may be due in part to a rational tradition in the west that looks with disfavor on emotionalism in religion where rationality and decorum are valued. Or is it simply because to the outsider glossolalia just makes no sense? And he cannot understand why anyone would want to make "non-sense."

If it is not clear from statements I have quoted that prejudice sours the words of many a writer, it should be documented from the study of Gerrard, a sociologist with many years of experience in the Appalachians (Gerrard 1968; also Tellegen, et al. 1969). Using the Minnesota Multi-Phasic Inventory (MMPI), he sought to compare the mental health of a group of glossolalist, snake-handling sectarians with a group from a "conventional" church in West Virginia. When three clinicians studied the responses, which were only labeled as belonging to Church A and Church B, they found that both groups were within the "normal limits." If there was any difference, in fact, the responses of the conventional group, as a whole, showed a little more neuroticism. But when the profiles were given to three other clinicians for interpretation, with the information that some of the subjects (not which ones) were Southern snake handlers, these analysts assigned most of the "normal" ones to the conventional church and the "abnormal" ones to the snake-handling sect. Clearly, then, these psychologists started with the bias that the snake handlers were abnormal. Others have found the same kind of bias among specialists who treat the abnormal (for example, Hine 1969:217).

People have also tried to account for phenomena that should not have been combined, seeing similarities when these were only superficial. All meaningless speech is not the same, even when the nonlinguistic behavior appears the same. And speech which appears the same can be associated with very different kinds of behavior.

It is crucial, therefore, that there be a clear understanding of what glossolalia is. Without it there can never be an answer to the question, "Why do people speak in tongues?" This is why we now leave this question to devote several chapters to a description of the nature and use of glossolalia, the unique contribution of this book.

3

ACQUIRED "SUPERNATURALLY"

LEARNING TO TALK in tongues is very different from learning to talk a natural language. It is not exactly like learning to talk for the first time, as a child, nor is it like learning to speak a second language later on.

Adults learn second languages principally for utilitarian reasons. Business, politics, tourism, and many other spheres of behavior provide motivation for acquiring either a smattering of, say, German, or complete fluency in it. No such practical goals motivate a person to seek the gift of tongues. Being fully aware of the unintelligibility of tongues, he cannot hope to use his glossa (or glossolalic "language") in any way familiar to him as a normal speaker of language although he almost certainly believes that tongues could be used intelligibly if God so willed. But this is never the explicit reason for wanting to speak in tongues—one of my questions dealt with this point—and it cannot be deduced from anything I have ever read or heard. (For a discussion of messages and interpretation, see Chapter 7.) The candidate may also be aware of certain social functions, discussed in Chapter 11, and it would be a mistake to deny they have an attraction for some people. Initially, however, what a person wants is the total experience of which glossolalia is a part.

Recruiting and Motivation

As glossolalists sometimes facetiously say, "A person doesn't buy tongues by themselves; they come with the shoes." Most of them therefore insist that tongues are only the consequence of being filled with the Spirit. One articulate respondent to my questionnaire deserves to be quoted at length:

In stubbing my toe, I yelled "Ouch!" Which was the experience—the "Ouch" I yelled or was it the actual encounter of my toe with some object? If I had not yelled "Ouch," would the encounter be any less real?

She then goes on to give her motive for wanting the baptism:

I had a great hunger placed in my heart for the baptism in the Holy Spirit. I could see so many places in my life that were not really controlled by Him. . . . I wanted the Holy Spirit to become the motivating force in my life. . . . The baptism in the Holy Spirit really is not complicated. On my part it was just a surrender of my will and accepting Him. The actual experience was a pouring out or a drenching in the love of Jesus—where I was able to actually respond and love Him with all my heart, soul and mind. "Tongues," present or absent, had nothing to do with this.

There are others for whom glossolalia is not simply a consequence, inevitable or not, of the baptism, but an evidence of this baptism, because it is a physical manifestation of an otherwise unseen event. It is, they say, like knowing from light that the electric current has been turned on. This, as we have seen, is part of the traditional Pentecostal creed.

It cannot be denied, however, that there are some people for whom glossolalia is attractive in itself. This is clear from statements like "I suppose people recommended it so highly that I was made to feel a little incomplete without it." Among the less educated, according to some reports, glossolalia is believed to make a person strong and to keep him from "backsliding." But one of my own college-educated respondents, a person with almost a lifetime's experience in the Protestant church, wanted to speak in tongues, she says, "so I could pray for our son who was ill with cancer. And there were so many others I wished to pray for in a better way."

This failure to clearly and consistently distinguish between the two experiences—the baptism and speaking in tongues—and their benefits is, in fact, rather common. It is found among Pentecostal leaders (for example, J. A. Cross, one-time Chairman of the Pentecostal Fellowship of North America, in W. Horton, ed.; and Oral Roberts, p. 43) and among laymen. Take such statements as the following:

During the two and a half years in which I was a seeker, I had been "encouraged" in many ways, from threats of missing the rapture of the saints [referring to the bodily ascension of Christians into heaven] to exhortations of the blessing and power it [that is, glossolalia] would bring.

As I sought for the baptism, I had numerous people tell me [to] do this or do that in order to receive the Holy Spirit and the gift of tongues. In thinking back over this period of my life, I realize I was seeking the evidence [that is, glossolalia] much more than I was seeking the gift of the Holy Spirit.

Notwithstanding some playing-down of glossolalia as independently important, people do not succeed in entirely depriving glossolalia of its own functions. Thus, the woman who was quoted as insisting on the consequential nature of glossolalia answered the question "Did you want to speak in tongues?" with the following: "I desired this if God wanted me to. Also I desired this if it would enable me to enter into real worship and praise from my heart. I have felt for years the inner sense that I could never truly express the worship which I wanted to." What she is saying is that she was willing to speak in tongues if (1) there was Biblical authority for it and if (2) it would contribute to her personal religious life. Becoming convinced in these two points is precisely what makes glossolalists of people.

Obedience to Scripture is a strong motive for seeking the charisma among people for whom the Bible is absolute authority in all religious matters. It is understandable, therefore, that charismatists seek to prove to others by their explanation of the Bible that they must or ought to have the experience. Most of this is done orally, in person-to-person contacts, or in small or large meetings. This is clear from statements such as the following: "I accepted speaking in tongues when I was fully persuaded that this practice is taught in the Bible" (from a middle-aged Presbyterian minister who on one occasion traveled eight hundred miles to attend a special class held in New York City!).

In traditional Pentecostal churches there is, of course, more or less regular teaching on the subject, and special meetings ("revival meetings") are set up where people can get the baptism. But one minister of the Pentecostal Holiness Church, considered by some to be the "Presbyterians of Pentecostalism" because of their less emotional approach to religion, told me that sanctification, as he called it, came up only periodically as a subject for special emphasis. In non-Pentecostal churches with upper middle-class congregations (for example, a Presbyterian church in New England) special "lectures" or "courses" on pneumatology may be given, sometimes discreetly announced in the church news sheet. (The use of the word pneumatology is class-linked. For this term, based on the Greek word which has as one of its meanings "spirit," Pentecostalists would simply say "the doctrine of the Holy Spirit.")

The way in which motives are expressed is determined by the extent to which Biblical teaching and Biblical language are used in conceptualizing religious experience. There are, on the one hand (and at one extreme), the Biblical literalists who seek to justify every assertion with proof-texts. One such person is a Texas evangelist, at one time a member of the Assemblies of God, who described his baptism in these words: "I received the laying on of hands (*as Paul practiced*) and immediately began speaking in tongues *as in Acts 19:6*" (emphasis added). On the other hand, there are people for whom only an "existential rightness" validates the charismatic experience. For example, there is a minister about fifty years old, educated (having a B.D.) and honored (with a D.D.) in his American Baptist denomination, who rejects what he calls revelational (that is, scriptural), ecclesiastical, and even experiential authoritarianism. For him "there is another system of communication beside that of sensory perceptions and reasoning upon them"; it is "a whole communications system which was commonly known before the Aristotelianization of the West" by which one can know "the realm of the irrational or the parasensory." This personalistic approach to religion, here very clear and well articulated, is however, apparent among many of my better-educated or (as far as I can tell) more individualistic respondents. They write about their experience with an emphasis on the personal, for example, "for me."

The importance and function of published material in the charismatic movement is variable. Among some people written material may be more convincing than the individuals with whom they are in personal contact. Among others the function of charismatic literature may be to reinforce immature beliefs. How much reading is done, by whom, and of what nature are matters that were not covered in my questionnaire, but some of my respondents indicated how influential had been John L. Sherrill's journalistic *They Speak with Other Tongues* and J. E. Stiles' pedagogic *The Gift of the Holy Spirit.* The psychologist L. B. Brown reports (1966) that of the twenty-five glossolalists he studied, there was none who had not read books on the subject. One of my respondents (the secret glossolalist referred to in Chapter 1) seems to have learned about the charismatic experience only from the printed page. This is how she came to speak in tongues:

I read an article in the [newspaper] telling about five United Church of Canada ministers who had had this experience. The way they spoke of it made me want it so much I cried. I began to read everything about it I could find and read and reread my New Testament. . . . The fact that these five ministers had experienced this, were willing to tell about it, thus risking their jobs, had a profound influence on me.

A more comprehensive report on the influence of Pentecostal literature comes from the research of L. Gerlach and associates (see Gerlach and Hine 1968 and 1970; Hine 1969). Using a questionnaire, they asked 239 Pentecostalists to rank in importance the factors that influenced them to seek the baptism experience and tongues. These factors were: an individual who talked to me about it privately, attending a small group meeting, attending services of a Pentecostal church, attending a large revival meeting, mass media, reading literature or tracts, parent's example or teachings, seeing the change in someone else's life, no influence at all, other. For the whole sample, literature ranked sixth in importance. It ranked sixth also for members of the established Pentecostal groups. For large independent churches involved in the charismatic movement it ranked seventh. For small groups of neo-Pentecostals who had started their own churches, it ranked fourth. But it is highest—second—among neo-Pentecostals scattered about in non-Pentecostal churches (for example, Episcopal, Lutheran, and Catholic). And in this last group what outranks the importance of literature is contact with an individual already in the movement.[1]

For some people, speaking in tongues is a condition for being baptized in the Holy Spirit. One of my respondents wrote that speaking in tongues was one of the requirements that God had given him. (He underlined the word "requirements.") Another person wrote that he had been seeking the baptism for about six months, but that he wanted it without tongues. "At that moment," he writes, "the Lord showed me how important it was *for me* to speak in tongues." The reason is explained elsewhere: "Because *for me* it was the 'last outpost' of self holding back from surrender." Both of these men disregard a scriptural authoritarian motivation for a personal psychological one: being willing to speak nonsense had for them become the last or most formidable hurdle. The willingness of another man, a Presbyterian minister, to do anything he could to get the blessing was indicated by lying on the floor. (This may have been, we imagine, a sign of self-humiliation for him.)

There are people, of course, for whom glossolalia is no obstacle at all. They are so impressed by the language-likeness of what they hear that they are convinced a person is miraculously speaking a language he does not know. Witnessing the supernatural dispels their doubts. Here is the testimonial of a civil engineer:

The service began as usual with a stirring song service. Then suddenly a real quiet came over that congregation and someone began to speak in another language, and after a short pause someone else began to speak some very wonderful words in English. It was most beautiful to hear. The pastor explained that this was the manifestation of tongues and interpretation spoken of in [the Bible].

For the first time in my life I had witnessed the supernatural in a church! I was 33 years old and had never heard anything said in any church about tongues or about the supernatural, although I had read of wonderful miracles in the Bible. In fact, one thing that made me doubt Christianity was that I had never seen such miracles performed today.

[1] This information is from V. H. Hine (personal communication).

In the midst of a group that was ridiculed and criticized by many, I saw the first manifestation of the supernatural! The apostle Paul says that tongues are for the unbeliever (1 Cor. 14:22). I must testify to that. I was an unbeliever and it was a tremendous witness to me! "This is what I want," I told myself, "I want to experience God" (*Voice,* May 1969, p. 25).

Prerequisites

Since speaking in tongues is a religious experience, its acquisition is thoroughly discussed in theological terms. But since there are so many different statements, among both Pentecostalist leaders and laymen, it will not be possible to give a careful synthesis here. Some of the issues, however, are: Does a person have to be a converted Christian before getting the baptism? Or, being a Christian, does he have to attain a certain degree of spirituality first? Can tongues come before the baptism? The traditional—or one traditional—Pentecostalist position is that sanctification, that is, personal holiness, must precede. If not, one preacher informed me, "tragic results might follow." Stiles, among other less dogmatic Pentecostalists, rejects this view (pp. 74ff). Similarly, Gee, dealing with the same problem, suggests (his own term) only three actions or attitudes: surrender, prayer, and faith (pp. 78–79). It is worth observing that these are all psychological in nature, comprehended by the word most often used as a prerequisite for acquiring both the baptism and glossolalia—*yield.* However, these leaders are addressing themselves to a Christian audience. Neo-Pentecostalists are less fussy about how a person comes into the experience, for it is, after all, a "gift of God."

Instruction

As human beings from childhood adopt the ways of their culture and learn to interact with others, they must learn to use the very complex verbal codes that are spoken around them. Put simply, every normal developing child must learn to make sense, and normal language is expected of him.

With such strong emphasis placed universally on the functional and cultural value of making sense, it takes strong motivations indeed for one to talk what society considers non-sense. We have looked at some of them in the last section. But being delivered from tradition and inhibitions is only the beginning. Once a person has decided to "blow it," what does he do next? If it is a language that he is going to speak, where does he learn it? What are going to be its consonants and vowels, its grammar and vocabulary? Is he to remain completely in the dark about these? In the Bible he will find no help. Nowhere is there a sample of glossolalia on which a person could pattern his own utterances. Nor is there advice on what one must do to begin. Indeed, there cannot be, glossolalists would say, because glossas are given by God as a special gift.

Instruction, of course, is not necessary. There are many people who seem to have "discovered" glossolalia on their own, that is, without having heard it from others. One of my respondents, for example, is a well-educated Dutch woman who, following a serious illness, began to have dreams and visions, to experience the "presence of Jesus," and to utter words whose phonetic shape she says was very different from her native language. Being a member of the Netherlands Reformed Church, she had had no contact with Pentecostalism; only years later, when she identified herself with the charismatic movement, did she improve this incipient glossolalia.

Another case was personally investigated. Among a group of intimate friends, all young married people who had become interested in occult and parapsychological phenomena through more or less systematic reading, there took place one day an utterance that was unintelligible to everyone present. The speaker had been in trance and could not account for what she said or why she spoke in this manner. I was called upon finally to try to identify this language and help to interpret the message. This is fundamentally the same kind of glossolalia one finds in Pentecostalist circles (a sample of which is found on page 255), and "cross-examination" supported the speaker's claim that she had not heard anything similar in her life. This is not surprising after one has understood the simplicity of glossolalia as a linguistic phenomenon and its occurrence in so many different forms (as noted in Chapter 6). Other "incontestable cases" are reported by Hine (1969:220); see also Kelsey (pp. 13,14,163) and Samarin (1969a).

These cases of spontaneous glossolalia, however, are probably rare. More often than not the seeker receives a great deal of guidance and instruction. Much of it actually contributes nothing to the acquisition of the skill, at least in its linguistic aspects, but it must be described, because the charismatic movement cannot be understood without an understanding of its folk linguistics.

The most common advice given to seekers appears to be "speak whatever comes to you," or words to that effect. This counsel is meant to reduce inhibitions; it assumes that the seeker is going to have an impulse to produce an utterance that is meaningless to him. The seeker already has been taught that these utterances are God-given, regardless of how they may sound (for example, Christenson, p. 15). In some people short utterances arise in conscious thought and are repeated internally before they are uttered. Once this has happened, some people at least are on their way to talking in tongues; for others there is much more to do. More will be said later about these initial utterances.

Some people are advised to "make sounds"—that, in fact, any sounds will do for a beginning. It is not uncommon, however, for the "teacher" to make some allusion to child speech. One of my respondents was told to "just begin to praise God in sounds and syllables that were not English, as you might make loving sounds to a baby." At one "baptismal session" of the Full Gospel Businessmen's Fellowship (described below, pages 58ff) the leader told the candidates about another seeker who was afraid that when she began to speak in tongues she would "talk funny" as she used to do when she was a girl playing with her dolls. He said that in childhood one pretended to talk a language; now, in the Spirit, it is real.

There are even cases where seekers are given some kinds of utterances, perhaps only a few syllables, to repeat after the leader, in one case, as given on a phonograph recording. It was also reported to me personally that in a meeting of a Dutch Pentecostal sect the minister prayed for two people without their responding in glossolalic prayers. Coming to the third person, he very softly uttered some meaningless syllables, whereupon the seeker broke out in "tongues." After the congregation had rejoiced at this success with "Halleluiahs" the minister said, *"Ik heb het niet voorgezegd, niet?"* ("I didn't say it first, did I?"). One of my own respondents wrote that she began to speak in tongues after having been instructed in the procedure ("to try to imitate the sounds they were making") and having "hands laid" on her (which is discussed below). This happened in the pastor's living room, with her own father, the pastor, and the pastor's wife praying for her. However, such mechanical procedures are condemned by charismatists like R. H. Hughes, a leader of the Church of God, Cleveland, Tennessee (in W. Horton, ed., p. 171).

Repetition leads some people from a brief meaningless utterance to really productive glossolalia. It is not surprising, therefore, that seekers should be taught to use repetition consciously. For example, "If you have a strange word form in your mind, then say it. . . . You will feel like dismissing the word and have many doubts, but keep speaking the 'words' in your mind." The same kind of advice seems to have been given by the Mormon leader Joseph Smith to his followers: "Arise upon your feet, speak or make some sound, continue to make sounds of some kind, and the Lord will make a tongue or language of it" (Cutten, p. 71, from J. H. Kennedy, *Early Days of Mormonism*).

Meaningful words, on the other hand, are also repeated. One of my respondents reported that a man in her group could only say *El Shaddai* (one of the Biblical names for God) for many months before he could speak fluently. (Apparently there was acceptance of this utterance as glossolalia although it does not fit my linguistic characterization of this phenomenon.) People have been advised, therefore, to "praise Jesus" (or some such phrase) and God would change their language. This is not difficult to comprehend when one has witnessed, as I have, Pentecostals repeating "Halleluiah" or "Jesus" with the greatest of emotion for a long time. (Observed also by Fauset, p. 111, at the Mt. Sinai Holiness Church; and Kelsey, p. 44, who mentions the use of the "Jesus prayer" in Russian Orthodox devotional practice.) Anything repeated at length may lose its meaning and become pure phonation, as the reader can demonstrate for himself.

There are many other kinds of instructions that are given to the seekers of the baptism, stated either as helps or conditions to realizing the experience. For example, at the Biblical Research Center (The Way, Inc.) directed by J. P. Wierwille, the very "mechanics of speaking [in tongues] (as we do in English)" is taught. So reports one of my respondents, an "alumna" of this institution.

Keeping one's hands lifted seems to be (or to have been) one of the traditional Pentecostal practices. Several of my respondents refer to instructions about how one was to hold his mouth and breathe. J. E. Stiles may have been the propagator of this form of inducement. He writes:

Recently I have discovered, through observation of a number of people, that those people who will open their mouths up wide will break forth speaking with tongues more clearly and easily than those who do not. Opening the mouth and breathing in constitutes a step of faith that God will honor (Stiles, p. 120; compare Wierwille, p. 59).[2]

Earlier practices of his own, practices that were quite common in his day, are ridiculed by Stiles in the following words:

I would say to [the candidate], "Now, brother, kneel down there. Lift up your hands and start praising the Lord." . . . But, I did not stop in my attempted help at this point. I could see that the Spirit was moving upon him, and I wanted to help him push over the hurdle, so quite probably I would shout, "Hold on, brother, hold on." One of my good assistants would say, "Now, just yield, brother, yield." While still another would insist, "Let go, brother, let go, let go." . . . I have had dozens of them tell me that they became so confused by all of this shouting and contrary instructions, and so discouraged through trying time after time, and always having the same results, that they finally gave up altogether and quit seeking the Holy Spirit entirely (p. 118).

Another Pentecostalist, with less humor, says that "A pack of jackals over their prey could hardly act more fiercely" than the "midwives" on these occasions of "spiritual child birth" (Bartleman, p. 47).

Although Stiles avows a change in the way he has instructed candidates, indicative of significant changes within the Pentecostal movement, his teachings are not entirely palatable to some seekers of the baptism. In fact, an understanding of the instruction that

[2] Since abnormal breathing patterns are known to affect body chemistry to a point where trance-like symptoms are induced, one might find in this practice evidence that glossolalia is a product of dissociative states. Indeed, I did observe that the possession of a Jamaican woman at a pocomania service was preceded by violent dancing and breathing (described more fully on page 11). However, there is no evidence that this is the kind of behavior that is prescribed in these Pentecostal meetings or, in fact, that ordinary deep breathing is usually followed by trance and tongues. One suspects that this advice was about as useful as a doctor's "Go to bed and drink lots of water."

they get must be complemented by an appreciation of how they respond to it. That many people do not become glossolalists is self-evident. It is more important to note that people do become glossolalists in spite of their initial reaction (disagreement, distaste, revulsion) to the teaching. Quite clearly many of these people are alert and critical students. They do not come completely open-minded and empty-headed to their teachers. They come with their own canons of judgment and interpretation, their own desires and inhibitions. In the end, the experience is molded to meet their needs.

It would seem, then, that there is very little about speaking in tongues that most seekers are really taught. This is indicated by their own testimonies and the very nature of the instruction they get. Beginning to speak in tongues is largely a jump into the dark.

Psychological States

What makes the acquisition of glossolalia a leap into the dark is ignorance—real or imagined—of exactly what is going to happen. It would seem that most people have little idea indeed of what their first utterances in glossolalia will sound like. There are some who never heard glossolalia before, as we have already seen, or heard it only very recently, sometimes just a few minutes before. Even when people have been exposed to it on several occasions, we cannot expect everyone to have acquired good impressions of what was happening linguistically. Initial impressions about glossolalia are generally quite superficial and extremely varied.

It is no wonder, therefore, that seekers approach the experience in various frames of mind: uncertainty, anxiety, fear, expectancy, pleasure, and so forth. The variety is the result of what the person has been taught about the experience, what his response has been, and the setting for the experience.

The most common state of mind is expectancy. This is natural, of course, in people who earnestly want something to happen and believe that it will happen. But it is important to note how this expectancy is nurtured (as in the teaching of "faith healer" Oral Roberts, pp. 5–7) and how it becomes as much a part of the situation as the physical environment. This is why one of my respondents described the setting for his first experience as having an "expectant atmosphere," as if it were palpable, a force that would descend on him.

This "atmosphere" issues from the nonverbal and verbal behavior of the participants in a situation. Like the audience at a dramatic performance, there are things one does and does not do before the curtain is drawn. In neo-Pentecostal groups, where glossolalia is acquired very often in small meetings, there may be a great use of silence and hushed speaking. But in other groups the denouement may be more flamboyantly announced. In some cases there is a parallel in the way a religious leader acts and the way a master of ceremonies introduces the next star at a variety show. In both cases the message is the same: "Great things are going to happen."

What has just been said is but a weak description of an experience that deserves more space. For a clearer picture to emerge one would also have to be freer of scientific rhetoric than one is inclined to be in a book of this kind. A novelist would do a better job than I. It must suffice to insist that I am not making too much of the expression "atmosphere" nor do I uncritically accept the rhetoric that glossolalists use to describe the psychological aspects of participation in religious meetings. Personal observation convinces me, however, that the rhetoric used to describe ecstasy is sometimes appropriate in these circumstances, although ecstasy, as rigorously defined, is not what they always experience. In other circumstances, of course, there are more reasons to admit the possibility of ecstasy. We will come back to this topic in Chapter 10.

In religious meetings of the more active kind, language plays an important part in developing expectancy. At the meeting described above (page 37) the sermon was only one part of a three-and-a-half-hour service that was meant to culminate in the experience of the baptism. The choice of the Biblical text itself permitted the development of expectancy: "If any one thirst," Jesus said, "let him come to me and drink" (John 7:37, RSV). The pastor was explicit in saying things like, "I know that many of you are expectant"; "My greatest desire is to see the Spirit of God work in our midst tonight"; "Will you let [God] manifest himself in you tonight?" "Open up and enjoy yourself this evening"; "Let the Spirit do what he wants"; "Be pliable clay." He used verbs like "knock," "seek," "ask," and "wrestle." (The last verb implies importunity, as noted above, and invokes the image of Jacob wrestling with a "man" all night long at the place he named Peniel, because he saw God "face to face," Genesis 32:22–32.) With this much invested in expectancy, there were bound to be some returns.

In a group, expectancy can be narrowed down to a point in time and focused on a single individual. As in other experiences where physical contact seems to be the trigger for important effects, acute expectancy is fostered by "the laying on of hands." Although manual contact for religious purposes is not restricted to the Christian religion, here it definitely has its precedent in the Bible. For example: "Then they laid their hands on them and they received the Holy Spirit" (Acts 8:17, RSV). In charismatic circles this act apparently never functions as the means to transmit a spiritual gift from one person to another. It is generally believed to be nothing more—although some behavior suggests more—than a sign of special concern for the individual. Thus in some groups the seeker may sit on a chair in the middle of a room while everyone within reach touches him, preferably on the head.

Whereas the custom of laying on of hands has not been dogmatized in Pentecostal doctrine, it is quite clear from actual practice that it is not taken lightly.[3] It is performed more by the clergy than the laity, and among the latter there are some who consider themselves, or are considered by their group, to have more right to do this (perhaps by being spiritually gifted) than others. Even at the Pentecostal service referred to above, the pastor invited members of the congregation to come to lay hands on the seekers, but only if they felt "led" to (that is, led by God). There were only a few such acts in this meeting, all by men old enough to have some stature in the church. Women charismatists also perform this act, and it is used also in healing, exorcising, and in special prayer.

Up to this point expectancy has been described only in positive terms, but it is not pure delight. Some people feel very embarrassed at the prospect of speaking in tongues, because it sounds silly to them. Some even experience fear that they will not be able to con-

[3] Compare the report about the FGBMFI meeting where "About twenty ministers requested the ministry of laying on of hands for the Baptism in the Holy Spirit" (*Voice*, January/February, 1969, p. 29) and the statement by Charles W. Conn that "The laying on of hands is significant as a token of confirmation, of encouragement or blessing, but not as a means of dispensing any grace" (in W. Horton, ed., p. 52). Both statements issue from traditional Pentecostalism.

trol their speech or themselves and will do "some strange thing."
The detractors of glossolalia encourage this fear, going so far as to
suggest that a person may come under the influence of the Devil
and blaspheme God. One glossolalist told me that his first utterance in tongues was /kada nagoma/.[4] When he asked an African if
he knew these words, the reply was that they reminded him of the
word for "evil spirit" or "Devil" in another African language somewhat familiar to him. In telling me this, the glossolalist ended by
saying, "It kinda shakes you up, doesn't it?"

Social Setting

Understanding the phenomenon of glossolalia has been seriously
hindered by associating it almost exclusively with the public meetings (church services or revivals) of traditional Pentecostalists.
These meetings, however, have never been associated with all the
glossolalic activity that people experienced; and this is more so
today than ever before. There is a wide variety of situations in
which people have uttered their first glossolalic utterances.

The following is a sample of a new type of public meeting:

This was a public baptism session supervised by a charismatist leader
of international renown. It was held at a regional week-end conference of the Full Gospel Business Men's Fellowship in a hotel in one of
America's largest cities. There were over a thousand people in attendance. The baptism session itself was held in the afternoon, following a
plenary session at which those who were seeking the baptism in the
Spirit were invited to go to an adjoining room. This was filled with over
200 people; all the seats were occupied and people stood along the
walls. Outside the room there was a noisy, milling crowd like that at
any large hotel conference.

Only a small proportion of the audience consisted of candidates (as
they were called). The clergyman asked them to occupy the front rows;
three rows were filled.

There was very little structure to the meeting, the whole of which

---

[4] Material within diagonals is in rough phonetic transcription. The
letters are used as in English, or in pronouncing dictionaries, with the exception that "r" has the value of standard Italian and the vowels of *beet,
boot, bait, boat, body, bit, bush, bet, bought, sofa,* and *bat* are represented
as/bit, but, bet, bot, bari, bĭt, bŭsh, bĕt, bŏt, sofă, and bât/. Acute accent
indicates a stressed syllable.

was supervised by the one clergyman. Throughout the meeting he kept up an almost uninterrupted stream of speech that went from one topic to another in a very fluid manner. Most of what he said was directed to the entire audience. He started by forbidding anybody but the candidates to speak out in tongues. This exhortation was accompanied by general instruction on the use of tongues in public. Then he addressed the candidates. He said that he was going to pray for them, not that they would speak in tongues, but that they would be filled with the Spirit. Here came a considerable amount of guidance that pertained to speaking in tongues. He then prayed, first in English, then in tongues. At this point people throughout the room began to pray audibly (presumably for the candidates), and the leader went up and down the rows praying for and encouraging each candidate. He then addressed the whole audience again, saying "And now I say the river is yours. Swimming time," thus permitting an outburst of glossolalia from the audience. This was finally cut off by "Let's be quiet now." The final part of the session was devoted again to general exhortations about the use of tongues.

In the clergyman's guidance to the candidates we find the following kinds of remarks. He wants them to be "absolutely relaxed," so he asks them to put down pocketbooks and other things that might bother them. He asks them to close their eyes and "Just begin to talk. Just lift up your heads and talk to Jesus standing right here listening to you. . . . Don't talk English. Stop praying. Stop begging. Stop pleading." He tells them, "Let your tongue flip. . . . Your tongue will be taken over by the Spirit." He warns them that their speech will sound funny and childish, but that "Unless you become like a child, you can't enter the kingdom." He anticipates that some will stammer and stutter. This, he tells them, is because they will be speaking too fast. They should slow down and say the syllables "one by one." He tells them that they may feel a trembling of the body. This is the Holy Spirit nudging them, saying, "If you speak, I'll give you a language." Nor was it necessary to raise one's arms. Then, somewhat facetiously, "There's no Scripture to say He wants to shake hands with you."

After the prayer for the candidates, when the leader addressed himself to each of them, his behavior resembled that of a rooter, like someone, for example, who paces along the swimming pool cheering a swimmer on in a race. Here are some of the things he said: "You cannot talk in tongues when you're talking in English. You're still begging. You must stop using English"; "Come on now. Speak out"; "There you are. He's talking. Keep talking. Say it again. Come on. Halleluiah. He's praying a new language!" "There you are. That's the

Holy Spirit"; "It isn't you making up the words. Your mind says you are, but you can't do it"; "That's right, Sister. Keep talking"; "You start off, and He gives the language as soon as you begin. The beginning is all you do."

It should be observed that nothing has been said about the use of music or chanting, because in this meeting there was no attempt to build up the emotions of the candidates. One could, of course, argue that the whole conference—and certainly the meeting that preceded this session—might constitute the emotional build-up. Nevertheless, this particular leader, very responsive to criticisms laid against traditional Pentecostalism and active in the ecumenical movement, publicly denounces the artificial inducement of an event that he insists comes only from God. Regardless of how social scientists might view this whole event, it must be admitted that there are important departures from old-style Pentecostalism.

There are, of course, many different kinds of public meetings. At Pentecostal "tarrying services" there need be no attention given to an individual since the whole group is verbalizing at the same time. Group meetings seem to be part of the technique used at The Way, Inc. (already referred to). In writing of her experience there, one respondent said, "This was a receivers' meeting in which everyone spoke out loud at once to encourage those who were being led into speaking in tongues. Speaking all at one time aloud is only used when receiving and at the will and discretion of the leader." In smaller meetings, the attention of the group may focus on a single individual, and the first utterances might follow the prayers or might be delayed until somewhat later in the meeting.

Included among small meetings, or constituting a special kind, are encounters between just two individuals: one of these persons has already had the experience, and the other is a seeker. At some point, perhaps after Bible study or discussion, at one's suggestion or the other's request, there is prayer that the seeker will receive the baptism. Such intimate meetings are especially common, from all reports, in the neo-Pentecostal movement, and they take place in a great variety of places: hotel lobbies, restaurants, and, in one case, even on board an airplane. At testimony meetings members of the movement seem to take great pleasure in hearing the novelty of such experiences.

Sometimes the delay in producing glossolalia for the first time is one of hours or weeks, and the person may find himself alone or in a public but secular environment. Thus, people break into tongues driving home from a meeting, at private prayer, or while they are about some menial chore. The account of a middle-aged Congregationalist housewife is instructive in many ways:

On . . . I received a real baptism. Two weeks prior to that I said four words at the close of a prayer, while alone in my home. They sounded so foolish to me that I was ashamed and did not mention it to anyone. [In the following incident] I did say these four words out loud and then received [the infilling of the Holy Spirit dated above]. . . . I was making my 9-year-old son's bed. He had been injured a year before in an accident, [and had] broken back and neck. Through prayer, and good medical care, he was out of the hospital in 21 days and back to school that fall. It was a year to the day that I made the bed and realized I'd never thanked our Father for this blessing. I started to pray and suddenly I was speaking in tongues.

Another far-from-religious setting for the acquisition of tongues was reported by one respondent. He said that he was "completely relaxed" in his favorite place for relaxing—in his bathtub!

The frequency of such solitary experiences of the Spirit baptism with tongues is certainly higher than people have imagined, evidenced by my own study and that of Gerlach and Hine. Of their 239 interviewees, 23 per cent reported it (Hine 1969:218).

Being relaxed is certainly no necessary condition for acquiring glossolalia, but it should be observed that many people report that their first experience with tongues was in a semi-wakeful state or even in sleep. In the latter case they awakened to find themselves talking in tongues or to have their spouse tell them they were. Of course, we have no way of determining the linguistic nature of these first utterances.

It should be noted that incipient glossolalia always seems to be associated with praise to God. (As will be seen in Chapters 7 and 8, there are several other functions, and practiced glossolalists may be versatile in their uses. The development is recognized by many of my respondents.) The setting appears to be irrelevant. One man reports that he first experienced tongues after he had delivered a message and just when the "altar service" had begun: "I began to praise [God] in a language I had never learned"

(*Voice,* March 1968, p. 14). He could know that he was praising God, of course, only by the way he felt.

Acquiring Glossolalia

The initial experience of speaking in tongues comes in many forms. One is immediate and fluent. The following is typical of such an experience. It is described by a well-educated Lutheran minister, fifty years of age, writing of what had happened four years before: "I was praying alone in my church. Something seemed to say, 'The gift is yours; reach out and take it.' I stretched my hands out toward the altar (while kneeling) and suddenly be' gan to pray in tongues."

It is the immediacy of the experience that so often is emphasized in these reports. While there is no reason to doubt this, understanding the relative ease with which a pseudolanguage can be produced, the rhetoric of these reports suggests that glossolalists attribute considerable value to this kind of baptism.

Others acquire glossolalia gradually and in different ways, apparently independently of the kinds of inducements described above in spite of the obvious similarities.

There are those who experience an unconscious switch from their normal language (say, English) to glossolalia. Here are two such reports, the first from a 67-year-old "retired Wall Street executive" (about what happened six years earlier), the second from the wife of a Methodist minister:

Three days previously I had asked Jesus to baptize me in the Holy Spirit out loud by myself. Nothing appeared to happen. But on this night I was completely relaxed in my favorite place to relax and was quietly praying and praising God in English when suddenly I realized I was not speaking English anymore, but a language unknown to me.

Two hours following my personal baptism in the Holy Spirit, I was alone in my bedroom. I was so overflowing with His love, I began to thank and praise Him. To my—almost shock—surprise I suddenly realized I was not praying in my native language.

These people seem to have been speaking in English when the switch occurred, but in the case of another person it happened while "singing [God's] praises" as he was driving home from a communion service. This was about three months after "hands" had been laid on him.

It would be of considerable value to know exactly how the switch occurred in all these instances. Was there an abrupt end to English when glossolalia was turned on? Or did non-English (that is, meaningless) bits first mix in with the English? The latter would be quite easy in singing, for it is common (if not universal) for people sometimes to use nonsense syllables like *ladada didi* to carry a tune. Some of my respondents, in fact, report that they sang before speaking in tongues.

In some people glossolalia appears first as a form of "inner speech." That is, meaningless bits of speech are conceived in thought. A Church of God minister remembers, for example, that his "initial language sounds" came as "sounds to the mind" before they were "deliberately spoken out." They were, in his spelling, *kum, te, la, lalasa, έ*. (The use of the letter ε derives from his having studied Greek; there is no way of knowing what the accent mark over it signified. The use of commas, by indicating pause, may mean that the "words" came as independent units rather than in this whole phrase.)

In the experience of a young practical nurse, a glossolalist of only a few months at the time of writing, inner speech was used as a means to improve her fluency in tongues (about which more will be said below). She says, "At first I had trouble pronouncing the words, and remembering them to speak them when they formed in my mind." This was after her first experience which she described in these words:

I had the "laying on of hands" for the Baptism in the Holy Spirit several minutes before but no tongues had come. Then we were praying for someone else [presumably for the baptism], and one word came. At first I thought I might just be repeating someone else in the room, but then several other words came completely different from the other people's tongues.

Another respondent reports that the word *thánatosána* "recurred in my mind when praying with others *before* I 'spoke in tongues.'" It reminded her, she says, of *thanatopsis,* a word whose meaning she probably knew: "a musing about death." Maybe she was even familiar with William Cullen Bryant's poem of this title. However, the word may be a fusion of two Biblical words, namely, *thanatos,* Greek for "death," and *hosanna.*

There does not seem to be too much of this kind of neologizing in glossolalia. One wonders if it may take place more often early in one's glossolalic experience than later—if what my respondents report is any fair indication. And when it does occur, one would like to know what linguistic, social, and psychological features go with it. What emotional stresses or other psychological problems might explain such words? We return to this topic shortly.

Whether in anticipation of the experience or in trepidation, the acquisition of tongues does not always come easily. One of my respondents, the same one who lay on the floor to express his submission to God (page 49), said that he sought the experience three years before getting it, and there are those who never succeed in getting the gift in spite of repeated and sincere attempts while following all the guidance that is given them. Pathetic reports from such people are found in J. E. Stiles' book.

Glossolalist leaders explain the difficulties of acquiring glossolalia in theological terms. They say that a person has not fully yielded himself to the Holy Spirit. Yielding includes more than faith and submission. It also implies that the person must persevere with expectancy. This is certainly good advice, because it may take some people a while before they catch on to what linguistic improvisation really is (see Chapter 4).

Differences in initial performances are therefore due at least in part to the kinds of psychological differences that account for success or failure in acquiring any new skill, like ice-skating. With glossolalia there is more reason for anxiety: the stakes are higher, because it is believed that the experience is supernatural. This is illustrated by T. B. Barratt, the founder of the Scandinavian Pentecostal movement: "The reason why it took such a time was because I *doubted* whether I could receive the tongues, and the thought of such a strange thing taking place; *that I should suddenly speak in an unknown tongue,* this alone was sufficient to hinder the work of the Spirit in me" (quoted in Block-Hoell, p. 133). There does not seem to be good reason, therefore, to explain what I call abortive glossolalia by saying that it is evidence that the conscious will is asserting itself over automatisms (Lombard, p. 26). Or if there is any truth in this suggestion, it does not account for every-thing.

Content and Effects

The rubrics "baptism in the Holy Spirit" and "glossolalia" comprehend a great variety of religious experiences, as has already been suggested in the preceding pages. This fact needs emphasis.

People experience everything from euphoria or ataraxia (a state in which mental serenity is combined with physical well-being) to frustration and disappointment. Glowing accounts of the initial event are frequent in the charismatic literature. Some people, for example, particularly those influenced by traditional Pentecostal rhetoric, talk about "a mighty baptism of the Holy Spirit," where the word "mighty" may indicate a definite physical or psychological experience, not merely an evaluation of it. But the measure of one's experience is in the nature of the speech event. Derek Prince, a popular and influential speaker in the present charismatic movement, even turns this around: "If you want a real in-filling, a real good in-filling, then you've got to have a real good overflow." (He seems to be alluding to the words of Jesus recorded in Matthew 12:34 which were paraphrased by one Pentecostalist as: "When the heart is full, it overflows through the mouth.") It is not surprising, therefore, that some people take pride in having acquired the gift.

A "mighty" experience may also be "miraculous" in some respects.

Xenoglossia, speaking in an unknown but real language, is frequently reported. (This topic is treated more fully in Chapter 5.) Accounts of deaf-mutes speaking are also known. One respondent wrote: "I once heard a deaf-mute man speak and sing in tongues, afterwards he could only make strange noises, write notes and do sign language to his friends to tell them what happened." Perhaps in these reports people seek a kind of fulfillment or replication of what is read in the Bible (Matthew 15:30–31) or sung in Protestant song:

> Hear Him ye deaf, His praise ye dumb,
>   your loosened tongues employ.

Ye blind behold your Saviour come,
and leap ye lame for joy!

From a psycholinguistic point of view, glossolalia on the part of deaf-mutes seems highly unlikely. All glossolalia so far studied is based on the phonology of the language (or languages) known by the speaker. A deaf-mute has not stored up in himself any set of sound patterns or developed the necessary muscular control prerequisite for glossolalia. If a deaf-mute did produce sound that was taken by witnesses to be glossolalia, I would expect it to be quite differently organized.

Equally miraculous in the estimation of glossolalists are visions, such as this one experienced by a Japanese Christian. After being prayed for,

... strange and unknown words poured from my mouth. I saw a vision —a light was streaming from the tomb in which Jesus Christ was once buried. Then I prayed: "Oh, Lord, let my mouth be the mouth to praise our Lord."

I prayed in tongues for two hours. This was the baptism in the Holy Spirit for which I had been longing! Since that time, everything I see looks very beautiful and peaceful. It is as though I were wrapped in mild spring mist and walking in a bright, beautiful flower garden (*Voice,* November 1967, p. 21).

Less "miraculous" perhaps, but equally mystical is the following account:

One summer day three years ago, while my family was away visiting, I was alone in our home, at ease in a semi-reclining chair. In one hand was a book I was reading and in the other hand a Bible in which I was looking up references cited in the book. As I closed my eyes in meditation, the centuries seemed to roll away and I was transported back in time to the early days of the Christian movement. It seemed as though I could commune with men and women who had seen and talked with Jesus.

I became oblivious to time. The next thing of which I was aware, was that I was moving through the house, walking up and down the hallway, in and out of the rooms, moving my arms as though propelling myself through a mighty stream of God's infinite love and grace. Wave after cleansing wave washed over me and the purifying, refining fires of God's redeeming love coursed through my entire being—body, mind, and spirit. All the while I was praising the Lord in a marvelous language that I had never known. In my school days I had studied Latin, French, German and Spanish—but it was none of these. It was a heavenly language that expressed my feelings more than any words of mine could do.

Eventually I fell across my bed, exhausted but happy. When I awakened the next morning, I was indeed a new creature in every sense of the word—in body, mind and spirit. For the first time in my life I felt whole, and free, and clean inside. (*Voice,* June 1969, p. 14).

Many glossolalists do not experience such authenticating events, so some are inclined to doubt that glossolalia, which itself is supposed to be a physical evidence of the work of the Holy Spirit, had actually occurred. One respondent wrote that she had "occasional doubts that everyone has at first. The Devil tries to make you think it's not real. But you *know* it is and nothing else matters." Another respondent who, after two years, still prays in tongues every day and "most days several times a day," lost her ability to speak two days after the initial experience, but "after talking with my minister [I] realized it was because of doubt."

These people have to have reassurance. When they have their problem diagnosed as doubt, they may deal with it by further commitment, that is, asking God to remove their doubts. Others are helped just by being told that what they utter is real. A teacher wrote that she had the experience in the fall of 1966, "but the joy of continuing was replaced by doubt from Satan until January 1967 when another friend overheard me praying and came to assure me I had received [presumably, the glossolalic evidence of the baptism]."

Reinforcement of belief comes in other forms. One person writes:

I just began talking as naturally as if in English—no prayer or praise or worship. A stumbling block in my mind had been removed so I tried to speak words other than English and found I was speaking what seemed like gibberish of my own making. I persisted because I wanted to find out what would happen if I kept it up and if it were really me or God.

She was able to talk in tongues "any time—just for fun and experimentation" for a while. It bothered her that it was so easy; it seemed silly. In her case belief was confirmed by what appeared to be the effects that glossolalia had in other areas of life: "I was plagued for months with [the] thought that it could be me even though I saw some things fit [providentially] that never had before."

These doubts are so common that charismatic leaders deal with them as they teach seekers. Reinforcement of the experience is also given as soon as meaningless utterances are made with shouts of "Halleluiah" or "Praise the Lord" or direct confirmation with "There! You're speaking in tongues!"

Control

Practice and improvement. For most people facility in speaking in tongues comes gradually and with much practice. While some people seem to experience fluency in improvising pseudolinguistic utterances at the very beginning, others, caught up in the emotion of the event, only confuse the joyous repetition of a limited number of syllables with linguistic facility.

Improvement in glossolalia comes not only in what people call "freedom" (that is, feeling more at ease), but also in being able to speak longer and to do more with glossolalia: there is greater variety in the general appearance of what is said. Although changes in sentence-melody are part of this, variety in the makeup of the segmental phonology (how consonants and vowels are put together and segmented) is equally important. As one respondent put it, "Most people [among us] with well-developed fluency in tongues speak with a definite rhythm [and] inflection, and stop and start as in natural speech." Several of my respondents noted repetitiousness or "a limited vocabulary" in their glossolalia. There is sometimes even a note of apology about this. It is surely never considered a desirable state of affairs, and one person clearly condemned "getting into a rut." (She says that unless she "adjusted [herself] to humility [she] would just ramble on.") This repetitiousness, as we will see, is the high frequency with which certain phonetically similar fragments recur in a discourse.

If there is a difference between people's ability to begin talking in tongues, what is the explanation? Perhaps some people just accidentally discover the technique for improvising language before others do. Others might have initial facility because they are less inhibited. These same people might be better mimics in language learning. Moreover, amount of education and knowledge of languages other than one's first language do not appear to determine either the facility of initial glossolalia or the quality of later glossolalia. Although one respondent who was more or less knowledgeable in nine foreign languages deplored repetitiousness in glossolalia, our sample text (page 77), which is certainly repetitious in some respects, is produced by a man with an enviable ability to mimic people, a very good memory, and knowledge of Spanish, Greek, and Hebrew.

The explanations given by glossolalists themselves for imperfect or undeveloped glossolalia are notable for the absence of supernaturalism. For example, "monotonous repetition" in inexperienced speakers is compared by one person at least to the speech of a "baby learning to talk." This explanation fails to take into account, however, that the child is learning by storing up information about his linguistic environment and will eventually speak just as the people around him; whereas a glossolalist, in spite of his claims, is receiving no linguistic models from God: no vocabulary, no grammar, and no syntax. So when a respondent explains improvement by saying "like anything else, the more you use it, the better you become at it," he is comparing glossolalia to a skill, like walking or playing golf or, of course, learning a foreign language.

The principle that "practice makes perfect" is clearly what glossolalists have in mind. This is certainly why some people are taught to make daily use of tongues (as in Oral Roberts, p. 40). Others, when they first begin to speak in tongues, do so whenever possible for fear that the gift might be lost. This is how a secret glossolalist of a main-line church in Canada describes her own experience:

It was a Sunday evening. I was lying down in the dark just relaxing. My family was downstairs watching TV. I had been asking God for this gift for several months. Suddenly from my innermost being a single sentence came. I buried my head in my pillow, and whispered it over and over again, for I thought I must memorize the sentence for future use. Also I could hardly believe that it had really happened.

And according to an evangelist from Texas, the reason that some tongues sound better than others is that the speakers "practice talking and therefore they improve upon God's language." (He surely must have known the meaning of "improve upon" when he wrote those words.) Another respondent is specific about how this is done: "Whether men, women, or children, they all run the words together as one long sentence until they are properly taught. You can make yourself slow down and make phrases or words at will."

If fluency and quality come with increased use, one might suppose that disuse would result in their opposites, but there is no information to support this assumption. There is evidence, however, that in spite of frequent and long use some people produce glossolalia that is inferior (that is, less like language) to that of others.

Planning and thought. When fluency does come, it is easier to speak in tongues than it is in one's natural language. This is what 53 per cent of my respondents answered to a specific question. (only 34 per cent gave answers that might be summarized as "more or less the same"; 6 per cent gave ambiguous answers.) And many of them explained why: "I do not have to put the words and sentences together"; "I just don't have to think. The words just come out"; "No thought is required for choice of words"; "I find it easier to speak in tongues because it bypasses my mind"; "No thought is required in connection with the formation of words." They are saying, in other words, that they are free of the constraints of language, namely, producing speech only when it is linked to specific concepts. Language users start with messages or concepts related in complex ways, but glossolalists start with sounds.

One of those who said that speaking in tongues was easier than speaking in English went on to add that "it is not a subconscious mechanical 'doodling' such as whistling aimlessly or drumming the fingers." Yet this is exactly the impression one gets from others. For example, when Rev. d'Esprit (see below) had stopped recording some glossolalia for us, he said, "I could have gone on and on; it's just like drumming." This is the same impression given by respondents who wrote "etc. etc." after the samples of glossolalia they sent me. Others describe the ease with which they can speak in tongues by saying they can "turn it on or off" at will. It is, in fact, so easy that one can even read while speaking in tongues; but this, to one person, is proof that the speech comes from outside himself.

The great facility with which glossolalia is produced has led some linguists to imagine—and assert for a fact—that there were *no* pauses, hesitations, false starts, and repetitions (as in *I saw . . . saw . . . what's-his-name yesterday*). If these features are absent in some glossolalic discourses, this is not to say that they are absent in all glossolalia. One instance of a false start is that of Rev. d'Esprit who started out with /ăp/, stopped, then resumed with /ashĕndă păkuyĭn/ and so forth. It would appear that he either blended the sequences /ash/ and /ăp/ or else got to /ăp/ (in /ndă pă/) before he wanted to. Given the word-like status of the segment /shăn/ (with other vowels) in his glossolalia, the latter is more likely. An undeniable mistake, as we would call it in ordinary language, was also observed in a woman's tape-recorded prayer. I transcribed it in this manner: /nasutilímini . . . limíndiya/. The main feature here is in the placement of the stress (from the syllable /li/ to /mi/); the alternation between /n/ and /nd/ is the kind that occurs commonly in glossolalia. Perhaps we are dealing in both these cases with a phenomenon that is found in ordinary speech. Intending to say *freshly picked flowers,* one might say instead *fleshly pricked . . . er,* and then go on.

What accounts for the "flow," as glossolalists themselves describe the ease with which they talk, is the very simple task they have to perform. This can be demonstrated by stringing along the syllables /ba/ and /da/ in a language-like way: /bádada dábaba dadabá/. No thought is necessary to produce such a discourse and one does not have to be conscious of the encoding process. The speech will come so easily that the syllables seem to run together.

Although there is no apparent reason for a person not to "know what he wants to say" in tongues, fluency is sometimes reduced by emotional factors. One teacher, for example, reported that when she is "upset over a situation, [she] may not speak too smoothly." The act of speaking can also be affected by thinking about it. One person who had noticed that there were no "b" and "p" sounds in her speech "once tried to invent words containing these two letters, and the words stopped coming." Another woman said "when I concentrate on words, I just can't talk." All that they are saying is that one cannot, at the same time, be aware and not aware of "what words and sounds will be made before they are spoken." This is no more surprising than what happens at the dinner table. Knowing what one will do next requires planning, and planning requires time; and if every act at dinner is planned, the whole event of taking one's meal becomes abnormal. But as one can choose to chew longer and more slowly, so can one choose to use only certain sounds and sound sequences if he wants to; some people obviously find the restriction a little more difficult than others.

This chapter should have put glossolalia in sharp contrast with the picture that was presented by the psychological explanations discussed in Chapter 2. We have now seen that the tongue speaker is the product of considerable instruction. Whether or not glossolalia comes suddenly or gradually, it takes the seeker quite a period of time before he learns what this baptism experience is all about. In some sense, then, glossolalia is learned behavior. It is not learned as real language is learned, however. But that is not necessary, as we shall now begin to see, for the most important information that the seeker needs to have is already part of his linguistic resources, even if he knows no more than one language. Understanding this point requires a description of glossolalia from a linguistic point of view. This is to be found in the following two chapters.

4

DESCRIBED
LINGUISTICALLY

THERE IS NO grammar for glossolalia, because it is a phenomenon, like human language in general, and not like a specific language. Only English, Dutch, German, and Norwegian—to name only a few and closely related languages—have grammars, for "grammars," in the sense employed here, are sets of "rules" or conventions that account for what people within a given speech community say and understand. And within certain bounds, they account for everything that could possibly occur as "language" among these people, even when there are no grammar *books,* as in preliterate tribes.

In glossolalia, however, nobody can learn a set of rules that would enable him to speak a "language" that is the same as someone else's. Even what one person speaks on different occasions is not the same in the linguistic sense.

If there is no grammar in the proper sense—as it is used in linguistics—that will account for the totality of a person's glossolalic output or even one particular form of it (a *glossa*), this is not to say that a glossa is entirely devoid of pattern. It is the purpose of this chapter to describe these patterns, and it will finish with the suggestion that anyone—whether in trance or not, whether religiously motivated or not—has glossolalia, one might say, on the tip of his tongue.

First Utterances

We have seen that although glossolalia seems to come easily to some people, others—by their own report—begin speaking tongues by stammering, babbling, or uttering syllables repetitiously. One man reported that his first words were *ab, ab, abba, abba;* another, that his first utterance consisted of "only two words or sounds."

So common is "abortive" glossolalia (statements about it are ade by writers in the beginning of this century), that some peo ple make a distinction between what they call "evidential glossola lia" that reveals the arrival of the Holy Spirit and fluent glossolalia that is used as a means of grace (a "tool" as we shall see). Some Pentecostal groups are satisfied with evidential glossolalia, but others make fluent speech the ideal. This difference in acceptability seems to be correlated with social differences: the lower the linguistic demands, the lower the socio-economic ranking of the group.[1] (Although degrees of competence are noted with respect to glossolalia, there are no such differences with xenoglossia: "When God gives a human language, it is *always* a pure cultured language even though the speaker may not be educated," wrote one of my respondents, a leader in the FGBMFI. The explanation of this difference is perhaps that only the fluent discourses of practiced glossolalists are heard as real languages.)

If glossolalists accept certain kinds of verbal activity as glossolalia, this is because they approve it on nonlinguistic grounds; the person's total behavior is accepted in the immediate religious context. For example, he has gone through the indoctrination period with understanding and sincerity and now displays complete yieldedness. The same utterances, however, would be rejected if they were associated with behavior that was not approved. This is true even of fluent glossolalia. Thus, glossolalia is identified as genuine by "evidence of a deepened prayer life, of a heightened sensitivity to the demands of the Spirit who dwells within, of a moral transformation of an enduring quality" (McDonnell 1966:614).

[1] This impression is based on all my sources of information. But since I did not investigate this matter in a systematic way, there is no statistical information to measure the correlation.

The possibility of false glossolalia, that is, something linguistically indistinguishable from genuine glossolalia but not inspired by God, puzzles many glossolalists. Very few of my respondents had definite answers to my questions about "fake" and "demonic" tongues. Some suggested that a person might be able to imitate tongues, but more common was the belief that the imitation would be accomplished by the Devil. This was the explanation for a glossolalic outburst I witnessed at the FGBMFI meeting already referred to (page 58). When a man in the balcony began to shout and groan in a way that led many to believe that he was demonically possessed, a woman near me leaped to her feet and burst out in fluent glossolalia introduced by ejaculations like /kăt, chăt, tăt/ while grimacing terribly and twisting her arm in a serpentine manner. It was in my opinion the woman's general behavior and untidy appearance—and not so much the way speech was constructed from consonants and vowels—that led one of the responsible men in the meeting who had also seen her from nearby to deny that she had been led by the Spirit. Her speech was not well-cadenced, gentle, and melodious but very fast, jarring, and strident. Unlike the other glossolalic discourses at this session, this one was not interpreted. (Interpretations into ordinary language of glossolalic messages are discussed in Chapter 7.)

Many glossolalists, nevertheless, claim that it is indeed possible to distinguish Spirit-inspired glossolalia from that which is Devil-inspired or is simply produced by human effort in imitation of the real thing.[2] This ability is a Spirit-given "gift of discernment" with which some people are endowed. It occurs in the Pauline list of spiritual gifts that includes speaking in tongues: "to another the ability to distinguish between spirits" (1 Corinthians 12:10, RSV). (A passage frequently referred to in this connection is in 1 John 4:1—"do not believe every spirit, but test the spirits to see

---

[2] This was the predictable explanation of a Pentecostal minister (presumably traditional) on seeing W. Cohn's cinematic record of an experiment with drums (1967:278). He "felt that the portrayed behavior may be called glossolalia, although he attributed it to spiritual sources which were not divine." Although the sociologist reports that all of the six volunteers "spoke in tongues to one degree or another" and that this behavior "seems indistinguishable from glossolalia," my own viewing of the film, confirmed by that of other observers on one occasion, leads me to a different conclusion. There were various kinds of vocal activity (one person made a pseudo-Indian ejaculation like /yahu/), and only one person uttered anything resembling glossolalia in the sense used here.

whether they are of God," RSV). This Biblical authority, it might be added, leads to the use of this "gift" for the ferreting out of evil-doers in a congregation, a practice also found among some independent African sects that have been influenced by Pentecostalism. In fact, it would appear that when the gift is exercised, it is people—not spurious cases of glossolalia—that are the primary targets. In any case, there is no claim, as far as we know, that the discernment is based on linguistic evidence.

If glossolalists were tested for their ability to distinguish religious (to them, real) from imitation glossolalia entirely on auditory perception (using tape recordings, for example), would they be able to do so? It is not certain.

Hine makes a contrary assertion: "The difference between the glossolalic behavior of psychotic individuals and that of nonpsychotic individuals was perfectly clear to the normal Pentecostals in Kiev's study" (1969:214). Unfortunately, she misunderstood Kiev, who only says that the *delusions* of West Indian sectarians "could be recognized as abnormal by most West Indians" (1963: 362; the same material in 1964). He is in no way talking about glossolalia. His study, however, is valuable for another reason, namely, that it shows how much a person needs to know before identifying delusions among people of a different culture (or subculture, one might add). Where delusions parallel cultural beliefs, "One must look for exaggerations, misinterpretations and distortions of culturally acceptable beliefs, which ultimately necessitates familiarity with the culture or consultation with representative members" (p. 363).

The only experiment I know of (by A. Carlson) used nonglossolalists as subjects, thirty university students in elementary psychology. They listened to twenty-two samples of pseudolanguage, half of which were religious and the other half imitation, with many different speakers in each group, and were asked to judge the resemblance of all the 45-second samples to real language, based upon sound content rather than style of delivery. The two groups of utterances were graded so much alike that Carlson concludes that there is potentially little difference phonologically between the two types of pseudolinguistic material, that is, religious and nonreligious. This is confirmed, as we shall see, by the production of nonreligious pseudolanguage in "real life," that is, outside the context of experimentation. In any case, the conclusions of this experiment cannot be extrapolated to Pentecostalists in general. What we would like to see is to what extent different groups of tongue speakers—traditional and neo-Pentecostal, poorly educated and well educated, etc.—are able to distinguish authentic from artificial glossolalia in the same "style," say, prayers.

Form[3]

What glossolalia is like is suggested by the sample text, a complete prayer said in isolation by a Presbyterian minister whom we call "Rev. d'Esprit."[4]

    1. kupóy shăndré fîlé sundrukumă shăndré lása hóya tăkí. 2. fozhŏn shĕtírĕloso kumó shăndré palasó shăntré kamóyĕntri. 3. só-zhăndri kága sómbo póyĕntrĕ lapatsómbo kóyshăntrala só. 4. fîlă săndrúzhăntrăkămălă sĭndrí patató săntrăkú zhăndré. 5. kílă só zhăndrámăndrăfulu sú shăntrí lĭmétăki. 6. mozăndro folĕsĭtĕrá sumprúturut fulĭsĭntráyindri kămpåtăkă fulăsó. 7. kézhăndri tarasómbo kayandré. 8. fíli sĭndrí tărotú săntrăkádĭ shin drĭpĭti píli săntró. 9. nésăntro fîlé săntrí káyăntroposhăntră méri kílisu. 10. fíli sĭndrí káyĕntro móshĕntrĕ pĕlĕsŏndo. 11. shĭndrí katári pilí sĭndrí kízhăn drúpu lăsúnt. 12. kambóyăntre filasín zhíndra mú. 13. fálasun drúshăntă káli síntratirăl súmpăke. 14. fîlă sózhăn drómă tărípili síndri kí. 15. kúzhăntray pilisín zhăndrumăndára fîlĭsĭntrú. 16. sazhándĕrĕ kélă sĭntrú pătăsámbo kóyăntay. 17. sizhăndrepí tărú shăntrăkó. 18.

---

[3] In this book the description of religious glossolalia is based on the speech of those whose primary language is English since no other first-hand data were available. It will be necessary eventually, of course, to compare glossolalia from places like Japan, Finland, Iceland, and Israel. I feel rather confident, nevertheless, that glossas from different parts of the world will have striking similarities, perhaps even more similarities among themselves than each does to its source language. This view is based on my own observations of glossolalia among native speakers of Dutch, Russian, and Spanish and on the observations of others. Further evidence is nonreligious glossolalia, discussed in Chapter 5, illustrated by some utterances from Turkey (see Appendix C).

[4] Rev. d'Esprit, whose name appears several times in this book, is not by any means an unusual representative of the neo-Pentecostal movement, and we have used data obtained from him only because we were fortunate to have his generous help over a period of several days. Besides, he has a very good recording voice, and he is an intelligent, articulate person. For other samples of glossolalia see Appendix C and the studies by Jacquith, Motley, and Wolfram.

kélăsăndri valasómba kóya. 19. vezíndre fílă săndrú shăntrámănă trufukú shẫntri pikí. 20. săzhẫndăr kóyĕntĕrĕ pĕríki. 21. mésăntro sezhẫndri kílă săntrú patasŏ. 22. sezhẫndru múli sĭntrĕ̆, tĕrĕpíli sĭndrí bité pătără pokó. 23. kóyĕntre pilisí gambóy yambóy hambóy zhăndrí pelăsăntrú kúnya păké. 24. zízhă drú víshindrămănătă kóyăntre sizhĭndri pilisĭndri kézhăn trupukú yĭndrí pălăsú. 25. sozhándre kélă săntrú zhĭndrámănă . . . shíntar ké. 26. sŏzhondri bíshăntăr kimbătărató súntră kó. 27. săzhẫndrémăt . . . tíli síntrăké. 28. sontó.

It is like the scores of glossolalic discourses I have heard in person or on tape recordings, many of which have been transcribed as this one was. On analysis these transcriptions will always expose the linguistically deviant nature of a glossolalic discourse (made explicit in Chapter 5), notwithstanding a charismatist's claim that glossolalia is neither repetitious nor meaningless banality, no "jabber-babble or twattle-twaddle," but clear, distinct, precise, and uncluttered speech (L. J. Willis, in W. Horton, ed., pp. 258,259). Neither is it interjectional behavior mixed with inarticulate sounds, as its detractors have insisted (for example, Lapsley and Simpson, p. 4). This topic is treated more fully in Chapter 10.

⟨A glossolalic discourse appears to be divided into units of speech that might be called "sentences" (more accurately "breath-groups") because of the rather natural use of volume or accent, rhythm, intonation (or melody), and pauses.⟩These features will naturally vary between speakers and for the same speaker on different occasions, depending on several factors (discussed below). In discourses of more than a few breath-groups there is often a somewhat monotonous use of a few intonational patterns (or sentence-melodies, as one might call them) that recur with only minor variations again and again. But this is not a necessary quality of glossolalia. This statement is made only to give the reader an impression of what a text sounds like. The rhythm, whether monotonous or not, is, of course, the product of a certain style. Even the ordinary prayers of these people, for example, are droned or "chanted" in typical ways. In the sample text, for example, the highest pitch is quickly reached, then the plateau may be maintained for a short bit, but always the level of pitch gradually drops toward the end.

A monotonous discourse is not, of course, necessarily said in a monotone. In fact, if a glossolalic discourse has any "meaning" at all, it has to be conveyed in part at least by the prosodic features.

(Monotone chants, however, are theoretically possible; but that is music, and we are talking about speech.) This was borne out by an experiment with Rev. d'Esprit. When he was instructed to speak in a musical monotone, he gave up after one false start and the successful utterance /e: la ka: yan ta: yan tri:/, saying that it was just too hard. (The colon marks length, as with musical long notes.) He had no difficulty, however, in slowing down his speech. The following breath-groups are examples of such:

1. /fi: ló: yâ shín dâ te shâ ta la hó: yĭn de ke. . . ./
2. /li: ya: pó: yĭn dâr lí som bó/
3. /ke yá: shĭn drí: tă ro pó: yĭn drí: zhĭn drí: pi li yá: lo. . . ./

They are interesting, because they contain the vowel /â/ (as in *cat*) that is otherwise rare in his glossolalia, and also because of the rhythmic distribution of accented syllables.

One sees in these specially elicited samples the nature of the rhythm that is so common in glossolalia (see also Motley, p. 98) and that is so pleasing to its practitioners. In rapid speech this pattern is not so noticeable, because several syllables may be unstressed. This is in evidence here in /tă ro/, in the third breath-group. With this description of the metrics of glossolalia, it should be noted, we have rejected the suggestion that glossolalia is always metronomic in timing—as if each syllable were being measured out to a beat. Neatly-timed glossas do occur, of course, but they are not necessarily the rule.

The breath-group itself can often be divided into subgroups like those set off in written English by a comma at points where phonological features like temporary pause and "suspended" pitch level occur. That they occur in glossolalia is not surprising when one remembers that even before children are able to talk they use intonation in a realistic way (see Laird and Chapter 6).

The rest of the material of which a breath-group is made consists of a series of syllables. The arrangement, however, is not random in a technical sense. Certain segments of speech always occur in any given text more often than any random segment one might pick. Notice the frequency of something like /shand/ in the sample text. There are phonetic variations, of course, but these are described below.

The occurrence of syllable-sequences in glossolalia can be described in terms of syntagmatic and "paradigmatic" (or associative) relationships. ("Paradigmatic" is a useful term. Its sense here is slightly different from its usual one in linguistics.)

The syntagmatic relationship of syllables (that is, their relation in a string) is one determined by the environment: given one syllable, what can be said about the syllable that precedes and follows it? Thus, if we take the syllable /so/ from the sample text, we find that it occurs ten times, including three times when it is /som/ before /bo/ (# means absence of syllable, that is, silence):

lo	so	ku
la	so {	shǎn #
lǎ	so	#
lǎ	so	zhǎn
#	so	zhǎn
ra ga pa }	so	bo

In other words, once a speaker decides (unconsciously, of course) to use a syllable like /so/, what is he going to do with it? This sample shows that he can combine it with other syllables, some preceding, some following, or both—producing sequences like /losoku/, /lasoshǎn/, /sozhǎn/, /lǎso/, and so forth. It is these syllable-sequences that give the appearance of words in glossolalia. Rev. d'Esprit's favorite "word" consists of /s-ntr-/ (different vowels occurring in the spaces marked by hyphens). The five most frequent "words" in Motley's speaker are /la/, /sian/, /tiada/, /siando/, and /xia/ for "Spanish" and /vish/, /vesh/, /tra/, /vaish/, and /rish/ for "Russian." A sample for each of these is given below, with the spelling slightly altered.

Sample of a glossolalist's "Spanish" tongue

travioxóta xiá exítamakapasán denisisiantiáda. ainimóta iamemóte exitakantráo exitakantraviande. livísta lavasiándo nemórta meporpampïrándara sontinisisian tiáda kepáltala patrabas tinisisiantiádadevioxóta.

Sample of a glossolalist's "Russian" tongue

brŏsh abríshĭn bărevésh alavorót dăravíshikararvát talbedírĭsn drovés drováishdi bráshadráividivish akapărevét arivishĭndara váslĕvĕriv. vedísh atraveda díshatrobodiásh atravedivéshni pĕrísh.

The illusion of word-structure is destroyed when one tries to dissect all the breath-groups of a text. Apart from the prominent syllable-sequences, the others must be grouped together rather arbitrarily, taking cues from the accent, rhythm, and melody of the breath-group. But since the organizations of these two patterns— syllabic and melodic—are largely independent, one feels like dividing syllables /... abc .../ sometimes into /... a bc .../, sometimes into /... ab c .../, and so on. So it is not surprising that a linguistically trained respondent was no more successful in "breaking down" her speech than I was. This was confirmed by an experiment with Rev. d'Esprit. When his own prayer was played back several hours later, he was unable to fulfill the function of the normal speaker of language. In other words, he could not, listening to his own speech, repeat for me what he had just said. It is possible, of course, that he was embarrassed by the task, although he certainly revealed no other symptoms of embarrassment.

The difficulty of finding "words" in a text can be illustrated by looking again at the sample. Although I have written the first breath-group as if it started with three different words, I must confess that I was undoubtedly influenced by the rhythm of the utterance, making each "word" come out with a final accented syllable. But there was no good reason for not beginning as follows: /ku póyshăn dréfĭ lésundru/. Other linguistically trained persons have looked at this text, and none of them arrives at exactly the same results that are presented here. Nor would they ever be expected to do so, no matter how well trained they were. Linguists all recognize that their ability to record utterances in a foreign language improves the more they know the meaning of what they are writing. This, for linguists, would have to be stated in a more sophisticated manner, but the point is simply that in natural languages the most important thing about speech is the meaning behind it. Without this meaning in glossolalia, where can "words" come from?

Nevertheless, in listening to recordings, one gets the feeling that words are almost emerging but are constantly being tampered with. This impression characterizes the general ambivalence of glossolalists about this matter. Harold Horton, for example, says that because glossolalic words are unknown (that is, in an unknown language), "they are quite indistinguishable in the phrases of which they form a part" (p. 166). Some people deny that they are speaking words at all.

Repetition is one of the most common features of syllables. This may be the repetition of complete syllables, as in /pititi/, /mimimi/, and /vana vana/, but more often it is a repetition of a consonant, as in /kika/, or vowel, as in /piki/. There may be patterns of syllable-sequences like *abracadabra,* where /d/ replaces /#/ (that is, nothing), and *ca* joins the two elements: *abra-ca-dabra.* (This illustrates a pattern, not religious glossolalia!) The result is consonantal variation, as in Rev. d'Esprit's /káyan táyan/ and /gambóy yambóy hambóy/. Samples from other speakers are: /lámomom ámomo/, /háynikichi áylikichi/, /káya mantáya/, /pára fára/, /shíbi híbi/, /kíni kíti/, and /hóriala háriala/. (Vocalic variation is also illustrated in the last example, where /o/ is replaced by /a/.)

Complete repetition, the recurrence of identical elements after each other, as in *xyzzyxx,* is not too common; and when a syllable-sequence is involved, even a longish one like a breath-group, repetition seems to have special significance for the speaker, like emphasis. There is, however, a more subtle kind of repetition that reveals the improvised nature of glossolalia. This is revealed in the use of consonants and vowels.

In any body of texts for the same speaker there is always a small number of sounds and syllables that are far more frequent than others. In one tabulation four sounds accounted for 40 to 50 per cent of the total as compared with 25 per cent for an English text.[5]

---

[5] English is used in all our discussion only by way of example, because it is best known by the readers. Glossolalia is not being compared with English, although specific features of certain texts are compared with the native language (sometimes English) of the speakers. There would be no advantage in a book of this type to compare sample glossolalic texts with texts from, say, African languages. We do not know, of course, what specific family of languages glossolalia should be compared with. Hence, when generalizations are made about human languages, these are considered opinions based on what is presently known about languages all over the world.

In Motley's "Spanish" five sounds, /t, s, n, a, o/, account for 49 per cent, and with three more, /r, d, i/, 68 per cent of the total is accounted for.

In texts of three different glossolalists analyzed by Wolfram, consonants were compared with vowels. Here are the percentages, all rounded. The top figures represent the percentages of vowels to consonants, 100 per cent being the total of segmentals (consonants plus vowels) in each text. In A, for example, a little over half of all the sounds are vowels (more precisely, syllabic nuclei, of which there are ten different ones), and the consonants (seventeen in number) represent slightly less than half of the total number of sounds. In addition, the vowels /a/ and /i/ are in all three texts quite high in frequency of occurrence, except /i/ in Text C. In A again, these two vowels together represent 38 per cent of the total number of sounds in that text. By contrast, the common sounds of ordinary English *sit* and the second vowel of *sofa* (that is, /ĭ/ and /ă/) together are represented for A, B, and C as follows: 1.8 per cent, 20 per cent, and 1 per cent. Notice how different B is with respect to this feature. It would naturally give quite a different impression than the others.

	Text A	Text B	Text C
vowels	52%	48%	45%
/a/	20%	15%	23%
/i/	18%	11%	5%

In Rev. d'Esprit's texts (not merely the sample given above) 52 per cent of all the consonants are accounted for by /t, k, s, y, p/. What is interesting, moreover, is the dominance of sounds made by the tongue tip. They represent 56.7 per cent of all the consonants that occur at the beginning of a syllable. But it should be noted that in one tabulation of English consonants alveolar sounds (made with tongue tip touching the gums behind the teeth) also represent 56.7 per cent. The explanation for this similarity is, to put it simply, that Rev. d'Esprit is "doing what comes naturally"! In other words, he and every other creator of extemporaneous pseudolanguage tends to use what is common in his native language. In fact, it is more common that he maximizes what is already most frequent.

One most curious kind of repetition is found in a text sixteen seconds in duration with four breath-groups. When the initial consonants of each syllable are listed in a series and allowance is made for intervening syllables, there is a considerable amount of matching of sounds in point or manner of articulation. For example, the seventh consonant from the end in breath-groups 1–3 are /b/ and /p/, that is, both made with the lips; the eighth consonants from the end, /n/ and /dr/, are made with the tip of the tongue; and although the ninth consonants, /v/ and /s/, are made at different points in the vocal tract, they are both fricative sounds. In the following display *O* indicates the absence of a consonant at that point (there was a simple vowel), *X* marks an unintelligible section, and hyphen indicates a gap created by stretching out the lines for maximal fit. In the first line, therefore, a syllable with /l/ was immediately followed by one with /s/, but immediately below /l/ (in line 2) there is a /t/, likewise a tongue-tip sound, which is followed by a syllable introduced by /p/.

1.	O	f	sh	dr	m	n	t	t	s	dr	k	y	t	f	l
2.	—	s	zh	dr	p	X	X	X	s	t	k	sh	d	v	t
3.	—	s	zh	dr	—	t	X	X	s	b	k	y	—	—	—
4.	O	k	sh	d											

What this text seems to suggest is that the speaker is using a similar sequence of sounds each time he produces a breath-group. No such pattern emerges in the vowels. They are the following:

1. ĭ ĭ ĭ i i ă ă i ĭ u u ă e ĭ ă i a ĭ i i i u u
2. ĭ ĭ i i X X X ă ă e ă ĕ i ă ă o o u u o ă e o
3. ĭ ĭ i i X X u u ă ă ă ă e ĭ e i ă u o ă
4. ĕ e ă i

If syntagmatic refers to *how* a speaker strings along elements in an utterance, paradigmatic refers to *what* he can select from. I use this term in talking about the speaker's linguistic resources. The difference is illustrated for English by showing, first, the following elements at his disposal.

neo-	Pentecostal		are	very	r
anti-	charismatist	-s	were	somewhat	devou.
non-	glossolalist		have been	rather	fanatic

The paradigmatic relationship between the members in each column is defined by their grammatical function. Their precise function is irrelevant at the moment. The syntagmatic relationship between these elements is defined by how they go together. Thus, one can select different pieces and make strings (sentences in real languages) like: *Anti-Pentecostals have been very fanatic* or *Neo-Pentecostals are devout.*

In glossolalia a kind of paradigmatic relationship is revealed in that there are syllable-sequences in every text that bear a strong phonetic resemblance to each other. This might be called a kind of "disguised" repetition. In the Bronx I heard /hozakiya/ (from the name of the Biblical prophet Hezekiah?) and /hozangiya/, /mamanda/, and /babanda/. From an Episcopalian prayer meeting

—	s	k	v	n	b	d	s	g	—	—	—
p	t	k	s	—	b	—	—	k	y	t	zh
p	t	r	s	dr	p	t	s	y	—	—	—

(see below) we find /sante/, /shantc/, /sante/, and /kante/. And from Rev. d'Esprit we have /shandre/, /zhandre/, /shantre/, /yandre/, etc. These phonetic variations on a base are generally similar in articulation: /s/ and /sh/ (voiceless and made with tongue-tip), /b/ and /m/ (voiced and made with both lips), and so forth. The extent of such variations in one text is seen in the following array of syllables found in the "Russian" glossa of Motley's glossolalist. I have arranged them to reveal how, by changing the first consonant (reading vertically) or by changing the vowel (reading horizontally), a large number of "words" is easily made. The dashes indicate the absence of a filled-out pattern. In other words, /fesh, faish, fosh, fos/ did not occur in the text. It is quite possible, however, that some of them would have occurred in a longer text or in a different one.

fish	----	-----	----	---
vish	vesh	vaish	vosh	vos
----	----	-----	posh	---
----	----	-----	bosh	---
----	----	-----	prosh	---
----	----	braish	brosh	bros
dish	desh	daish	dosh	---
tish	----	-----	----	----
----	----	-----	trosh	----
----	----	-----	krosh	kros
rish	resh	-----	-----	----

It is obviously possible to have elements from a paradigmatic set related syntagmatically. This is implied in sequences like /shibi hibi/ where two units differ only in the initial consonants. So the man who in 1707 reported hearing *vaugh daugh faugh raugh raugh faugh daugh vaugh* (with consonantal variation) at a Quaker meeting may not have been far from the truth (quoted by Mackie, p. 79).

Glossolalic syllables themselves, of course, consist of consonants and vowels. For the most part these are simply taken from the native language of the speaker although sounds learned in other languages may be introduced: /x/ from German or Spanish (as in *Buch* "book" and *ojo* "eye") in an American's speech is an example. It is surprising, however, how little of this goes on. This might be explained by inadequate exposure to or imperfect learning of other languages among the people from whom we obtained samples of glossolalia. Another explanation might be the tendency for a person to "regress" to his "easiest," "most natural" sounds, that is, the ones he learned in childhood (in real language, however, not babbling).

Not all the sounds of one's native language are used, nor are they selected—unconsciously, of course—in a systematic way. The only English sounds absent from Rev. d'Esprit's texts, taken as a whole, are the fricatives represented by "th": as in *thistle* and *this*. But another speaker had only /t, k, m, n, s/ for her consonants, and no others. Some speakers recognize the phonological poverty of their glossas; one person even tried to do something about it, by introducing a consonant, and failed! (That is, she consciously made a modification. Given time a person can, I think, do so.) Perhaps one's inventory of sounds increases as he becomes a more proficient speaker. This hypothesis needs to be tested.

If a person's native language is the source for his glossas, we should expect his dominant dialect to determine their form. So if the vowel of *bought* and *saw* were to occur in the glossas of people from Philadelphia and Minneapolis, cities that are distinguished dialectally with respect to this vowel as well as in other features, we would expect to hear a similar difference reflected in glossolalic speech. But we have no clear examples of such dialect interference. Thus, neither the glossa of a person from Mississippi nor that of a native from eastern Texas, whose normal English in each case is characterized by what the man-in-the-street calls a "broad accent," revealed the speaker's normal English dialect. In both cases I also heard samples of the speaker's casual English speech. Although this gave them away as "Southerners," their glossolalic speech did not.

Perhaps there is a kind of levelling of speech that produces a common denominator of sounds. This would result, for example, from filtering out pronunciations characteristic of one's native variety of language, especially if it were considered nonstandard or of low prestige. Since a delicate control of one's speech is normal for most people, no matter what variety of language they may speak, it is not surprising that it would occur when a person switched from natural to pseudolanguage. This ability to modify one's speech according to circumstances, among other factors, implies a certain degree of consciousness about speech differences. Thus, middle-class natives of New York City, who do not normally have an "r" in words like *floor* (when followed by a vowel) and *fourth* (suggested by *fou'th floo'*) in casual speech, tend to introduce this sound when they are talking more formally. And this is done unconsciously. This kind of speech modification, so neatly described by William Labov for New York, could be illustrated by many other examples.

What makes a person's glossa different from his native language is how he uses its sounds. In Rev. d'Esprit's form of English the vowel of *bought* is always followed by a consonant, but in his "word" /patasǒ/ it is not. Moreover, as all speakers of American, he has an /h/, as in *hat,* but when speaking in tongues, he usually makes it with a great deal of friction.

American English also has a sound like the one represented by "r" in Spanish (*pero,* "but"), as in a common pronunciation of "t" and "d" between vowels (*Betty, laddie*). But in the glossolalia of native speakers of American English it is an extremely common sound, sometimes even lengthened (technically, trilled), as in Spanish *perro,* "dog." In ordinary English this Spanish-type sound never occurs at the beginning of a syllable, except in some styles of singing. It is, however, common in American glossas, for example, /rasiyat/. This same sound also occurs in some styles of religious speech, at least in the United States. I have heard it in sermons and prayers in fundamentalist circles, but its distribution is probably more widespread than my own experience would indicate. Not every "r" is said in the Spanish manner, however. For some people only *spirit* and *spiritual* are said in this way. (I am not suggesting, of course, that this "r" has the same function for glossolalists as it does for speakers of English in other religious contexts.) In contrast, the "r" of *rabbit* is rare indeed in the glossas of Americans.

Meaning

Meaning in language is the *systematic* relationship that exists between segments of orally articulated sound and brain-stored concepts that relate to subjective and objective experience cognitively perceived. Meaning is associated with single words like *seed,* affixes like *-s* in *seeds,* phrases like *hot-dog* (a frankfurter), and so on. Of this kind of meaning—recognized as "linguistic" in a narrow sense—there is virtually none in glossolalia, nor can there be as long as each glossa is improvised more or less at random. Not random in the mathematical sense, of course. But even if the vocal output is here-and-there correlated with something else in the individual's universe, we just cannot often establish the relationship in a consistent way.

The absence of systematic sound-meaning correlations is illustrated by the Shaker song presented on page 185. If the English is meant as any kind of translation at all, there ought to be a pretty close fit between the glossolalic and English words. But one seeks in vain for, among other things, the glossolalic marker of futurity (as with *I'll come* and *I'll take*) and for the second person pronoun (*thou, thee, thy*). It would appear, however, that glossolalic *me* and *I* represent English *me* and *I,* presumably pronounced the same way. (The use of the capital letter may be fortuitous since the only place this "word" occurs is at the beginning of a line.) We do not know, of course, what came first, the glossolalic utterance or the English version, or, indeed, if they somehow came at the same time. In any case, it surely is not accidental that both the glossolalic and English lines rhyme.

How much meaning attaches to sound certainly depends in part on how the speaker conceives his glossolalia. Should a person not care if his glossas are like languages, he would not be inclined at all to attach meaning to "words" that may appear again and again. The same would be true of one who believed that the meaning of glossolalia was "para-intellectual," as one leading charismatist puts it. A less sophisticated tongue speaker informs me that glossolalia bypasses the intellectual processes that are contaminated by the "curse of our language due to vocabulary structure"!

Another factor is the amount of borrowing from languages known to the speaker. Not considered among these are proper names, mostly from the Bible, that the speakers frequently recognize as such. These often have an exotic form that is different from the one in the person's own language: *Yezu* or *Yeshua* presumably referring to *Jesus;* and even a friend's name is deformed from *Marshall* to *Masha,* as suggested by my respondent. Clergymen use other words which they say "resemble" those in the Biblical languages: one man cited (and misspelled) *agaliasthē* (Greek *agalliaomai,* "rejoice exceedingly") that was "just a happiness word" for him. And a housewife who had studied some Spanish in school used *Yay-sō ē-say amoy anā* and *tā amō* (in her spelling) with the feeling that she was saying "I love God" with these "sounds." She recognized that they resembled Spanish, but she seems to have forgotten that in Spanish *te amo* means "I love you"; *Yay-so,* which she writes with a capital "Y" and translates as "God," is probably a modification of *Yezu* already mentioned.

Another interesting example was provided by a nonreligious glossolalist about whom more will be said in Chapter 6. He recorded samples of his own speech, obviously not realizing that *et cetera* (in English usually seen only in its abbreviation *etc.*) provided him with some of his glossolalic speech. The following is in his own spelling and "translation" (Le Baron, p. 290).

Etce ce Tera. Lute te turo scente.
Inke runo tere. Scete inte telee turo.
Oru imbe impe iste. Simpe, Simpe, Simpe.

Love now has been sent!
The light of the earth! The joy of the day!
The light of all the world!

Notice that here too the syllables are grouped in different ways to produce different "words": *ce Tera, scete, scente; Tera, tere, turo.*

The unconscious use of material from a language known to the speaker is, in the opinions of some who study the human psyche, a revelation of the content of the subconscious.[6] If this is true for ordinary language, they would find it true of glossolalia. Freudians would therefore find it interesting that one of my respondents, a Lutheran minister, recalls having used *Maria* in tongue speech on several occasions.

A Freudian, in fact, did try to psychoanalyze a tongue speaker early in this century (see Pfister), a subject (named "Simon") who had guilt feelings as a consequence of certain sexual acts and who had been recently involved in Pentecostalist religion. In the course of the investigation Pfister obtained the following sample of glossolalia. It is, however, not typical of the kind being described in this chapter, because it was first "written down" (in thirty-eight seconds) in Simon's own exotic script (see below, page 186). The oral value of this text was then said for Pfister's convenience. The original spelling, which followed German conventions, is here changed for readers of English.

> *chin chumi kraso chimaino cholúr epshunor eleshúor vechu flizishur flizishu bléshur ígvishu séneshu akvidáshu kvintidashu senushu fridishu tokishu machushu bikingshu yeffeshu varashau elimshu libanshu arashu leshu gayonshu saylonshu saylondúshu ínoshu egolorshu menogolorshu endishu.*

It turns out that most of these words, as Simon explained them one by one, have some correspondence to other words—German,

---

[6] Something similar, cryptomnesia, is taken up more fully on pages 115 and following.

French, and English—known by him (pp. 38–41). And the words do in fact reflect some of his concerns. Thus, *chumi* suggests the name of Franz Schumi, a writer of novels Simon had read, but considered by him to be "a great seducer." (He makes a mistake in naming the novelist, however, and this mistake comes out in the glossolalia. He pronounced the name as Franz Tschumi. This is interesting because the "ch" sound consists of "t" followed by "sh," as in German "nz" and "sch.") Of *kraso* Simon says that the novelist talks "crass nonsense" (*krassen Unsinn*). *Chimaino* consists of *chi* as in the German attempt at the English pronunciation of the name Jesus, and *maino* means "opinion" (*Meinung*): Schumi in his own opinion, says Simon, takes Jesus' place. The syllable *shu* takes on two meanings in this text. On the one hand, it represents "shoe" (*Schuhe*), which is a prominent symbol in Simon's discussion of his own problems. On the other hand, Pfister suggests, it may come from "Manchu" (German *Mandschu*), since Simon had at one time planned to go to China as a missionary, using his gift of tongues for preaching. Travel is suggested in several place names: Peking (*bikingshu*), Jaffa (*yeffeshu*), Elim, a Biblical word (*elimshu*), Lebanon (*libanshu*), Arabia (*arashu*), and Ceylon (*saylonshu*).

This is an interesting case, but it must be repeated that it is not typical of glossolalia as a religious speech event. A similar study for Pentecostal glossolalia would not be impossible, but it would have to be done differently. (For my own participation in such an investigation, see below.)

The most interesting kind of meaning from a linguistic point of view is that which emerges in the course of a person's use of glossolalia independently of any known language. Meaning is associated with what a person first said in tongues or with frequently recurring expressions. The latter are the more common, and if the sample from my respondents is representative, they are more expressive than denotative in meaning. Of the first kind is *shalmaneka* "praise the Lord"; on the other hand, because *otī* is frequently used, a speaker says it must mean "Lord," "God," "I," or "you"; and *lē lō,* repeated at the ends of sentences, for another person "must mean 'Praise God' or something similar."

It is easy to see how repetition and predictable occurrence—either at the beginning or end of a sentence or discourse—can help a segment of glossolalia to take on meaning. In the sample text, for example, /nésăntro/and /mésăntro/ both introduce sentences (9 and 21) with a slight pause and suspended pitch as if the speaker were saying "I told you . . ." And /sontó/ occurs in the last sentence with a falling intonation that definitely gives the idea of completion; it might mean "It is finished" or "Amen."

Frequent occurrence alone, however, is not sufficient to make glossolalic expressions take on meaning. What is necessary is an emotional state that is significant or meaningful to the speaker. This is why the very first utterance, expressed when a person is having a "peak experience," is so often of great personal value. The "meaningful" utterances cited by glossolalists are therefore charged with emotional meaning. The following examples illustrate this point. One housewife now uses *woo* as "a loud exclamation of rejoicing," but she only heard herself say it "very slowly and softly at first." Another housewife reports that the "words" *shăndah alanna macouria shiela ala mosiea* (in her spelling) "have come many times when I feel a sudden burst of praise or joy." For this same person *onna tai dĭ dennechie* means "honor to Jesus." Another respondent clearly remembers that *nee-show eel-ee-oh, hush-eye shawn-dye* (/nisho iliyo hăshay shŏnday/ in my orthography) came to him one day (while driving his car) with "a great volume in spiritual outpouring." But it was not until several weeks or months later that he perceived its meaning: "sufficient always— Saviour Jesus." One observes that the speaker divides the "translation" into two parts that reflect the two portions of the glossolalic utterance. It is not unreasonable to suppose that he predicates the meaning as "(My) Saviour Jesus is always sufficient." This utterance is another good example of the kind of alternating repetition that so frequently occurs in glossolalia.

These examples, however, appear to be quite uncommon. Most of the meaning that the speaker of tongues associates with his speech activity is not encoded linguistically. Instead, it is expressed by switching from natural language to glossolalia. The choice itself is as communicative—or meaningful—as choosing to wear one set of clothes instead of another for dinner with company. We will return to this point in Chapter 12.

But there is another kind of meaning that lies behind the choice and the form that a glossolalic discourse may take (like the motivation for choosing one tie instead of another): it may be joy, concern, anxiety, etc. One might say that a specific glossolalic discourse "means" joy; it might be translated into a single predication: "I am happy." This is why we should say that a glossolalic discourse alludes to meaning rather than specifies it.

The emotions that tongue speakers associate with glossolalia are fewer than one might expect, and it is interesting that they should be stated so often in appositive terms: for example, praise (or adoration) and petition, love and command. But one can also cite sadness, peace, and assurance. Some emotions are probably associated with speech directed to God and others when speech occurs as a "message" in a social setting (see Chapter 7 for discussion of uses), but there is clearly a great deal of overlapping. Thus one can feel assured in private prayer and pronounce a message of assurance in public. More interesting is the fact that although exhortation is appropriate in a message addressed to a group, it should also be characteristic of prayer. The sample text, for example, was described by a number of nonreligious persons who heard it as being argumentative; the speaker sounded as if he were trying to prove something. If this is so, it is only because "free-prayers" (especially in nonliturgical churches) are frequently insistent in nature. There are, of course, many Biblical texts that could serve as justification for importunity. One of them is Luke 11:5–10. (Emotion is dealt with in another connection in the section that immediately follows.)

Varieties

Although many people see no variation in their glossolalic speech, except perhaps for the improvement that might follow the initial experience, others perceive differences so great that they distinguish different "languages." A person may have just two more-or-less uniform glossas, like Motley's subject, who had a "Spanish" and a "Russian" variety (page 85), or, if we are to believe others, a large number of them. One Pentecostalist reported on his own varieties in the following way: "I am sure that I spoke seven or eight different languages. They were clear and plain, and the different positions of the tongue, and the different tones of the voice, and the different accents, made me understand how different the languages were, one from the other" (quoted in Bloch-Hoell, p. 134).

The number of glossas in a person's inventory obviously depends on what he thinks makes them different. One that had a high incidence of /shm/, /shr/, and /ts/ would sound quite different from one with /nd/, /nt/, and /ng/.

If changes take place in the same discourse, they may not be noticed. That such changes do in fact take place is clear from my own study of long glossolalic texts (say, one-half hour or more in duration), noted also by Motley (p. 9), and from what respondents report. One housewife says, "My language has changed many times while praying. It sounds like dialects to me—dialects of the same language." If this is anything like what I have heard, it may be nothing more than the occurrence of a new intonational contour or a new sound or cluster of sounds after a period of repetitious speech.

That varieties do in fact occur is clear when transcriptions of texts are compared. Although all of the discourses recorded for us by Rev. d'Esprit are remarkably alike, even texts recorded five months apart, the two varieties of Motley's Pentecostal subject, labeled "Spanish" and "Russian" by him, have interesting differences. The Russian variety has many recurrent segments that end in consonants, particularly /s/ and /sh/ (see page 86 above), whereas the Spanish variety has far fewer. Moreover, the "Spanish language" has segments like /siando, tando, sando/ that look like the Spanish present participle, as in *hablando,* "speaking," whereas /tiada/ and similar words look like the past participle (feminine form), as in *hablada,* "spoken." But in the two "languages" of one speaker presented in Appendix C there are fewer differences signalled in the syllabic structure. There are differences, but these are of the type that are not easily presented in writing, sentence-melody, for example.

What is particularly interesting about glossic variation is that it is correlated oftentimes with emotion, context, or use. Rev. d'Esprit has an oriental glossa similar to his first glossolalic speech. Sometimes when it recurs, which is not often, he feels "a tremendous flow of emotion" going through him. (It might be noted that at his first experience the oriental one was almost immediately replaced by another because of doubts about what was happening:

he said, " 'God, I don't want it if it's merely an aberration. I don't want it.' And I moved right from that oriental [tongue] . . . to something completely different.") Emotion figures also in the following event reported by someone else: "I experienced one shift maybe a week or two after I started and seemed to be speaking a different language since the only feature I can pinpoint is a high frequency of final *a* formerly and a high frequency subsequently of final *e*. The day the shift occurred I experienced a kind of 'drying up' though I didn't actually lose the ability to speak." Another person observes that her glossolalic speech is different depending on whether she is alone or in a meeting. One person has to be "under special compulsion and a certain spiritual tenseness" to speak his "special tongue." This is a form of glossolalia he associates with something he uttered early in his experience: "Shortly after the baptism, while preparing to retire, [I] seemed to be seeking a confirmation of the whole matter, when something within, like a geyser, began bubbling, spouting then erupting into a tremendous outflow of praise and worship, almost an agonizing experience; [it] seemed to be a special language." Another person, a Foursquare Gospel minister, actually manipulates the differences until they fit his emotions: "Sometimes I have to 'shift gears' in order to find the 'tongue' which gives vent to my particular burden of prayer. . . . I switch to the sound which gives me the greatest sense of fulfillment in praying." Since this man would certainly believe that, in any case, his glossas came from the Holy Spirit, there seems to be a contradiction between his beliefs and his practice. Incidentally, he is undoubtedly using the word "sound" in a very general sense, referring perhaps only to cadence and melodic patterns and not to any selection of consonants or vowels. The case mentioned on page 86 is therefore a different one.

The differences that manifest emotional states—and therefore convey the different meanings—are to be found in a number of vocal features: voice quality, pitch contours (that is, voice melody or intonation), pitch intervals and degree of stress on accented syllables, speed of utterance, clarity of articulation, etc. Glossolalists are less precise in their identification of these features but nonetheless instructive about their function. One person has a "fluent and melodious" glossa that is used for adoration and another "quite guttural and primitive" one that "seems to have more power for intercession." Similarly a minister has a "harsh, brutal command language" and a "soft, gentle love language." (Notice how the varieties are contrastive as with the functions.) But even when people do not report two definite varieties of glossolalia, they are remarkably consistent in positing either one or the other of the varieties and ascribing values to them. On the one hand, "richer sounds" are used when one respondent feels "nearer to God" (and this speech has a high incidence of what she considered the "noun" *i*); and when the speech is "gentle" another person says she is expressing love to Jesus; a particularly "beautiful" variety of glossolalia is used by one woman when she prays for people with emotional problems. On the other hand, a "harsh and commanding" variety of glossolalia is used by an evangelist against the Devil.

One might suppose that some of the emotion conveyed by particular varieties of glossolalia might be manifested in certain sounds; this is the impression one gets from the use of terms like "gentle" and "harsh." But experiments with speakers of both religious and nonreligious pseudolanguage (and in the latter case the person had used pseudolanguage for over fifty years) indicate that such correlations are unlikely. For example, in an experiment conducted by Dr. J. Laffal and myself, Rev. d'Esprit was asked to respond to a number of concepts: strength/weakness, emptiness/fullness, beginning/ending, leading/following, death, and anger. An analysis of these discourses that averaged twenty-three seconds in length reveals nothing phonologically significant. However, when the texts were played to a group of subjects who were asked to identify from the above list the concepts with which they were associated, there was considerable consistency of response. It is clear, therefore, that something besides consonants and vowels conveyed the meaning the speaker was encoding.

There are general behavioral differences depending on the situation and the function that the discourse appears to have. These differences did not escape one of my respondents. She noted that men speak more forcefully as a rule, and some women have a crying or weeping tone (something I have observed as well); even voice quality may be different. Kelsey reports having heard a man's voice "with almost overpowering strength that was like being grasped physically" (p. 91).

A woman who used a "gentle" variety, as she describes it, while praying for people who are discouraged or worried could very well switch to a "harsher" variety if she were exorcising someone in prayer. However, it is not clear that the glossas for messages are consistently different from those used in prayer or praise. It should also be noted that there appear to be no significant differences between the glossas of men, women, and children. My questionnaire dealt with this point.

If speaking in tongues is fundamentally an emotional experience, it is also an esthetic one. The most common response to glossolalia among Pentecostals is to judge it beautiful. Is this so because of the phonological characteristics of glossolalia, because of the nonlinguistic features that characterize glossolalic discourse, because of the emotional state of the hearer, or because of the religious context? Probably all of them to some extent. A person from our cultural background who hears someone speak with a strident and loud voice, with extreme ranges of pitch and strong, stressed syllables is not going to be favorably impressed, particularly if the behavior is not in harmony with the emotional tone of a meeting. But if other things are equal, some forms of glossolalia would be more appealing to native speakers of English. I (with my own cultural-linguistic bias) should imagine that /bayana/ would sound better than /byakrapu/. In other words, there are rather definite notions about speech that go into judging—as well as producing—glossolalia. (This point is taken up again in the next chapter.) This is why "demonic tongues" are reported to be guttural and harsh. Since we only have the statements of glossolalists to go by, we do not know whether they are considered demonic because of certain vocal characteristics or whether the characteristics are attributed to them because, for other reasons, as noted on page 75, they are judged to be demonic.

These evaluations of glossolalia must be related to evaluations of natural languages. Among speakers of English the German language is considered less pleasing than a Romance one (for example, French or Italian) precisely because it is "guttural"; but the Germans in turn consider Dutch ugly for the same reason! Whatever the terms "harsh," "grating," and "guttural" might mean to speakers of English (or perhaps for all West Europeans), it is clear that these are low-ranking terms on the scale of linguistic esthetics. Even in England, urban speech is sometimes deprecated for having these qualities whereas rural speech is considered "soft" and "musical" (Halliday, pp. 163–4); and in science-fiction a nonearthly language is usually characterized as harsh, strident, grating, and very often "guttural" (Krueger, p. 77).

Diaglossic "Words"

Most of the learning associated with glossolalia, as we saw in Chapter 3, is nonlinguistic: for example, that there is such a phenomenon, how in general it differs from natural language, when and how to use it. It is possible, however, for one to imitate another person's glossolalia in the use of "favorite" sounds or sequences of sounds, and there is indeed a remarkable amount of such learning in the glossolalist community (Motley's statement to the contrary notwithstanding, p. 24). A term is needed to name this "pan-glossolalist" phenomenon; it might be *diaglossa*.

Even glossolalists are aware of the similarity that exists in the speech of different people. (Interesting is the fact that all observations to this effect were made to me by ministers or lay leaders.) One man says: "It seems that there are certain similarities of tongues and some of these words seem to be common to a number of people. I travel a great deal and [I have] heard tongues in New England, California, Texas, Sweden, and Germany, and many times there *seems* to be a similarity between tongues in a given area and even between areas to a lesser degree." A minister observes that "there seem to be a few 'established patterns' among public tongue speakers," and he even cites *shon dai* as an example, a segment that appears all over the United States (see below). A minister of the Assemblies of God denomination explains similarities by the fact that "those under the influence of strong personalities sometimes tend to speak similarly in tongues just as they may imitate mannerisms." And a Southern Baptist evangelist authoritatively declares, "When I hear others sound as I do, it is my duty to warn them that God never made two leaves alike on a tree. God is God and should never be reduced to human habit."

Evidence for diaglossa is seen in the similarity between the utterances of several members of a single Episcopalian charismatic group and in the widespread occurrence of a single segment. In the latter case we observe that many people throughout the United States and Canada use a "word" that consists of an initial /s/ or /sh/, then a vowel, followed by /nt/ or /nd/ and another vowel: in other words, /shanda/, /santi/, and so forth. What is remarkable is that it should appear in a tenth of the responses to my question: "Do you recall any words from your tongues or from the tongues of other people?" The recurrent segment is here written as it was given in the questionnaires:

(*ka*) *shun di*	Seattle, Washington
schone do (*ka*)	California
shunto-	?
shan-da	Michigan
shawn-dye	Connecticut
shandah	North Carolina
ah-shon-da	?
shanda	New York

This segment also occurs in the glossolalia of a neo-Pentecostal from Toronto (in the form of /shănti/), by Wolfram (texts 2, 5, and 7), in samples obtained from Rev. d'Esprit, in the Episcopalian samples, and even from the snake-handlers of Scrabble Creek, West Virginia—/shăndămăsaya/—(as seen in the documentary film by P. Adair).

Although I am suggesting that this "word" has been passed on from one glossolalist group to another, we must consider other explanations for its wide distribution. Pure chance is one of them. Given the limited number of sounds and syllables used by English-speaking Pentecostals, we can expect some segments to recur. Obviously, the shorter the segment, the more likely its recurrence: for example, /sa/. But what is interesting about this segment is that it is disyllabic, that it has a restricted number of consonants that occur in the two positions, and that in the first syllable the vowel tends not to be /ĭ, i, ĕ, e/.

Another explanation would combine accident and learning. Some people may have started, unconsciously of course, with a syllable derived from a word like *Sunday* or *sanctum* and improvised on it. My own attempt easily produced this bit of glossolalia: /săndi mătăndi kiliyándi/. Or perhaps, having heard themselves use a syllable like /san/ in, for example, /sanakapari/, they would capitalize on it because of its resemblance to words with which they were already familiar, that is, words from a natural language. This much similarity with the speech of other glossolalists would be fortuitous. But once the similarity was recognized, the utterances would be reinforced and might in fact tend to become more alike.

It would appear far-fetched to relate this "word" with any similar one found in another language unless it could be shown that some glossolalist at some time in the past was familiar with this language. This kind of reasoning is not convincing to the Christian glossolalist, because he believes in the supernaturalness of tongues. Therefore some of them will be awed (or would be in certain circumstances) by the fact that in India many people begin and end a conversation, even in a "secular" context, by repeating *Santi santi,* "Peace peace." It probably would not matter to some glossolalists that these are devout Hindus.

I find all of these alternative explanations a bit forced. The most reasonable explanation, it seems to me, given the amount of interaction that goes on among participants in the charismatic movement, is one of learning. This is somewhat substantiated by further cases, such as the following.

From a group of people who had been meeting together for some time in an Episcopal church we have the following sample of a much larger body of similar segments. They are extracted from transcriptions of tape recordings of glossolalic prayers uttered at a single session. The hyphens set off the segments being compared.

Speaker A: *shonda-dĭdiya, shănto-riya, shănti, shăntiya-tiyâ, săntetidiyă, siyawto-shŏnte, ta-shanda, tiya-shănte.*

Speaker B: *ila-shante, ilăpa-sănte-kă-shante, kilăpuchă-shunte, kashĕtĕk-sĕnte, tĕ-kănte, ikă-sante, tukopa-sante, săntĕk-shut-sănte, ikeshunte, kiko-sănte, teka-shănte.*

Speaker C: *shandi-ăporătiyanămĭniyăda, shandi-ĕnăniya, sănte-tĭtiya, nĭpĭti-yănte, porată-sande, tăriyăpo-sănte, kă-rănde.*

Speaker D: *shĭnte-tĭtiyatiysĭ, tiyăponăkĕrăta-shănde, tiyopo-sŏnde.*

The important thing to notice here is that four out of a group of eight or more people use the segment /shande/ or /sande/ in some form, and that this is the same segment that occurs in other parts of North America. In other ways, however, their glossas do not look alike. This would be clear only if we gave the complete texts of each speaker. Neither do they sound alike, for each person has his "favorite" speech "styles" (consisting of speed of utterance, sentence-melodies, and so on).

Similar but somewhat less convincing to a nonlinguist are recurrent segments heard in the glossolalia of four different young people at a Puerto Rican meeting in the Bronx (described in Chapter 9). These should be read as Spanish; in the dialect of many of these people, words with "ll" (for example, *calle,* "street") are pronounced with /j/ as in English *June* instead of /y/:

/hurrara . . . shanta/
/huja . . . mamanta/
/hozakiya . . . mamanda/ and /babanda/
/hukiya babando/

To a linguist, however, there is more than accidental similarity in the first syllables of these utterances. There may have been more examples of diaglossa at this meeting, but there was so much noise that only a few isolated utterances were heard clearly enough for accurate transcription.

With this chapter the reader should begin to have a notion of the simplicity of a glossolalic utterance, that is, the part of glossolalic behavior that consists of a stream of speech with its consonants, vowels, and—to a lesser extent—its accentual patterns. To produce such an utterance, all that the reader needs to do is draw some syllables from a language he knows and string them along realistically: it does help to try to *sound* as if one is saying something. The experiment is made a little easier by actually visualizing some syllables like the following:

mi	*ti*	*li*	*ni*
ma	*ta*	*la*	*na*
mo	*to*	*lo*	*no*

But this is not necessary. In my experiment with a group of college students who had never even heard of glossolalia before, one very realistic glossolalic discourse was produced by a man who imagined himself speaking to a United Nations committee. One can, of course, add all kinds of frills to one's language, making it as exotic as he wants, by using strange sounds and sound-combinations and eerie sentence melodies.

The next chapter will make the description of glossolalia more precise by comparing it with natural language. There are interesting similarities and differences.

5

CONTRASTED WITH LANGUAGE

THERE IS VERY little reason for human beings to invent a language that is unlike any that is already found on earth. Artificial languages, like Esperanto, are no exception, for although they are in a sense new languages, not being genetically related in a normal way to other languages—as, say, English is to German—they are decidedly like natural languages; they were purposely made so, in order to serve as communication bridges for people, like a Turk and a German, who did not know each other's native languages.

Nonhuman languages, on the other hand, occur outside "normal" cultural behavior. Examples are found among people who claim to communicate with beings from another world (like the medium Helen Smith and her "Martian" guide, for which see Chapter 6) and writers who try to imagine what another kind of communicative system would be like, for example, the other-worldly language of the schizophrenic girl of Hannah Green's novel *I Never Promised You a Rose Garden* or nonhuman words in science fiction (see Krueger). In such attempts, where humans have to say or write something that somehow represents speech, authors cannot get away from human language: their most daring neologism will in all likelihood be similar to something found somewhere in the world, although writing permits the representation of unpronounceable words, like *wgooqxbb*.

It is understandable, therefore, that glossolalia should be very much like human language in spite of its supposed divine source among Pentecostals, for they are as bound to their language and culture as every other human being.

In this chapter we shall examine this similarity to natural language as well as some significant dissimilarities, both from a linguistic point of view. But first we shall consider the superficial similarities, observing glossolalia naively, from a nonlinguist's point of view. It is in this connection that xenoglossia and cryptomnesia must also be discussed.

Superficial Similarities

It has been implied in much that has already been said that glossas often strike people as being quite like languages. I once tested this fact in a casual experiment with a group of unsuspecting Dutch linguists with whom I was wont to "talk shop" at coffeebreaks. "What do you think this is?" I asked them. And then I began reading the following lines (originally obtained by Wolfram and further discussed in Samarin 1968:75):

yamana kita siyanayasi
yamana kita siyanayasi
anakiyana tiyasanaya anakiyatana, siyanayasi.

Their response was that it sounded like a prayer or poem and that it could be some Malayo-Polynesian language, a group of languages with which they were particularly familiar. This is not surprising when one finds dance-song lyrics in New Guinea like:

Meyana li nimibo, nolilube
Meyana li nimibo, nolilube
Sehuyanagu sefo sefo agolamemo
Meyana li nimibo, nolilube

"Give me that over there, that *agolamemo* (a kind of betelnut) from Sehuyanagu" (R. Young, p. 215). It was only after I continued my reading of the text that they began to feel uncomfortable about their first appraisal, because the sentences go on somewhat repetitiously for eighteen more breath-groups:

asakina, anakisa, asakiyana tiyanayasi
yamana kita, siyanayasi.

Another sample, like the preceding one a glossolalic prayer, was played in its original tape-recorded form to a group of young doctors, all being trained in psychiatry and psychoanalytic techniques. Without knowing precisely what they were listening to, their responses were something like the following:

A reading of poetry or lyric prose on a sentimental subject (homeland, childhood, etc.) in a strange Eastern language.
A middle-aged man reading an old saga of a far-away land.
This poet is remembering beauty, perhaps his homeland, through a veil of nostalgia and sadness.
Scriptural reading by a man in a foreign language.
Religious ceremony in Russian.
Poetic, Slavic language. Declamation, perhaps sad, perhaps patriotic fervor.
Not a Slavic language, perhaps Indian or Afghan. Poetic, pleasant.

However, there were a few people whose responses were, for example, "Is it a made-up language?" and "It's not a language; it just sounds monotonous."

People differ, of course, in how critical they are of what they perceive; they are also critical in different respects. The last responses were given by individuals whose intuition about real language was good or who did not care to pretend, even in an experiment, that this was a language. But some people are less critical, perhaps by temperament, but especially—in the case of religious glossolalia—as a result of teaching about the phenomenon.

Nevertheless, glossolalists do have some notions about why they think their tongues are like languages, a matter that was probed in my questionnaire. Most of the answers to my question give linguistic reasons like those below, although a housewife's affirmative answer was followed by a psychological reason: "I don't know why, but I do not feel I'm the type to just rattle on making 'sounds.'" Another person, a prominent leader in the charismatic movement, cites lack of redundancy (which is contradicted by recordings of his speech) and speed and ease of utterance as evidence for his glossas' being real languages.[1] Many, as would be expected in a religious group, give the Bible as proof; and one person knew that his glossa was a language "by faith." This conviction was expressed by a Southern evangelist in the statement that glossolalia has to be different from normal language or it would not be from God. The fact that glossolalic messages are interpreted was cited by only one person; perhaps a different population of respondents would have used this reason more. More interesting are answers like the following: "It sounds too much like a language not to be"; "I speak just as if I am speaking my own language"; "One speaks as though it were a language"; "Not just a lot of sounds." Similarities to other languages in sound or full identification ("Someone told me I was speaking Hebrew") also constitute evidence. The latter, the case of xenoglossia, is taken up below. Generally, the answers are more specific. The phonology is recognized as containing "a variety of sounds" that are grouped into "many different" or "definite syllables."

A kind of grammar is apparent to many people in that they recognize the "same words" (or "recurrent partials" as one linguistically trained respondent sophisticatedly put it). One person even recognized "short words that connect others" like conjunctions and prepositions. Words, they say, are also used with different endings (or suffixes), and in glossolalic poetry "words" rhyme. (This is recognition in a vague sense, of course. Glossolalists recall very little of what they have said.) Indeed, pseudoinflection or what glossolalists could interpret as inflection appears in all the glossolalia that has been recorded for native speakers of English. Notice the various ways in which the "stem" /tata/ takes on "endings" in seven different breath-groups of one particular text:

    tata-sa
    tata-sa-tarishti
    tata-sa-te

[1] This is in an answer to a question of mine about "fake" tongues (see above page 75f): "I believe that, in their desire to speak in tongues, many people unwittingly concoct languages through a cerebral process, but in such cases they cannot speak them with ease and rapidity and without great redundancy." Charismatist leaders are apparently sensitive to criticism about repetitiousness (which is what he means; redundancy is a technical term that really does not apply here), for similar statements occur with some frequency.

tata-vate-sa-taristi
tata-tava-sa
tata-tatasitiwi

These could be divided differently, as we have already seen (page 81): for example, /tata-tata sitiwi/, producing different "stems," different "affixes," and different "words." Lombard also noted the simulation of inflection in the occurrence of "words" like *booros, boorin,* and *oorin* (p. 33).[2]

Syntax is recognized in the statement that "words seem to phrase themselves in groups," and both sentences and paragraphs (in speech, of course) are also identified. Other features of spoken language used as proof that glossas are languages were variety and change and what the linguist calls intonational features ("inflection and modulation," "cadence," "rhythm," "rise and fall of voice and tone"). Other proof is found in there being pauses for breath, continuity, repetition, and slowness and deliberateness. Real meaning, of course, cannot be used as evidence, yet it is reported that glossas "seem meaningful" and they "express para-intellectual meaning." It is interesting, although not surprising, that one person should give as her proof, "Because I seemed to learn it," meaning, of course, that she had become more competent in producing pseudolanguage.

Although the majority of my respondents are convinced that their glossas are languages, they are uncertain about what languages they might be compared to. Only nineteen out of sixty-nine (or 27%) were not convinced that their glossas were languages: eight did not know, three were not interested, four doubted that they were languages, one said that they were "at times," and three said that they were not earthly languages. In response to the question "What languages have your tongues resembled?" 50 per cent of the

---

[2] What would happen in the glossolalia of native speakers of an uninflected language who had no familiarity whatsoever with an inflected one is uncertain but certainly intriguing. Since suffixation, as here illustrated by accretion to the "stem" /tata/ (the alternation in English speakers of /a/ and /ă/ poses no problem), is more common in natural language than prefixation, we may have here further evidence to the universal dominance of suffixation in human language (Greenberg, pp. 86ff). On the other hand, this kind of accretion may have other motivations. For example, saying the same "stem" first may give the speaker more time to think up (unconsciously, of course) a new suffix.

respondents (43 out of 85) either said that they did not know or provided no clear answer.[3] And many of the remaining respondents qualified their answers with words like "guess," "probably," "possibly," and "seemed like." The following list of languages or language types is nevertheless interesting; the numbers indicate how many times each was mentioned by the forty-two respondents. Names in quotation marks are supplied by myself to classify the responses.

29	"Oriental"	8	"Semitic"
	Oriental, 13		Hebrew, 5
	Chinese, 8		Arabic, 1
	Hawaiian, 2		Aramaic, 2
	Japanese, 2	6	"Germanic"
	Polynesian, 3		German, 4
	Vietnamese, 1		Scandinavian, 1
24	"Romance"		Yiddish, 1
	Spanish, 12	5	"Slavic"
	Italian, 6	4	Indian (Western Hemisphere)
	French, 3	3	Greek
	Latin, 3	2	Eskimo
8	African		

Even though these comparisons are nothing more than guesses by (with one exception) linguistically naive people and are in some cases based on accidental exposure to the language mentioned (for example, one person had heard Eskimo in Alaska some months before speaking in tongues and another person heard Vietnamese on a television newscast), it is nevertheless striking that the "oriental" and "Romance" languages stand at the top of the list. The reason for the high rank of the former may be that, like African and Indian languages, they are exotic to westerners. This linguistic characterization of glossas as "oriental" may be an-

[3] Excluded from the tabulation are two responses that are obviously wild guesses and two of unqualified identifications as specific natural languages (that is, reported cases of xenoglossia.) In response to another question, 50% of the repondents said that if someone could show that tongues were not like human languages, they would have to be considered heavenly, spiritual, or angelic languages (see Samarin, 1970b.) They are apparently following Paul's reference to "languages of angels" (1 Corinthians 13:1). In the Corinthian congregation, it should be noted, different varieties of "languages" occurred (in Greek *gēnē glōssōn*, 1 Corinthians 13:12,28), but they are not limited as they are in Acts 2:8–11.

other manifestation of the attitude among westerners that has led people for a long time to study or dabble with oriental religions, leading even to the creation of pseudo-oriental sects. (Orientalisms also seem to figure prominently in western spiritism; see, for example, page 135f for the case of the medium Helen Smith.) It is also not unlikely that there is to be found here some influence of the notion held by many occidental men-in-the-street that oriental languages, especially Chinese, have no grammar.

It is also possible, however, that the oriental and Romance characterizations reflect a superficial but rather accurate observation of the phonological patterns of the glossas that were being uttered. In both cases one finds languages with words whose syllable structure is somewhat simpler than that found in, say, Germanic languages, like English. Not all English words have as many consonants clustered together as *fifth, thinks,* and *strength* (CVCC, CVCCC, and CCCVCCC, where C and V represent consonant and vowel), but there are many of them, and these are quite different from Spanish *manteca* and *gato* (CVCCVCV and CVCV). One person actually said that "the syllables sound like French or Spanish."

Intonation may also have played an important part in the comparisons, because it is a part of western folk linguistics that oriental languages have a sing-song quality that is different from western languages. Since the speakers could not identify their own intonational patterns with anything they knew, they could only call it oriental. One person, in fact, was explicit in saying that her glossa sounded like "an oriental chant." Indeed, some tape recordings of glossolalia make one imagine romantic scenes from nineteenth-century plays of the exotic Far East.

Xenoglossia

Since most glossolalists believe that their glossas are real languages, it is not surprising that they find confirmations for this belief. Thus, there are supposed to be numerous cases, if never their own, where utterances have been identified as Hebrew, Chinese, German, etc. What makes this belief religiously significant is that these were languages unknown to the speakers; they were participants in a miracle. If glossolalia is a sign, then xenoglossia is God adding to the impressiveness of the sign. So states one doctrinal book by a traditional Pentecostalist:

Although its [glossolalia's] chief purpose was for communion with God in prayer and praise, yet it could also provide an arresting sign to unbelievers if any were present. Divine providence could add to the impressiveness of the sign by causing the language uttered to be the mother-tongue of the unbeliever, as on the Day of Pentecost. This was apparently incidental, however, and was not inherent in the gift (Gee, p. 58).

The belief in xenoglossia is obviously based on a passage that is crucial for Pentecostals: Acts 2. It is recorded that when some of the disciples were together in Jerusalem, on the occasion of the annual holy day, they began to speak in "languages." Other Jewish pilgrims in the area came to see what this sound was,

and they were bewildered, because each one heard them [the disciples] speaking in his own language. And they were amazed and wondered, saying, "Are not all these who are speaking Galileans? And how is it that we hear, each of us in his own native language? Parthians and Medes and Elamites and residents of Mesopotamia, Judea and Cappadocia, Pontus and Asia, Phrygia and Pamphylia, Egypt and the parts of Libya belonging to Cyrene, and visitors from Rome, both Jews and proselytes, Cretans and Arabians, we hear them telling in our own tongues the mighty works of God" (verses 6–11, RSV).

As in the Biblical account, moreover, glossolalists do not themselves claim to have spoken such-and-such a foreign language (or do so rather uncommonly), as the following cases illustrate. Generally, it is someone else who identifies the supposed language. In view of this fact, it is inaccurate for the psychologist Janet, writing under the name of Pierre Saintyves, to describe glossolalia as the result of fraud and pious deceit (1912:380). He asserts that claims regarding the miraculous are the result of deliberate or unconscious attempts at making others believe something. Although his observations do not apply to Pentecostal glossolalia—where the social unit merely supports its own beliefs in the miraculous— they are undoubtedly appropriate for individuals with delusions. But believing in linguistic miracles can be as much a part of normal cultural tradition as it is of pathological delusions.

Early in the century, when glossolalia was almost entirely restricted to groups of poorly educated people, the belief that tongues were real, earthly languages seems to have been stronger than it is today. It is reported that some people even went abroad as missionaries in the firm conviction that they were speaking Chinese, for example, or some African language. A. B. Simpson, one of the founders of the holiness-oriented Christian and Missionary Alliance denomination, is quoted by Bartleman (p. 40) as having said the following: "We are to witness before the Lord's return real missionary 'tongues' like those of Pentecost, through which the heathen world shall hear in their own language 'the wonderful works of God,' and this perhaps on a scale of whose vastness we have scarcely dreamed." But this evangelistic function is rejected by Charles W. Conn, important leader of the Church of God (in W. Horton, p. 44). A similar change is reported for the Catholic Apostolic Church or Irvingism by M. O. Oliphant where tongues were first considered xenoglossia, then a sign of the baptism of the Spirit (as stated in Cutten, p. 105). For another reference to such evangelistic xenoglossia see Bloch-Hoell (p. 87). Nowadays, especially among neo-Pentecostals, it is only believed that tongue speakers pray for foreign people in their own (that is, foreign) languages.

Here then is one such experience as described to me by a man who is now an influential leader in the charismatic movement. When he first spoke in tongues, he expected his fellow clergymen to say "you got mixed up with some very emotional people who worked themselves up into a frenzy and then let off steam with this form of jibberish, which of course is not articulate speech,"

So I said, "Lord, if this is an actual language, please reveal to me what it is," and so I walked deliberately away from the tabernacle [tent] where I received this experience down a path through the woods, with this language still flowing up within me like an artesian spring. A little girl about eleven years old came walking up the path toward me, and when she came to me she stopped, listened, and laughed. "Why, you are speaking Polish," she said. "Take me to a Polish man," I replied. I was afraid to stop speaking in tongues for fear I might never be able to start again. She led me to a man standing on the stoop of his cabin. The moment I saw him I said to myself, "Just think—this man is a complete stranger to me—I have never met him before—but in Christ we are brothers." *"Baratcha, baratcha, baratcha,"* he replied. "You called me *baratcha,*" which means "brother" in Polish.

Usually the languages identified are currently spoken somewhere in the world, but occasionally someone describes a glossa as an old or "primitive" form of a modern language or even an extinct one. Reports of such cases of xenoglossia very often have two features. The first is that the language in question is spoken perfectly, fluently, or beautifully. The respondent who was just quoted even informed me, "I was told once by an interpreter for the United States Air Force that I was speaking pure patrician Greek." The second feature is that the person who identifies the language hears a message in it for himself. This might be called "miracle reinforcement," because the second miracle that confirms the first consists of a close matching of the message to the person's experience—like the sometimes funny, sometimes eerie, relevance of the message of a fortune cooky to what one has been thinking or doing.

Not satisfied with simple miracles, some glossolalists entertain double miracles as we saw on page 65. Although Jesus only made men able to talk (Mark 7:31–37), there are many reports from charismatists of deaf-mutes speaking a language unknown to all of their acquaintances and relatives (for example, Sherrill, p. 105).

Authentic cases of xenoglossia would be miraculous indeed, unless one accepts parapsychological explanations, since language is by definition learned behavior. Some students of psychic phenomena accept the possibility of xenoglossia, as did Charles Richet, the inventor of the term (*xénoglossie* in French), who reported a case of automatic writing in a language unknown to the speaker. But a case of xenoglossia could be proven real only if, on the one hand, it were demonstrated that the speaker could not possibly have learned the language in any normal way and, on the other hand, that the language spoken was incontestably a real one. Fulfilling these requirements is difficult, hence the number of cases of xenoglossia is negligible or nil, depending on how much credibility one attributes to the investigations.

It is extremely doubtful that the alleged cases of xenoglossia among charismatists are real.[4] Any time one attempts to verify them he finds that the stories have been greatly distorted or that

[4] Dr. Ian Stevenson suggests that genuine xenoglossia is unlikely among glossolalists, because their verbal behavior is not usually accompanied by a marked alteration of consciousness (1966:302). Since this statement assumes that genuine xenoglossia does occur and that it will always be accompanied by trance phenomena, both of which have yet to be proven, it cannot be taken seriously.

the "witnesses" turn out to be incompetent or unreliable from a linguistic point of view. The first-person account already cited illustrates the latter point. Although the word *baratcha* is given as proof that this glossa is Polish, this is too little evidence. That is, one cannot prove that a stream of speech is from a real language just because several syllables remind one of a real language. (Incidentally, *baratcha* is closer in pronunciation to the plural form of the Polish word.) In the text already referred to (page 104) there are more examples. Several sequences of syllables can be interpreted as Japanese:

ama kita	"the nurse has come"
sina kita	"the merchandise has come"
asa kita	"morning has come"
yana kita	"awful north"

Another case is the following, reported to me in person by someone who had grown up in a traditional Pentecostal church but had never been a tongue speaker herself. When a man arose to give a message in tongues, she immediately recognized it as the language she had learned in Africa as a missionary many years before. And as he spoke, she understood the sense of what he was saying. Immediately the meeting was over, she met with her husband and son, who also spoke this language. All of them had been amazed to hear it from the lips of someone who could not possibly have had the opportunity to learn it as they had.

Probing as politely as I could, I found that she apparently had some knowledge of this language but she spoke it with quite an accent, in addition to the fact that she ignored the tones that are a part of this language's structure. I could not, of course, determine for myself whether the tongue speaker had in fact made a discourse in this language (the length of which she was uncertain, maybe a minute or less), but I did ask her if the man spoke as an African, or with a "missionary's accent." She said it was the latter, but she had obviously never thought of this point before. In my opinion, this man's glossolalia, based on English sounds, resembled the version that she and her family spoke, also based on English sounds.

Moreover, although she claimed to understand what was said, all that she could report was that the man was praising Jesus, the same kind of message that was given in the interpretation. In other words, cross-examination destroys the credibility of this sincere person who claimed to hear a language she personally knew.

It might be added, somewhat parenthetically, that this case is typical in another respect. There were present in the meeting two girls whose parents were very reluctant to see them leave for Africa as missionaries. This allegedly miraculous experience, with a message of comfort and assurance from God, dispelled their fears and subsequently sustained them during times of great personal danger experienced by the girls in Africa. One sees here the religious value of the glossolalic event—something shared by a rather large group of people—and the way that religious experience sustains belief in the functions of glossolalia. This is a topic that we will return to in the final chapter.

The features that lead one to identify a glossa as being this or that language may be very subtle. On hearing the glossolalia of a schizophrenic patient, I had the distinct impression at first that it was a Slavic language. It was only after a deliberate effort to learn why this was so that I discovered that it was because of the syllable that sounded something like /lyud/ which occurs in the Russian word for "people."

Such accidental resemblances can be so strong in normal behavior that native speakers of Thai, while in the United States, avoided words in their own language that to them sounded like English vulgar expressions. Thus, Thai *chid,* "to be close," and *cid,* "heart, mind," both of which begin with a sound similar to that in English *chip,* were taboo in polite speech because a four-letter English word beginning with "sh" sounds so much like these Thai words (Haas 1957).

The unreliability of witnesses in identifying glossolalic languages is beautifully illustrated by Edgar Allan Poe's *The Murders in the Rue Morgue.* Several people hear shrieks from the fourth-story residence of Madame L'Espanaye and her daughter. On being interviewed, they give very different interpretations. They all heard a shrill voice, but one French witness identified it as a Spanish one; the Dutch witness maintained that it was French; the English witness said it was German; the Spaniard insisted, on the basis of the intonation, that it was English; and the Italian said it was Russian. Having no reason to believe otherwise, they took the shrill voice to be that of a human; but being unable to identify the nationality of the speaker, each witness identified the voice as being characteristic of a language unknown to himself. The voice turned out to be that of the murderer, a creature unfamiliar to all involved —an orang-utan!

Illusions in this way always disappear on close examination, and it is not surprising that one of my respondents should report that he had heard of cases where xenoglossia disappeared (or as he put it, the speaker "lost the ability to speak [for example, German] via tongues") after the person began to study it "in the usual hardwork manner." What apparently happened was that what the person thought was German proved to be something entirely different when compared with real German.[5]

Cryptomnesia

Some alleged cases of xenoglossia might be explained by cryptomnesia which is the appearance in the conscious mind of what was once stored in the memory and then forgotten. While such cases of "hidden memory" are not unusual, something more common is remembering a language under certain kinds of stress. Thus, an eminent botanist who in his younger days used Malay while conducting field work in Indonesia is able now to make sentences in this language only when in the hearing of a language that is unintelligible to him, and then the Malay appears involuntarily and instead of the intended sentences. This is just another case of the even more common type of language mixing, as when, for example, a hostess asks her French-speaking dinner-guest "Voulez-vous du *mapa?*" translating English "Would you like some bread?" but using the local African word instead of the French *pain*. I probably was borrowing from this same language when in a moment of silliness I wrote a glossolalic thank-you note to my Alakinki-speaking friend (page 141) who had sent me some material:

Makari Dipyo,
Dorondo mo kadastayante, kidarupa wenta, kedara wenta.
Kiparku na torostante, i valakantu wamemi.

[5] Investigation might reveal that the more a group of people is familiar with foreign languages, the less will it claim cases of xenoglossia—or the more far-fetched its claims will be (for example, not German but Hottentot). This is just a hypothesis. At the moment there is no evidence to show that this is indeed true.

As I wrote, I was thinking something like "Thank you very much . . ." and in Sango *mo* means "you." I think *i* on that occasion meant "and," probably coming from Spanish.

Similar is the case of the middle-aged school-principal whose sample of glossolalia in the questionnaire, with diacritics he provided, has Spanish-like elements:

> *Pōrō vandō rō, lē kăbănzō,*
> *Dăndolé se lă fă măsē,*
> *Yē carră, mucho mando,*
> *Pēpé la, kumē randō,*
> *Gō lavandō, selăgă yă,*
> *Te dala püka, sē răseka soonă,*
> *Mē äkă rändo mandorō, etc. etc.*

They include: *mucho,* "much," *le* direct object pronoun (masculine), *la* direct object pronoun (feminine), *-ndo* present participle suffix, *dando,* "giving," *lavando,* "washing," *se* reflexive pronoun, and *me* first person singular object pronoun. The respondent speaks Swedish and has studied Latin, German, "and a little Spanish."

There is no evidence, however, that glossolalic discourses are characterized by the amount and kind of mixing that one finds in the speech of some bilinguals. The following, for example, might be said by a French-speaking person: *Je suis allée, you know, au cinéma, et puis—what's-his-name?—Dick, the guy from work, was there. Pas de chance, tu sais?* Not only is there no evidence to suggest this kind of mixing (and glossolalists have made great efforts to trace the origins of their "languages"), but it is also something that cannot happen. The glossolalist cannot put words from different languages together to make sense, because the lack of sense is, among other things, what characterizes his speech. This fictitious example, however, both makes sense and can be put into either English or French with very little trouble. (The instance cited on page 191 is different enough not to be considered an exception. In any case, we have little more information about it than what is given.)

It is theoretically possible, of course, for a person to make polylingual nonsense by haphazardly stringing together real but perhaps slightly altered words from several languages, but there is no documented case of this ever having occurred in glossolalia. To put it simply, a glossolalist does not select freely and extensively from the vocabulary that he may have acquired in Latin, French, Spanish, German, and English, for example. To do this extemporaneously and extensively would be quite an accomplishment indeed, even for a skilled polyglot. There are linguistic reasons for this that we will not go into here.

If "word salads"—ungrammatical arrangements of words—characterize the speech of some schizophrenics, this is no evidence that the same kind of thing goes on in glossolalia. The two phenomena are incontrovertibly different.

This is not to say that polylingual nonsense is impossible among human beings. We were just talking about extemporaneous—in a sense, unrehearsed—speech. But in traditional texts, like songs or spells, one can expect words from different languages to be collected. There are several reasons why this should happen, but they do not interest us now. What is relevant, however, is that such texts can eventually become meaningless even to the specialists who utter them, even without the changes in pronunciation that might occur after a period of time (like *hocus pocus* which allegedly comes from *Hoc est corpus meus,* "This is My body," pronounced in the celebration of the Christian eucharist).

A good example of this kind of traditional language mixture is found in the Sinhalese *mantra* used in addressing the demons that are supposed to be responsible for a person's illness. These spells, referred to as the "language of the demons," are compounded of Sinhalese, Tamil, Pali, Sanskrit, Malayalam, Telugu, Bengali, and even Persian. It is no wonder that the spells are unintelligible (Tambiah 1968:177).

What does happen in glossolalia, then, is that words or phrases from known languages are used rather sparingly and sometimes, even, in a rather systematic way. A glossolalic prayer might begin or end in English; in the middle of such a prayer, after a breath-group is completed, there might be a full sentence in English. This natural-language material, moreover, consists of clichés in the technical sense: they are set phrases like "Thus saith the Lord." Here is a sample from the glossolalia of a West Indian (that is, Caribbean Negro), inexplicably identified by the reporting anthropologist as an ejaculation (Calley, pp. 78,163, slightly altered from the original in spelling):

He shall be my *amajuka*
He shall be my *atandoboine*
He shall be my *adala shilama pando baka shai bahikasai*
He shall be my *adai*
He shall be my *a hekobai*
He shall be my *blandahopendalabai*
He shall be my *dahoken salabai*
He shall be my *dasarabai*
He shall be my *dahokentaia hokentai*
He shall be my *dahokal*
He shall be my *hokensala lipos salam*
He shall be my *umbabadala shilama.*

Real cases of cryptomnesia would be quite startling in charismatic behavior, but they would be difficult to document because the linguistically naive are insufficiently critical.

Many people do not seem to realize that the occurrence of words from languages known to them is evidence against the supernatural nature of their tongues. My respondents provide several examples of their credulity. For example, a Texas housewife reported that "[her] language that sounded like Eskimo was spoken soon after our return from a trip to Alaska where we heard some Eskimo singing." A former missionary to West Africa recorded the phrase *alla kamaiya* in which he identified the word *alla* as "God" without noting that the Islamicized peoples of Africa use the Arabic word *Allah* with this meaning. A well-educated minister reports using *tetelesthai* "or something like that" which meant "that something was finished." This, in fact, is an incorrect spelling (with "th"—for Greek θ—instead of "t") of the third person passive perfective of the Greek verb *teleō*. It is uttered by Jesus just before he dies on the cross: *tetélestai*, "It is finished" (John 19:30).

Similarities to language

The great variety of evidence cited at the beginning of this chapter and earlier reveals how glossolalists, who claim to experience a single phenomenon, fail to agree on what it is that demonstrates that their glossas are languages. Their proof has different kinds of motivations. They behave somewhat like people would if they proved that a cow was an "animal" by saying that it had four legs, or lived on land instead of in the water, or had a hairy covering to its body, or fed its young with mammary glands. In determining what X is, we have to know what it could possibly be assigned to. In the one case, the question simply is "What is an 'animal'?" and in the other "What is a 'language'?" For the latter it is better to ask "What is 'language'?" since all languages ever known to man share fundamental features. Having defined "language," we use this canon to decide whether glossolalia is to be admitted as one of its manifestations.

Language is identified as such because of its form and function; moreover, given one, we assume the other. If we discovered non-terrestrial creatures vocally interacting with each other in what appeared to us as a patterned way, we would assume that they had "language." Language is not simply communication, but a *system* of communication; that is to say, it has structure. This is why the recent discovery of pulsars led some scientists to speculate that these might be communicative: they seemed to appear in a pattern.

The systematic nature of language is apparent even without the reassurance of its meaningfulness. Language is so systematic, in fact, that man is hardly ingenious enough to disguise it to the extent that another human cannot decode it. What this means is that language consists of an inventory of units of several different orders each with its own patterns of distribution. The elements—sound units, "words" and affixes, phrases and clauses, etc.—are not put together in random order. Thus, in language one would not expect the sound units *t, m, a,* and *i* to come out in sequences like the following: *aimt taim mtai tima tmia tmai* etc. (as produced by throwing four cards with these letters up in the air). It is, in fact, impossible for man to produce anything truly at random.

Nonrandomness and pattern, however, should not be emphasized at the expense of two other characteristics of language, arbitrariness and contrast. A board equally divided by horizontal and vertical lines is certainly patterned, but it communicates practically nothing; however, when some squares are red and others black, the checkerboard becomes functional. If, in a four-lettered word, the elements *t, m, a,* and *i* can occur in all positions (as in *tmai, mtai, itma, iatm,* etc.), then there is no contrast between them: they are all members of the same class. But if *a* and *i* can only follow *t* and *m* (as in *tima, mati, mita,* etc.), then these two sets of sounds contrast with each other.

Arbitrariness, the other feature, is illustrated, for example, by the fact that the sound represented by "ng" occurs in English at the end of a word, as in *sing,* but never at the beginning. There is no reason why it should not occur in a word like *ngis*; other languages, like Vietnamese, have words beginning with this sound. So this is just one of the quirks of English.

But arbitrariness is found in a more important place: in the relationship that units of sound have to what is outside the linguistic system. It is completely arbitrary that the structure people live in is called *house* in English but *tuwa* in Gbeya, an African language.

Language, therefore, to put it rather simply, is a system of vocal symbols internally organized in a patterned way and related arbitrarily to the external world. It is also a system that is transmitted by learning, that is, from the older members to the new members of society. It is not like the "dance-language" that is inherited by bees. If language were inherited, there would not be the kind of change that we observe over a period of several centuries. Shakespeare's English is different from our own, and Chaucer's even more so.

If we operate with the linguist's canon of language, we can judge whether a glossa is like any human language extant or extinct. And we find that all of the glossas we have examined (recorded by ourselves or others) do have some, albeit incomplete, resemblance to natural language. To recapitulate what has already been suggested, glossolalia is verbal behavior that consists of using a certain number of consonants and vowels in the constitution of a limited number of syllables that in turn are organized into larger units that are taken apart and rearranged pseudogrammatically. One might call these "words." These again are strung along to make longer utterances that are set off by pauses or silence of various durations and co-occur with variations in pitch, volume, speed, and intensity. These breath-groups or "sentences" with their intonational patterns, paralinguistic features (such as voice quality), and accompanying nonverbal behavior (like posture and gestures) all resemble, if they are not identical with, the kinds of features one finds in societies known to the speakers. Indeed, there is no doubt that a practiced glossolalist, in contrast with a beginner, really sounds as if he is talking a language.

It is this superficial resemblance to language, surely, that reinforces the glossolalist and helps him maintain the fiction that he is really talking. The meaningfulness of the immediate experience must also be a factor. That is, he has thoughts and feelings that are real, and the authenticity of this experience validates the verbal phenomenon that accompanies it. All that is missing is a "translation system," a semantics, that relates the two sets of phenomena. The glossolalist bypasses this, not simply because it is not existent (he has one available in his own language), but because it is at the moment irrelevant. There is more to say on this topic in Chapters 10 and 11.

What is interesting about these similarities as far as linguists and other social scientists are concerned is the all-pervasive influence of one's linguistic knowledge. A human being simply cannot avoid being influenced by the patterns of language once he has acquired its use. One might even speculate that there is no vocal activity produced by man that is not at least partly language-controlled.

To these verbal similarities with language must be added one more, equally important and equally derived from one's linguistic experience as a human. It is that glossolalia acquires different social functions that parallel those of language. In other words, glossolalia is not just sound produced in a certain way but sound *used* in socially meaningful ways. We will not say more about this here, but it ought to be kept in mind while reading Chapter 7. It is worth pointing out, however, that form and function are somehow interdependent. Important for the whole social function of glossas is the fact that they should *sound* like languages.

Dissimilarities to Language

It is on looking closely at glossas that their artificiality becomes apparent.[6] This is as true of their construction as it is of their function.

---

[6] Sherrill's book *They Speak with other Tongues* is frequently cited by laymen as having proved the contrary. But all the author did was to play some tape recordings to a group of people to see if they could identify any languages in the texts. He reports: ". . . although no language known to these men was recorded, they had frequently identified language *patterns* on the tapes. The 'shape' of real language, the variety of sound combination, infrequency of repetition and so forth, is virtually impossible, so they said, to reproduce by deliberate effort" (p. 113). Although some of these people are

The function of language is, among other things, communication. It might be more proper to say that man uses language for communication, and that language makes this possible by "translating" experience—which is everything man perceives—into sound waves in a way that another person can retranslate them into a comparable experience. This feature of language is "semanticity," and one of its characteristics is that at one level of language "words" denote parts of man's experience: for example, *house, dog, tree.* There is very little of this in glossolalia, and the few meaningful words that occasionally occur hardly constitute an exception (see Chapter 4).[7] This basic difference between pseudolanguage and real language has many important implications, only two of which are now sketched out.

1. Glossas and natural languages are responsive to the world outside the speaker in different ways. In normal speech it is content, and not merely manner of delivery, that changes constantly in response to topic, person, setting, time, and so forth. Thus, at a certain point in time, say, August thirty-first, what one says might contain words like *hot, humid, muggy, tired;* on January first—in Chicago, for example—the words would be different. In glossolalia, however, it is the total speech event, not its parts, that is primarily correlated with the "world" or, more accurately, with a person's emotional response to experience.

This description of the meaning of glossolalia is based on statements made by glossolalists and from analyses of their discourses. It was even tested, as we saw on page 96, with Rev. d'Esprit. It was only with the concept of death that he had a conscious response: "Now that was the most meaningful thing that I've done thus far." Upon questioning he explained: "I had the feeling of

---

referred to as "linguists," there is no way of judging their competence or of separating their impressions from Sherrill's interpretations. Also, they did not analyze but only listened to the recordings. Another glossolalist writer would have us believe that a German linguist supposedly proficient in 45 languages said: "I would need at least sixteen pages of phonetically transcribed script to study and analyze before I could make a certain judgment (whether what was spoken is a true language)." (Quoted in McDonnell 1970:43n.) Only the credulous will accept this uncritically.

[7] A glossolalist might argue that this is no argument, because the semantics of glossolalia is different from that of human language. In the absence of any evidence, this is, of course, no counter-argument but just a statement of faith.

what was being said. . . . I sensed that I was talking about the fact that . . . there is no death, that we move from this life to another life, and that what many think of death is illusion. . . ." But this feeling has no linguistic significance whatsoever. Just a few hours before, he had met and talked with a couple whose child had recently died, and he had been sincerely grieved with them. It is understandable, therefore, that the word "death" would have a greater psychological effect on him, whatever it might be, than other words; and it would have a greater effect on him than it would on a student, say, who had just received word that he had been awarded a generous scholarship. So when Rev. d'Esprit says that he experienced something "meaningful" as he prayed in tongues while meditating on death, he may only mean that his emotions were more realistic, more marked than they would be when, say, he sat absent-mindedly at the wheel of his automobile, waiting for a light to change.

This is not to say that every time a Pentecostalist prays he is saying "the same thing." Far from it. After all, he has not memorized his speech. There are differences between each one of his discourses, but these are not systematically (in terms of rules of a system) related to what lies outside the speech. (This is what was meant by "linguistic" in the preceding paragraph.) The pieces in the speech are inconsequential when compared with general differences (for example, in speed of utterance, length of breath-groups, and degree of stress) between one "language" and another and between two discourses in the same "language" that have different "meanings" (say, joy and anxiety). In English, for example, one has to be careful what consonants occur before the syllable -*it* or what words follow *Did you have a look at her* . . . ? Ignoring rules of grammar or usage ("social semantics") can lead to misunderstanding or vulgarity. (Other facets of this topic are taken up in Chapter 10.)

As a transportation system that mediates between speaker and addressee, language provides a network of roads that can be taken, each with its own scenery and limitations. In other words, one can say "the same thing" in different ways. Put a little more carefully, in natural language some utterances (whether they be sentences or paragraphs) are paraphrases of others and are therefore equivalent in some sense. Language provides an infinite number of exam-

ples, but we can look at various English translations of part of John
I:I:

> Before the world was created, the Word already existed. (To-
> day's English Version)
> At the beginning God expressed Himself. (Phillips)
> When all things began, the Word already was. (New English)
> From the first the Word was in being. (Basic English)
> In the beginning was the Word. (Authorized Version)
> In the beginning the Word existed. (Williams)

Apart from one's tastes or prejudices there should be no difficulty
in accepting these sentences as equivalent. "The Word began before the world was created" would not be equivalent. In glossolalia,
however, all (or perhaps nearly all) utterances are interchange-
able. This first "sentence" from a glossolalic prayer—/diyăn
tekriyămo pandri talava shande/—could just as well have occurred
in the place of the fifth—/tekiyandĭ lăvosăndrama kayă shĕndĭ
lăvăsiyă/. We assume that this is true because of the way syllables
freely conjoin to make "words" and "sentences." Naturally, it would
be impossible for a glossolalist to tell you if his reordered utterances
meant something different or had any meaning whatsoever, because he was not aware of any systematic meaning to begin with.
The main exception to this rule of freedom is the use by some
speakers, as we have already noted, of formulaic ways of beginning
or ending a discourse in glossolalia.

2. In construction as well as in function glossas are fundamentally different from languages. For one thing, they have very
few elements that have fixed patterns of distribution such as are
found with affixes and words in natural languages. This is seen in
any analysis of a rather long glossolalic text. Enough has been said
about this topic already to preclude further discussion here.

If glossas do not have grammatical structure, we might nevertheless expect them to be like languages phonologically, because
they sound so much like languages. Even here we are deceived.

The total number of different sounds appears to be smaller than
one finds in most languages, and usually smaller than those in
the person's native language. Admittedly, however, the latter have
been European ones in most of the studies reported on. What
Hawaiian glossolalia would sound like (assuming that we could

find a speaker who knew no other language from which he could borrow sounds), we do not know. That language has only thirteen fundamental sound units (phonemes), five vowels and eight consonants. There are languages with as many as forty-five phonemes reliably accounted for, but it is difficult to be precise about an average. Some linguists guess at a figure around thirty (Hockett 1958:93).

There are glossas with only half a dozen consonants and two or three vowels. The actual number varies from speaker to speaker, in the glossas of the same person, and in a single text (as noted below). What determines the number is not always clear. It cannot be wholly attributed to the person's experience in other languages. That accounts for what sounds he uses, not necessarily how many. Two people who know only English can differ drastically in their phonological inventories.

This point can be illustrated (not proven) by comparing portions of three different texts. Below are listed the 105 or so consonants (*not* letters) that occur in the first verses of 1 Corinthians 12, in the Basic English Version (where more redundancy is expected than in ordinary English) as compared with the consonants of the first four breath-groups of two glossolalic texts, both from native speakers of English. Glossa A is that of Rev. d'Esprit. The frequency of occurrence of each consonant, as indicated by the figures, is also given for further comparison. The semi-vowels /w/ and /y/ are omitted from the glossas, because it is not easy to distinguish their consonantal from diphthongal function in these texts: /y/, for example, never occurred unmistakably at the beginning of a syllable, as in /ya/. The letter "r," it must be remembered, stands for the Spanish sound in the glossas but the usual sound of American *rabbit* for the Basic English text, as illustrating my own form of American. Other pronunciation cues are given in the table.

The reason that a reservation was made above ("not proven") is that many more texts would have to be compared before such tables could be taken as "proof." Nevertheless, I have compared enough texts, some more carefully than others, to make me feel thoroughly satisfied that this is a fair comparison. Part of the difficulty in establishing the difference, of course, is the fluid nature of glossolalia, as we have already indicated. A tongue speaker can drop some sounds, introduce new ones, and increase or decrease their frequencies at will, so to speak. We can hardly be certain that we are comparing the total inventory (or list) of sounds of any set of speakers at any time. In a natural language, however, the list is always definite for the whole language when studied within a restricted period of time. But there will obviously be different lists of sounds for different texts, no matter what parts of them are compared.

Comparison of consonants from three texts

	Basic English	Glossa A	Glossa B
p	2	6	6
b	6	2	—
t	18	10	30
d	3	8	5
k	2	9	11
g	1	1	—
θ (*thin*)	2	—	—
ζ (*this*)	6	—	—
ch	1	—	—
j (*judo*)	2	—	—
sh	1	6	5
zh	—	4	—
m	3	6	5
n	6	15	22
ng (*sing*)	2	—	—
f	3	3	—
v	3	—	—
s	5	11	5
z	7	—	—
h	—	1	—
l	2	8	3
r	15	14	10
w	9	—	—
y	6	—	—
	105	104	102

Glossas are strikingly unlike natural languages in the rank frequency curves of the sounds (see page 82f). There is generally a sharper break between the most and least common sounds than in natural languages, and the same is true of syllables and sequences of syllables. What this means is that certain units are being overworked. This cannot happen in normal language, because the occurrence of sounds is determined by the words they occur in, and the words are largely determined by the message that the speaker wants to encode. In a self-conscious use of language, of course, one can select from the language's total inventory of words to make a special effect, as with alliteration or rhyme.

Another aspect of this feature of language is that no matter how many sounds a language has, their function is to differentiate meaningful segments of speech. That is, sounds not only make up such segments (such as *she, ship, shrink, bush*) but also do it in such a way that speakers of that language can tell these units apart from others (such as *see* and *sip*). Since there is no such need in glossolalia, one can say anything he wants in any way he wants. Put in technical terms this is to say that the phonological system is not subservient and obedient to a semantic system; or, a semantic system is not imposed on the phonological system. This is why a glossolalist uses (and in some sense, plays around with) similar segments such as /sita, shita, sinta, chita/.

This discussion suggests another feature of glossolalia that has been mentioned once or twice before (for example, page 88). It is that glossolalia, even though it is lexically meaningless, is not a randomized collection of sounds and sound sequences. It is the result, rather, of some kind of principle of selection. The illustrative words with which the preceding paragraph ends also illustrate this point. This is selection because the glossolalist chooses—at any point in time—to use this instead of that syllable or sequence. The causes of the choices may be varied, and some may be more prominent than others at different points in time, but they are irrelevant to our present discussion.

This chapter has demonstrated that glossolalia is a derivative phenomenon. Its basic features depend on the linguistic competence and knowledge of each speaker. This will surprise no one who came to this study already convinced that glossolalia was some kind of gibberish. However, now he knows that it is not *simply* that. We have also seen that because glossolalia is not just gibberish millions of tongue speakers are led to believe that they engage in authentic speech. Now they can understand what led them to this conviction. They must realize, moreover, that when the full apparatus of linguistic science comes to bear on glossolalia, this turns out to be only a façade of language—although at times a very good one indeed. For when we comprehend what language is, we must conclude that no glossa, no matter how well constructed, is a specimen of human language, because it is neither internally organized nor systematically related to the world man perceives.

Not all that we know about language has been brought to the present examination. Nor have we mentioned all that we already know about glossolalia. That combination would have made this book larger and more technical than it is meant to be.

Yet there is one more aspect of this phenomenon that cannot be ignored. We must see its relation to other anomalous forms of speech. The next chapter, therefore, will show that apart from ordinary human language there are several phenomena that reveal close resemblances to glossolalia narrowly understood.

6

COMPARED WITH
OTHER FORMS

GLOSSOLALIA HAS BEEN misunderstood, because people have been too preoccupied with its psychological and sociological features. When it is examined from a linguistic point of view, one begins to understand how close it is to everyone of us.

There is, in fact, a wide range of verbal phenomena, most of it meaningless but some of it in natural language, that resembles glossolalia in interesting ways. The most closely related are those that (a) are produced extemporaneously, (b) are of rather long duration, (c) have no linguistic meaning (where sequences of sound are related systematically to meanings), and (d) bear no close resemblance in form to a known language. Some of these are used as if they were communicative (if only in play), but others are clearly not communicative in function. That is the easiest way to classify them. There are several subcategories, and their characteristics are sometimes overlapping.

Communicative

One group of tongues-like speech includes magical incantations, spiritistic medium speech, argots, double-talk, and the like. What these have in common is being, or pretending to be, communicative in nature. Some, moreover, are supposedly preternatural or supernatural in origin; others are not.

Preternatural. Glossolalia that comes from someone or something outside a person can occur in a religious or nonreligious context. The recorded cases of religious glossolalia are mostly Christian; that is, they are inherited through the Christian tradition and occur in a Christian context. What is now "Christian" glossolalia could, of course, be a Christianized form of a non-Christian or even nonpreternatural glossolalia. Some people, as we have already seen, used some form of pseudolanguage in prayer long before they knew of its institutionalization in the charismatic movement. Other people seem to have moved from a kind of spiritism, perhaps private and unsystematized, to Pentecostalism; some, in fact, never arrive at a clear distinction. (And others go from the charismatic to the psychic.) One such person is a woman who asked questions of the spiritual power that communicated with her. We have a recording of her questions (in English) and the answers (in perfectly good glossolalia). She was interested in knowing things like: "Are you the *niratangalo?*" "Am I a diabetic?" "Will Paul ever marry?" "Is the teaching about reincarnation true?" "Is the teaching about the rapture true?"[1] The answer to the last question was /yastanday koriyatay somila shanday/. (Compare the last word with those listed on page 99.)

If the Christianization of glossolalia can take place in individuals, it might happen on a broader scale. For example, in Russia how did the Khlysti of the eighteenth century and the Molokans of the nineteenth century acquire glossolalia?[2] Was there a tradi-

---

[1] The rapture generally refers to the bodily ascension of all believers at the return of Jesus Christ, but we do not know what this woman meant by this term. See 1 Thessalonians 4:16–17, "The dead in Christ will rise first; then we who are alive, who are left, shall be caught up together with them in the clouds to meet the Lord in the air" (RSV).

[2] The Khlysty, or the People of God as they called themselves, flourished from early in the seventeenth (if not even earlier) to late in the nineteenth century. Extremely heterodox by comparison with Russian Orthodoxy or other dominant forms of Christianity, this sect is considered mystical by Bolshakoff. Glossolalia appears to have taken place at secret night services where there were also ritual dancing and other "emotional" behavior. Samples of the utterances are recorded from earlier sources by Roman Jakobson

tion in eastern Christianity that paralleled the one in the west? Was the practice imported from the west? Did it have non-Christian antecedents, or did it arise spontaneously? The answers in such cases are of interest especially to the student of religious history, but the linguist is particularly intrigued by the last possibility because of what it might reveal about man's linguistic propensities (about which more will be said below).

Cases of non-Christian glossolalia, on the other hand, are difficult to document in spite of attempts, like May's, to do so. The problem, as we have repeatedly said, is knowing for certain what kind of speech was actually used. Plato's reference to ecstatic speech in ancient Greece is interesting, but it is not ethnographic. And even when modern ethnographers report the use of anomalous language, say, by shamans, they do not say enough about it.[3] I will try to describe one case from personal experience.

In the Caribbean there are several forms of folk religion some of which, for all their Christian trappings, reveal several features of the traditional African religions from which they descend. The best-known of these is Haitian voodoo. In Cuba, which is not without its African heritage, there is a *santeria* cult. It consists of local groups of initiated and their priestesses, that is, *santera.* (These are words of Spanish origin.) In a general way the cult could be described as a religious form of spiritism. It is spiritistic because of the *santera*'s communication with the *ser,* protective spirits of one

---

(1966:635–644): for example, *kindra fendra kiraveca, rentre fente,* and *natrufuntru.* The Molokans, another heterodox sect, are discussed more fully below (page 184).

[3] Like so much that has been written about glossolalia, May's article in the *American Anthropologist* has been used uncritically. Although it is only "A survey of glossolalia and related phenomena in non-Christian religions," people have cited it as having proved that "non-Christian glossolalia has been found on all continents," as one person wrote. May's survey depends on library sources, but a little investigation will reveal that observers have used the term "glossolalia" for a wide variety of vocal phenomena. All that May has documented, therefore, is that some kind of anomalous vocalizations occur in some religious behavior in different parts of the world. Sangree, for example, says that the African Church of the Holy Spirit (otherwise known as Dini Ya Roho) in Kenya uses glossolalia, but he describes it as *da-da-da-da-da-da-da-da-da* "and other broken syllables" (p. 176); this is hardly glossolalia. And when Eliade says that "the shamanic 'spirit language' not only attempts to imitate animal cries but contains a certain proportion of spontaneous creations" (p. 440, cf. pp. 62,96–99), there is no way of knowing what these vocalizations are; he also is using library sources.

type or another, who "ride" or possess her in trance; it is religious because of the emphasis on healing and because of the ritual that is used at the seances. As so often happens with possession, the spirit is believed to talk through the priestess.

I did not need to attend a cult service to hear a spirit talk. All I had to do was to have a consultation with a *santera*. The one whom I went to see practiced in the Bronx, ironically just a hundred yards or less from the Assemblies of God church where I had witnessed glossolalia (described on page 188). It was that same night, in fact, that I walked up the dingy stairs to her locked and burglar-protected apartment. When I arrived, accompanied by a social worker of the area who had joined the cult in connection with her research, the *santera* was ironing. There were more signs of "class" than one might expect in this neighborhood, such as copies of mass-produced paintings on the walls, a television set, and a nice but gaudy sofa protected against frequent use by a plastic cover. But the small "consultation" room was fitted out only with the bizarre paraphernalia of the cult. (The cult-room was in the basement.) The consultation began when I was seated in front of the *santera,* hands crossed on my lap, my knees just a few inches from hers. She touched various objects in the shrine, rubbed cologne over various parts of my torso, and blew cigar smoke over my head and face. Then she waited. Presently she behaved as if in trance: her body twitched and she made clicking and sucking noises. In a voice that sounded a little drunk she then began to ask me questions and to tell me about myself. All of this was in Spanish; my companion translated when necessary. The consultation ended with "prescriptions" about how to avoid getting headaches and how to get to sleep at night.

The fee was $3.00, but it was worth it. During the session one of her spirits spoke, not the African "Kongo" one I wanted to hear but a "Hindu." Although the voice was a bit fuzzy, whether from a trance-state or all the cigar smoke she had deliberately inhaled I do not know, the speech was clearly enunciated. It did not sound anything at all like a language from India, but neither did it sound very much like her Puerto Rican Spanish. In fact, it very much resembled religious glossolalia I have heard; and although there was less repetition than I have come to expect, there was no indication that this was memorized speech.

It is possible, however, that this "Hindu" speech was a deformation of an African language, because Efik, "Kongo" (some Bantu language), and especially Yoruba (known as Lucumí in Cuba, see Olmsted), play an important role in the *santeria* cults. Prayers and dance-songs, for example, are in Yoruba. Moreover, "as part of their training in the Afro-Cuban cults, even the newcomers acquire a vocabulary in an African language. . . . These vocabularies are systematically learned through instruction by those more advanced in the cults, and are copied by hand into note books or copy books" (Bascom 1953:163; see also Bastide). The extent of this knowledge is remarkable. Bascom reports that in 1948, when he was conducting anthropological research, there were Cuban Negroes "from one end of the island to the other" who could actually talk Yoruba (1950:64); this was eighty years after slavery was abolished. However, if my *santera*'s speech was close to an African language, my familiarity with African languages (including Yoruba) would have permitted me, I think, to recognize it as such.

The line from preternatural pseudolanguages to spells, incantations, verbal charms, and the like is not a very clear one, partly because these are not communicative in the same sense and partly because they may not be religious. In some instances, in fact, it may be difficult to distinguish the magical from the playful use of language.

Some nursery rhymes, for example, with or without a certain amount of "mumbo-jumbo," give an impression of the unknown and awesome if not the occult. The following Dutch pseudomagical rhyme gives the idea:

Hokus pokus pilatus pas
Ik wou dat jij weg [or *dood, groot,* etc.] *was.*

(The last line translates as "I wish you were gone [or dead, fat, etc.].") Other spells are *Ofano Oblamo Ospergo* and *Pax Sax Sarax* (from Malcolm Torrie's mystery story *Your Secret Friend* [1968] about death in a haunted house, p. 201). Alliteration, not lexical nonsense, was used in a charm of seventeenth-century England to avert evil spirits. A person was to say, very quickly three times in a row, "Three blew beans in a blew bladder; rattle, bladder, rattle" (Radford, p. 35). But nonsense, as well as rhyme, is

used in spell-like mocking taunts based on personal names. Here is
one from Surrey, England:

> *Joan to oan,*
> *Pepp-in-tus scoan*
> *Frastockadilla moan,*
> *Fring frang froan* (Opie, p. 158).

Some are adapted in metrics to a well-known cat-call, the melody
of which will bring back to many readers painful memories of
childhood troubles.

The following is sung out by a boy at a "Miss Runyon" in a novel
for adults.

> *Runyon todunyon*
> *Tianigo sunyon*
> *Tie-legged, tie-legged*
> *Bow-legged Runyon.*

It is clear, therefore, that magical language commonly if not universally uses linguistic devices that resemble those of glossolalia.
For example, a certain group of English witches were supposed to
have repeated, according to one of them who confessed in 1664,
something like *Thout, tout, a tout, tout, throughout and about* on
their way to their meetings and *Rentum tormentum* as they left
(Joseph Glanville, 1726, quoted by Mackie, p. 37).

Nonreligious but preternatural glossolalia occurs when people
are in communication with psychic phenomena, usually spirits of
human beings who once lived on earth. If the language is foreign,
whether terrestrial or extraterrestrial, a "guide," usually different
from the one who speaks, must interpret.

The distinction between religious and nonreligious glossolalia is
admittedly difficult to make at times. For example, one person who
sold recordings of his "Music of the spheres" described it in the

following words: This is a "musical creation in which those psychically trained or developed in this incarnation can see the aura of the Soul besides often those great Ascended Masters from higher dimensions; also recollections from past lives come to some during the revery of the singing as well as other revelations of the fourth dimension." Even without transcriptions one infers from the description that this is indeed glossolalia: "The songs are created solely for the audience—never heard before and never to be repeated by singer from memory—as the music is strictly a projection of the Soul from universal sources to the Soul of the listener." Moreover, this form of singing came to him "as a lad" and "always in relaxation or in periods of rest." In any case, this distinction between religious and nonreligious is one that Pentecostal glossolalists would probably want to make.

One of the best known cases of spiritistic glossolalia is that of a Swiss medium who was studied by the psychologist Flournoy for at least three years. This Helen Smith, a pseudonym given to protect her identity, was a very interesting and unusual person in many ways, but it is her language that we are concerned with. There were actually a number of languages: a "Sanskrit" in her "Hindu cycle" and "Martian," "Ultra-Martian," "Uranian," and "Lunar" in her "Martian cycle." They are all, however, to one degree or another, recoded forms of her native French, and, when she wrote Martian, as she often did in trance, the two languages are matched word-for-word. For example:

De	vechi	ke	ti	efi	merve	eni
Tu	vois	que	de	choses	superbes	ici

"You see many wonderful things here."

Astané	ne	ze	ten	ti	vi
Astané	est	là	près	de	toi

"Astané is there beside you."

The Martian is not orthographically similar to French, however, because a different system of symbols was used, one that resembles Devanagari of Sanskrit and other languages of India. Except for a couple of modifications, Helen had as many letters as there are in French, and she used them in the same way: her letters for "c" and "h" combined to represent the consonant of *chou*, "cabbage" (phonetically /shu/), and the letters for "o" and "u" combined to represent the vowel /u/.

Although Helen never produced a great deal of Martian—only 160 different words which occurred three hundred times altogether —she was remarkably consistent in their use over a period of three years. But this was after she had embarked on speaking Martian. That was about seven months after her first outpouring of a meaningless utterance. Flournoy was not able to write it down, because it came so rapidly and somewhat indistinctly. This, in my opinion, was (unpremeditated) glossolalia. It evolved into systematic Martian, even as Flournoy points out, because Helen was asked for the meanings of some of the words; so she was challenged to organize her Martian into meaningful units. There is no evidence, however, that she did this consciously.

It is in the way sounds are distributed in Martian that one sees why it should be considered glossolalia. Even though there is a strong influence of French in the sounds that are used, how the words are modified, and how they are put together in sentences, other rules independent of French are in operation. For example, *nini nini triménêni* is not a simple mirror image of French "Nous nous comprenions" ("for us to understand each other") where each sound would be represented by a single sound in Martian. (French *nous,* of course, consists only of /nu/.) Although there is some phonological similarity (e.g. /n/ for /n/ and /tr/ for /pr/), there is more repetition of sounds in the Martian than one finds in the French. In other words, the occurrence of one sound has an effect on what precedes or follows. This is so strong a tendency that it even makes Helen err: when she said *viche tarviné,* "*notre langue*" ("our language"), she was anticipating in *viche* the "v" that was to follow, because everywhere else the word is only *iche* (Flournoy, p. 208). This is the kind of alliteration, as we have seen, that is common in glossolalia. Notice the repetition also in *bana zizazi,* "*trois fois*" ("three times"): it would appear that *zi-za-zi* either indicates plurality or duration in time.

The high incidence of certain sounds in Martian may be due, therefore, to the repetitive nature of glossolalia, where the production of speech is simplified by using certain sounds and sound sequences with great frequency. But it also appears that Helen was interested in how her language sounded. Thus, although the sound

/ch/ as in English *chew* occurs in French only in a few words taken from other languages, it is common in Helen's Martian. (French "ch" is, of course, pronounced /sh/.) There is also an important difference in the occurrence of vowels. This is Flournoy's own comparison:

	Martian	French
"i" and "e"	73.3%	32.3%
"a" and "o"	18.6%	19.4%
"u," diphthongs, nasalized vowels, and mute "e"	8.0%	48.4%

Martian also has only a few words that end with consonants—such as /l, p, k/—whereas French has many (table, soupe, république, etc.). Helen made her bias in favor of open syllables, seen also in English-speaking glossolalists, explicit when her guide Astané called Ultramartian an "ugly speech" ("langage grossier"). In Flournoy's sample of this language only one word ends with a vowel. Finally, Martian seems to have been different from French in its "délicates nuances d'accentuation" ("subtle variations of accent") and "légère scansion des mots en brèves et en longues" ("slight scansion of words into short and long") vowels (Flournoy, p. 203).

Another published account is that of "Le Baron," an American contemporary of Helen, whose report about his own experience is published in the *Proceedings of the Society for Psychical Research*. His was pure glossolalia as the sample words and phrases reveal, but he always felt that he was talking a real language, and he went to a great deal of trouble trying to determine its linguistic affinities. This was a private language, however, used only when he was in communication with what he called his "psycho-automatism," a kind of mental force, he says, with which a person can put himself in rapport. Up to a certain point, conversations used to take place in English, with Le Baron obviously acting as the "sender" and "receiver" of his own and the psycho's messages. (In other words, he was talking to himself.) One day, in a hotel room, it simply switched from English to "unintelligible sounds resembling a foreign tongue," and when Le Baron asked for a translation, he got it. Although Le Baron apparently did not go into trance on these occasions, he makes it clear that a "worked up" condition was necessary for the experience and that "complete self-surrender . . . resulted in the communication of a loftier flow of verbiage" (p. 288).

I personally investigated the case of a young married woman who had spoken in tongues while in trance. She is a member of a very small and intimate group of friends who became interested in psychical phenomena as a result of reading and conversation. They discovered trancing accidentally (or so it appears) but learned to induce and control the trance after further reading and experience. Daphne (the name I give her) first spoke English in trance. Her English utterances were recorded by her friends on a tape recorder and later fully transcribed. This record is being studied for what it might teach the group. These friends believe that they are getting some kind of guidance from a source outside themselves, although they do not yet understand all the significance of these messages. Glossolalia came only a couple of times and already—after a few months—the group has lost interest in these messages, they said, because of their unintelligibility. It was the problem of their decipherment that led them to seek the help of a linguist. A sample of Daphne's tongues is given in Appendix C. The first part of the recording is untranscribable because of the speaker's condition. The rest of it is clearly articulated and quite normal in delivery. This speech is somewhat different from religious glossolalia I have heard in being richer in sound types. Daphne uses many sounds that are not native to English, some of them of French origin (which she has studied), and some of them are similar to German sounds (which she has not studied). It is significant, however, that she has excellent mimicking ability, as I learned by experimentation. In general, the recording makes one believe that Daphne had (unconsciously) exerted considerable effort in trying to produce a very exotic form of speech. Nevertheless, this is unquestionably glossolalia, another instance of someone "discovering" pseudolanguage without contact with Pentecostalism. It is worth noting that these crypto-cultists (as one might call them) have already been changed by their experience, tending to be more moral and more interested in a God-like supernatural being. They too are going through some kind of conversion experience.

Nonpreternatural. The anomalous forms of language that do not originate in a source outside of man are numerous indeed. Some have real or fictitious communicative value whereas others, as we shall see in the next section, do not have communication at all as their primary function. Among the forms of speech that we are considering here, some have more real (that is, systematic semantic) meaning than others, but all in some way or another resemble true glossolalia. The most important feature is that the phonological substance of language (the "shape of words," if one wants to put it that way) has been modified. This may lead to the deformation of individual words or the whole vocabulary and the creation of new words. The process is in the direction of simplification.

Special forms of speech that retain a lot of their meaning are used, as one would expect, in some kind of in-group, that is, a kind of microsociety. All of them might be called argots if the other meanings of this term are ignored. Some argots, just because they are used by an in-group, exclude outsiders by being incomprehensible to them. These are "secret" or "disguised" languages. "Pig-Latin" is one that most people in the English-speaking world know of. But these "languages" are not of too much interest to us, because their "grammar" is too dependent on a natural language. For example, Pig-Latin simply transposes syllables and adds another meaningless, redundant one to further conceal the process of deformation: *Where did you go?* becomes *Ere-whay id-day ou-yay o-gay?* (Interestingly, it is not the colloquial *Where'dja go?* that is used as the base form.) More interesting are things like the argots of Ethiopia where there is modification of several kinds, among which are augmentation and reduction, processes that witness to deliberate manipulation of the sounds of language (Leslau 1964).

Baby-talk might also be considered here even though the microsociety usually consists only of people of different generational strata, older and younger. A prolonged use of baby-talk might, however, result in a kind of pidgin (a simplified language), as among the Pilagá Indians of South America, where children use "baby-Pilagá" among themselves in certain cases (Henry and Henry). This is in contrast to our society where baby-talk is really a special form of adult speech used with children who have not yet mastered adult language. Other variations occur. Although baby-talk may affect only certain parts of the language, usually its vocabulary, it may, as among the Pilagá, become drastically different from it. Baby-talk can, on the other hand, be so "weak" in form that it affects only a few words. These might be hypocoristic terms like the pet name "Didi" for Diane[4] or family words like "strim bims" for *string beans* that are remnants of child language (Read 1962).

Private languages of multiple-born children, so-called "twin-languages," have been reported, but no description is available to me. One would expect them to be based on the language the siblings were exposed to, but there is reason to believe (such as the few words that have been cited) that a process very much like the one in religious glossolalia might account for some of the vocabulary. Children with this kind of special language might be bilingual, using the secret one amongst themselves and a normal one with "outsiders." It has been reported, however, that some, even single-born, children have substituted a private language for the adult language in every context: they understood what was said to them, but they spoke only their own language.[5] In every such case the child grew out of his private world and entered that of society.

When one turns to meaningless forms of nonpreternatural speech, he finds that they are not restricted to a microsociety and are for the most part ludic in function; in other words, they are used for the fun of it. The best-known example is that of double-talk. A person might pretend to speak German, for instance, by using a few German words and typical German sounds and by exaggerating the use of inverted verb forms and prepositions; nonsense would make up the rest of the utterances, like *Hebben sie die cowlein shmeck on die mut verkisst?* Charlie Chaplin did something like this when he gave a speech as Adolf Hitler in *The Great Dictator;* Danny Kaye, well-known in the United States for his skill at double-talk, led a group of Japanese soldiers in the film

---

[4] The man who called his adult but unmarried daughter by this term in my presence also used a peculiar falsetto that was drastically different from his normal speech. His predilection for affective (or affected) speech was also manifested in the nonsense he used (almost identical structurally with religious glossolalia) in talking with a terrier pup.

[5] In the two cases that were reported to me from personal experience the children were under apparent emotional stress. In one, reported by the father himself, stress was due to a bewildering polylingual environment on immigrating to Canada. In the other, two pre-school children were without their mother during the day while she worked. They refused to speak anything but their own language even though they were old enough to use English.

Up in Arms by speaking "Japanese" to them; and Arte Johnson, famous for his television performances, is a contemporary virtuoso of this type. Children in multilingual societies also engage in this kind of play.

It is only a step away from double-talk of this kind, where a known language is being imitated, to another kind where the imitation is more general in nature. If there is a model in the mind of the speaker, perhaps hidden in the unconscious, the hearer is not able to identify it. Pseudolanguages of this type are very similar to if not identical with religious glossolalia, and the differences depend on how the language is being used and how much conscious artifice there is in making it. For example, one anthropologist friend of mine has been speaking what he has only recently named "Alakinki" for over fifty years. He uses it now, whether alone or with others, to give expression to strong emotions like anger or frustration. However, it was originally practiced when he and a friend in their 'teens wanted to discourage adults from listening to what they were saying. Today Alakinki is indistinguishable from religious glossolalia when transcriptions are compared. Naturally, they sound different because their melodic features are different. But if he were to pray in Alakinki, I imagine that the similarity would be greater.

Another anthropologist, long addicted to mimicking other languages and other dialects of his own language, produces glossolalia when he wants to pretend ignorance of the language of the country he happens to be visiting. In this way he discourages guides from pestering him on his frequent trips abroad. His pseudolanguages, of which I have several tape-recorded samples, differ considerably from Alakinki. For one thing, the syllable structure is more complex. In a couple of the glossas, speech consists almost entirely of consonants, there being just enough resonants (like /m/) and fricatives (like /s/) and an occasional vowel to permit the escape of air out of the mouth. This is easier than one imagines. A similar kind of pseudolanguage, "Bosvidian" by name, is sometimes used by a certain small, intimate group of American students when they are high on marijuana. English vowels and consonants are used and it also has long consonant clusters. Its function apparently is to make the participants feel the group solidarity and it is partly just for fun. Unlike religious glossolalia, Bosvidian is used exclusively in "conversation."

A great many more examples of the adult use of pseudolanguage can be cited. Here are three where glossolalia ·is used privately. One man said that as a child on a Texas farm he used to talk to the cows this way: "There was no use talkin' to 'em in English; they couldn't understand anyway." A young man reared in a Baptist family where swearing was frowned upon expressed his emotions in nonsensical "Baptist swearing." A New York City psychiatrist, on the other hand, had all the profanity he needed and no inhibitions to express anger, but for a happy frame of mind as he walked down the street he frequently used glossolalia.

In the following example also, pseudolanguage was used to express strong emotion. An adult man in his fifties informed me that on one occasion when he was sixteen years old he burst out in a fit of anger at an older brother who had been taunting him. He remembers that while speaking he had no idea that he was not talking a language known to him (English, Yiddish, or Classical Hebrew). It was only after he had stopped speaking that he realized that he did not know what he had said. The experience was so bizarre that he wondered at the time if he had spoken a language of a preincarnation. It never happened to him again.

As one might expect, pretend-language is found more often among children and adolescents than among adults, unless the latter are freed from inhibitions by convivial inebriation. Bringing up the subject in public always raises new examples, but they are rarely reported in print. Here is one example from Heinrich Spoerl's *Die Feurzangenbowle* ("The Flaming Punchbowl"), published in 1933. Some high school boys meet a group of girls with their teacher out on a walk in the country. To tease them, the boys keep circling and confronting them on the path. Finally, the teacher asks the boys to stop bothering them, whereupon Husemann pretends not to understand a word. His friend Knebel takes up the cue, jumps forward and says, *Habushko zasafras chimborumbum ulahubi*; another, *Ruchi binuchi, tsampampel, takataka, pulida*; and another, *Kroklovaftsi takri, tsasku rü-rü*. When the teacher asks, "Parlez-vous français, Messieurs?" the answer is *Okasamolga shurliburli, elidarotspon leilolente panu*. And when she tries, "Do you speak English?" she is told *Lafraya diboldo neknek shtakabumbum, shtakabumbum* (pp. 102–104).[6]

[6] The spelling of the pretend-language has been slightly altered for readers of English to give a better idea of the sounds.

Pretend-language is for fun, certainly in nonreligious contexts, but is there some point in a person's life (for example, in early childhood) when it is "for real"—unless, of course, even a child perceives the difference between real and play languages? On the other hand, perhaps there is a bit of "play" in all pretense, even the religious form.

What we are alluding to is the practice of children to make up words and sentences that are nonsense as far as one can tell. A four-year-old child went through a stage when he quizzed Father and Mother with "Do you know what a . . . is?" This was a game, because he knew that the parents were unacquainted with his word. His language was not as well developed as that of his siblings at this age, probably, explains the father, because he had lived in Togo, Ghana, Spain, and Germany when he was learning to speak English! Another child used a make-up language in an apparent attempt to do what her father and older sister were doing, talking French and Fulani. This practice may go back to very early childhood, to a time when a child has not yet acquired language. One observant, scholarly grandfather has noted that when his granddaughter was only a little over a year old she indulged in what he called "Playing Grown-up Game" in which a stream of nonsense was spoken in very close imitation of adult speech. She could even carry on realistic "conversations" with him (Laird 1968; also Bloom 1968:202).

These anomalous utterances by children were just described as nonsense, but this may be begging the question in some instances. When a child mocks another with a meaningless epithet, as in "You're a *gigifanu!*" he is saying, "You're a you-know-what!" Although the abused child does not know exactly what a *gigifanu* might be, he certainly knows that it is not nice.

Noncommunicative

There is a strong difference between communicative and noncommunicative anomalous speech only when the intent is consciously different. But the lines between believing, pretending, and not intending at all to say something can be very thin indeed. For example, the nonsense of be-bop jazz is surely only for fun; it is playing with the sounds of language. Moreover, play is only one of the functions of "playing around with" language, as we shall see below. And if there is a kind of continuum in the functions to which nonsense is put, so is there a continuum in the forms it takes. Some be-bop utterances are almost indistinguishable from religious glossolalia, but be-bop is only an improved form of *trala-lala*-ing. There is, therefore, a lot of indeterminacy in establishing similarities, but we must make the attempt. To do so, we shall make the distinction between contrived and noncontrived nonsense.

Noncontrived. There is a lot of nonsense material in song, some of it put there intentionally. But some of it arises because we are inclined to hum a tune, or carry it with *lalala* or something more interesting. This kind of scanning appears to be universal and it is remarkably similar all over the world. The most common vowels appear to be /i/ and /a/, and the most common consonants seem to be those made with the tongue tip, like /l, t, d, r/. Anybody can provide himself with examples, and he will find that what he sings is like the *tialariri* sung by a Dutch bicycle repairman I heard or by a Korana bushman of South Africa when he sounded out the tune ordinarily played by a reed-flute. It went (with slight modification):

> *Ta tina ta / ta tanana / ta tina ta / ta tana ta tana ta / ta tanana / ta tina ta / ta tana ta tana ta / ta tana ta ta / ta tana ta ta / ta tina ta tina ta / ta tina ta tana ta*

Such vocal material is also found in refrains, of course, like *Fal-di-rw-di-lam-tam, tw-li-ri-dl-i, try-la-lam-tam, ty-lam-ta-ni* . . . of a Welsh Christmas carol (where "w" is a vowel) praising the holly bough (so transcribed by a newspaper reporter) or

> *wa-ya, ya-ya-ya, tiyon vous tombé*
> *wo-wo, wo-wo, tiyon vous tombé*
> *wa-wa, wa-wa, tiyon vous tombé*

from a Louisiana Creole song where *tiyon-vous tombé* means "your headkerchief fell down" (Courlander, p. 170).

Large sections of a song, as in yodeling, may be devoted to such nonsense material. In "mouth" or "vocal music" and be-bop jazz it may be its most important vocal element. Sometimes mouth music is primarily an imitation of musical instruments, as in the Hebrides Islands, but it can also be purely vocal. A good example of the second is found among Hungarian Gypsies. One particular recording sounds very much like be-bop.[7]

The use of meaningless refrains is very widespread in the world, as is documented by the folk-musicologist Sachs (pp. 51,69–70). The songs of North American Indians are especially characterized by this feature (illustrated by Boas), but there is an interesting convergence of traditional art form and religion in the case of the "peyote cult." This is an inter-tribal, syncretistic—but fundamentally "pagan"—religion organized as the Native American Church. Its chief religious service includes the use of the mind-expanding "button" of the peyote cactus (*Lophophora williamsii*). About one-half of all the songs of this movement are nonsense, and among the Arapaho peyotists almost all of them are (see Nettl for information about these songs). Moreover, these meaningless syllables are different from similar syllables in other songs. Here is part of one such song (Nettl, p. 23):

wi ni wi ci hay
yo wi hay
wi ci hay
yo wi ci ni hay
yo wi ci ni hay
yo wi how
wi ci hay.

Be-bop was a popular genre of jazz in the three decades following Louis ("Satchmo") Armstrong's first recording of it in 1926. It was always primarily a Negro specialty, going back, "Jelly Roll" Morton claimed, to the early years of this century. Some of the best-known pieces are Armstrong's *Heebie Jeebies* and *Skid-dat* and Ella Fitzgerald's lively *Stompin'* and *Oh, lady be good*.[8] Lyrics were not important to these musicians (as the bop song *Hey, Pete, le's eat mo' meat!* clearly illustrates), and the nonsense vocalizations merely provided a complement to what would have otherwise been a largely instrumental performance. Of course,

---

[7] *Folkmusic from Hungary* (Philips album #631.204 PL, Side 2, Number 2).

[8] The albums are CL 851 and MGV 8624 respectively. Other artists are Babs Gonzalez (Dauntless 4311 or 6311), Eddie Jefferson (Prestige 7619), James Moody, Sarah Vaughn with Cannonball Adderley (*In the Land of Hi-Fi,* EMRC 36058), Jackie Cain with Roy Kral (LPV 519 and 530), King Pleasure (Prestige records), and Henry Glover.

some played it cool, like Dizzie Gillespie and Joe Carroll in *Hey, Pete!* and others played it hot, like Fitzgerald in *Oh, Lady!* Whether hot or cool, the interpretation seemed to determine in some part at least the nature of the vocalizations. It is highly unlikely that there were lyrics for be-bop although each vocal artist may have had his own style with favorite syllable types. In one song the only nonsense lines (using our somewhat phonetic spelling) are

> *Bliyabada ulya,*
> *Bliyabada ulya ku.*

In another, the nonsense starts out with

> *Bap, bap, bup bup, dut dut. . . .*
> *Baba bobop, bop bop, bolye. . . .*

It does not take very much for scanning to become lyrics. (I am talking only about our own society; what happens elsewhere is unknown to me.) The process is one in which vocalization becomes verbalization: sounds take on the shape of words. This happens partly through the influence of real words in the environment of the nonsense. Rhyme is part of the process. In a simple form it occurs in be-bop as

> *Ey! Ey! I! U!*
> I'm be-boppin' too.

In the song *In the Land of Oo Bla Dee*[9] a more advanced rhyme is:

> I asked her, *Ubida ublu,*
>   ("Darling, will you marry me?"),
> She said, *Ubadiliya bla blila, iblu*
>   ("There's nothing in the land I'd rather do").

But rhyme can work on nonsense without the presence of meaningful words, because a rhyme is a kind of paradigm. It is this paradigmatic relationship between utterances that makes it seem as if words, with affixes, were being used. Here is a children's game-song from the Netherlands:

> *Oze-wieze, woze-wieze*
> *Walla kristalla kristoze*

---

[9] Copyright © 1949 Criterion Music Corporation.

Wieze-woze
Wieze wies wies wies wies.

(The vowel "o" is pronounced as in French *beau*, "i" as in French *dit*, final "e" as in the final vowel of English *sofa*; "w" is similar to English "v.") As one might expect, the two kinds of rhyme can occur in the same song. Here is a refrain from a Corsican lullaby:

> *Fa lu ninni, fa lu nanna*
> *Dormi, dormi, o car di mamma.*

("Sleep, sleep, Mama's dear one.") And from the Gullah Negroes of South John's Island, South Carolina, comes this children's dance-song:

> *Mama lama, cuma lama*
> *Cuma la bistay.* (Repeat)
> *Oh no no no no*
> *Tay bistay.* (Repeat)
> *Eeny meeny, jus' a teeny*
> *Ooka ama leeny.*
> *Atcha patacha, cuma latcha*
> *"X," "Y," "Z."*

Related to these musical "lyrics" are those that children use in chants and games. Here are two in English (Withers, pp. 86, 183):

> *Acka, bacca, soda cracka,*
> *Acka, backa, boo.*
> *If your father chews tobacca,*
> *Out goes YOU.*

> *Did you eever, iver, over,*
> *In your leef, life, loaf,*
> *See the deevel, divel, dovel,*
> *Kiss his weef, wife, woaf?*

The following one in Dutch is (today) complete nonsense:

> *Olleke bolleke,*
> *Rubi solleke,*
> *Olleke bolleke*
> *Knol!*

Contrived. It is not surprising that nonsense should occur in poetry and that when a poet deliberately uses language for the sake of sound he does what others do perhaps less consciously.

When a poet limits himself to real languages, he can use only what he is given. Although he can play with meanings, it is sound play—in some form of repetition—that resembles glossolalia. In poetry, patterned repetition occurs with consonants at the beginning of words (alliteration) or of vowel and consonants at the end (rhyme), stress, and so forth. Rhyme and "accent" are common enough to need no exemplification. Alliteration is less used in English than it once was; in other languages it is still an important device. Here is a sample from a Lapp poem by Pedar Jalvi (in Collinder, p. 202):

> *Vaarid viegam, duoddar duolmam,*
> *alla gaisa ala goarngum,*
> *Vuvdid vacam, gedgid gaečam ...*
> "I run in the mountains, I wander in the field,
> I climb right to the summit,
> I walk in the forest, I look at the stones ..."

There are poetic texts even in commercial advertising. Alliteration is part of the Diamond Lumber Company's slogan "For a gem of a job" (where /j/ is repeated) and rhyme in radio station CHUM's characterization of itself as

> Chum
> where the fun
> comes from.

Poetry, however, is a special genre of discourse, and in our society poetic devices are generally avoided in prose, whether of the spoken or written varieties. And if they are used, a little—like vanilla flavoring—must be made to go a long way. Nevertheless, in some contexts there is more tolerance, especially by certain groups of people. It is interesting, therefore, that rhyming talk should occur when people are free of their society's constraints. One finds it among people who are high on mind-expanding drugs; and the medium Helen Smith (see above) would occasionally "talk poetry" even when not in a seance.

Individual instances of "poetic prose" are not too difficult to find. Even more interesting is its use by a social group. Some groups of American Negroes apparently used (perhaps still use) what the musician Mezz Mezzrow called "viper conversation" or "street-corner poetry." He says, "This jive is a private affair, a secret inner-circle code cooked up partly to mystify the outsiders, while it brings those in the know closer together because they alone have the key to the puzzle. The hipster's lingo is a private kind of folk-poetry, meant for the ears of the brethren alone" (p. 100). Here is a sample as provided by Mezzrow with emphasis added by myself (p. 99):

> A: Solid ole man, pick up on this *rock,* and it didn't come from no mudkicker in the *block*—I had to bring time for it don't you *see,* so raise up Jack and let *me be.* How'm I *doin'* Poppa Mezz, am I *rhymin'* or am I *rhymin'.*
>
> B: You ain't *climbin',* you're really *chimin',* if you ain't *timin'* a hawk can't *see.*

This chapter has added evidence to demonstrate the "normality" of glossolalia by showing that there are several kinds of speech phenomena that are more or less similar to it. In other words, glossolalia is located somewhere in a list—perhaps even continuum—of speech anomalies that start with the most rudimentary and approach the most language-like. What makes them all different is the amount of "mix" of various linguistic "ingredients" that is determined mostly by how the user conceives the speech event he engages in. I do not say, of course, that glossolalia is poetry, to take only one of the examples. Rather, I say that these two seem to have two things in common: certain linguistic devices and a similar esthetic function.

I might go on to suggest that much of this "infra-linguistic" material may have a common motivation. In the nonsense forms, for example, there appears to be a reversion or regression to a phonologically simplified form of speech. But the examination of this "explanation" of glossolalia, enticing as it is, would lead us far from the immediate task into linguistic technicalities we should like to avoid in this book (but see Samarin 1970a).

Glossolalia is similar to some other forms of speech in function as well as in form. We therefore proceed now to an examination, in five chapters, of the uses and functions of tongues. These too will help the reader to understand *why* the glossolalist engages in speech he does not immediately understand.

7

PRAYED, PROPHESIED, AND INTERPRETED

NATURAL LANGUAGE is put to many uses. Its most obvious functions are communication (*I went to Portugal last year; Where is the post office?*) and the control of human behavior (*Don't cross the street now*), but speech is also used as an oral vehicle for music, to take up time (for example, telling jokes while waiting for the arrival of a banquet speaker), to conceal anxiety, as an accompaniment to more important activities (like speeches at commencement exercises and cheering at American football games), and so forth. It is not surprising therefore that we should find a wide range of overt and covert or explicit and implicit functions of glossolalia. Popular treatment has ignored the complexity of functions, like the newspaper article entitled "Is speaking in tongues the voice of God or schizophrenic babbling?" These are not the only alternatives, as this and the following chapters will demonstrate.

In this chapter we shall discuss two of the uses that glossolalists themselves recognize, praying and giving messages. We learn what these speech events are, how they are used, and—where relevant—how they are supervised or controlled.

But first we need to note that glossolalists make a theological distinction that correlates only in part with the functional one. They would distinguish between the "gift of tongues" (what L. Willis in W. Horton calls "ecclesiastical tongues," p. 264) on the one hand, and, on the other hand, tongues both as an evidence of the Spirit-filling experience and also as a means of worship. Here is the statement of one of my respondents, a Ph.D. candidate:

I distinguish two distinct aspects of Christian experience, which have tongues as a common factor. First is the "baptism in the Holy Spirit," which is a personal experience between the believer and God; a sign of the experience is tongues, and thereafter a believer may speak in tongues at will in a devotional way; that is, as a form of communication with God or prayer. Such speaking in tongues has no value to a hearer except vicariously as when one is happy because another is happy. Second, we have as one of the charismatic gifts of the Holy Spirit the gift of tongues. In this the Holy Spirit moves on a believer to speak in tongues and subsequently on some believer to deliver in the common language of those present the content of what was spoken in tongues. This cannot be done at will but only when the Spirit prompts and the believer obeys. Its purpose is to speak a specific message to those present, and thus contributes directly to the hearer's spiritual life. There is no relationship between these two aspects except that tongues is a common element.

This distinction appears to have a literary basis and not an empirical one. That is, it appears necessary for the interpretation of the relevant Biblical texts (e.g., 1 Corinthians 12:10 and 14:2). Almost every respondent who makes such a distinction is unable to see any linguistic difference. That there are a few who do feel that there is a difference—without being able to say what it is—is not surprising when we remember that there are other function-correlated differences.

For some people, however, no such categories exist. They insist that there is no "speaking" in tongues, just praying. It is not irrelevant that these people are among the better educated and from the traditionally noncharismatic churches. This is true for my respondents and, apparently, elsewhere. Thus, in an Episcopal parish in New Zealand 56 per cent of the tongue speakers who were interviewed said they used glossolalia only in private and 88 per cent of them agreed that tongues "could have a place as a communal act within Christian worship" (Brown 1967; see also Kelsey, pp. 149–150).

Prayers

We use the term prayer for one of the functions of glossolalia, because this is what glossolalists themselves say they engage in at times. It is also called "simple" or "devotional" tongues (see Roberts, p. 52; Frost, p. 24).

Objectively, looking at the whole speech act, it is easy to grant that the glossolalist is engaged in prayer even though the speech is unintelligible. The reason is that he *looks* and *sounds* as if he were praying. His eyes are closed; he may nod his head, if kneeling; he may lift up his head, if standing; his voice takes on the qualities that characterize prayers in the person's native language. Besides, when prayers are said in a public meeting, they occur at those places and times when prayer is appropriate. On such occasions, even the length of a glossolalic prayer is typical. Thus, when people are praying around in a circle, each person taking his turn, as described on page 176, almost everyone restricts himself to the average amount of time (about one or two minutes, but depending on the size of the group).

Some of these characteristics of prayer as a total pattern of behavior undoubtedly recur in private. The greatest difference would be at "formal" private prayer (my own term). On such occasions people pray for as long as three hours, they say. "Informal" private prayer is praying "on the run," so to speak: for example, when worrying about traffic congestion.

Praying in tongues is, as the above-mentioned study by Brown suggests, much more common than giving messages in tongues, and private praying is more common than public praying. This was confirmed by my own study. In response to my question "Do you speak in tongues more often in a group than in private?" sixty-eight out of eighty-five respondents (that is, 80%) answered no. One person used tongues only in private, five about equally in both situations, three more often in a group, and the rest answered equivocally. (Unfortunately, some understood "speak" to mean "utter messages" rather than my intended "employ.")

This predominant use of tongues in prayer, especially private, is to be explained in part by the nature of the contemporary Pentecostal movement. It is from a religious point of view primarily a "devotional" movement. So common is praying, both in ordinary language and in glossolalia, that McDonnell, a Catholic theologian, says that "a casual observer would be led to think that it was simply a prayer movement" (1970:44). Another explanation might be the fact that neo-Pentecostalism is still very much a lay movement in spite of the ever-present clergy. It would seem that as the patterns of leadership emerged in any local group, the relationship between praying and giving messages would change.[1] This is suggested by facts that are examined later in this chapter. How the present movement compares with the early period of traditional Pentecostalism with respect to glossolalic praying is not at the moment clear.

Glossolalic praying, especially in a group meeting, is not simply a substitute for prayer in natural language whenever it is appropriate. For example, even in a gathering of charismatists the ritual "opening prayer" is not in tongues. As will be seen below, there are rules which govern the propriety of using glossolalia. This prayer is naturally not the liturgical or rote kind (which could hardly be called glossolalia in any case) but is like the "free prayer" that one finds in Protestant groups of the "low church" variety (e.g., Baptist and traditional Methodist). A glossolalic prayer is therefore a spontaneous utterance spoken in isolation; sometimes, however, there may be unison prayer where all in attendance at a meeting pray at the same time—not the same prayer, of course. This practice is probably borrowed from traditional Pentecostalists who frequently pray together even in their native languages, although univocal praying among Protestants goes back at least as far as the holiness movement and revivalism of the nineteenth century.

Glossolalists consider praise and petition (including intercession) to be the most important uses of glossolalic prayers, in which

[1] For example, that the public use of tongues would become the function of leadership. The three respondents just referred to who said they used glossolalia more often in a group are male, thirty-six, forty-seven, and fifty-two years of age, all with above-average education, two undoubtedly much above the average of their churches. One is chairman of the board of his church (Church of God), one is a lay preacher (The Apostolic Church, England), and the other is a minister (with a Th.D.) of a Presbyterian church.

they claim to have greater freedom and efficacy by comparison with prayers in natural language. Glossolalia makes it possible for a person to express great joy or profound concern which one is otherwise unable to put into words. A person may find himself, for example, deeply troubled without knowing the reason. Taking this unease as evidence of God's prodding, he engages in glossolalic praying without knowing for whom or why he is praying. Many times, however, it turns out that someone known to the person or connected with his immediate religious group was in dire need at that very moment. Reporting such "miraculous" events takes a prominent part in Pentecostalist testimony meetings and in Pentecostalist literature (for example, Frost, p. 26).

After having prayed, the person's concern disappears and he feels that the matter is cared for. This is why glossolalists say that glossolalia takes the drudgery out of praying, that it enables them to pray when it is otherwise impossible (for example, in grief), and that it makes praying easier. Statements like the following could be supplied in great numbers: "Through the Holy Spirit I can pray easier and can pray either with tongues or my understanding [that is, in English]. I can pray even if I don't know what and how to pray, and I just praise and talk to God. It's refreshing and overflowing."

Praying in tongues is also better, because a person is able to focus on the object of adoration, God, rather than on the means of adoration, language; one person says that rather than concentrating on the mode of communication, one concentrates on the communication itself. The result of this freedom is experienced physically as well as psychologically: one feels more relaxed and rested even though one may have prayed "all night."

The freedom that supposedly characterizes glossolalic praying is significant by comparison with the strain that is said to accompany earnest prayer outside this experience.[2] This contrast has significant psychological and sociolinguistic implications. In the rhetoric of the holiness movement—which includes Pentecostal-

[2] Further study is needed to compare the nonlinguistic behavior of traditional Pentecostalists and neo-Pentecostalists with respect to such things as intensity of action. The former, in my opinion, commonly act as if in pain while engaged in "praising God" in a natural language whereas non-Pentecostal behavior is restrained and calm. In other words, in one case a person learns to act out or show how much he really cares.

ism, one of its extreme forms—earnest praying is described as a kind of struggle: one "prays through" and "wrestles with God," as noted earlier. Nowhere, to my knowledge, is this rhetoric applied to glossolalic praying.

This freedom is described in terms of a dualism that is only partly consistent with a common Christian concept of man as consisting of body, soul and/or spirit. To glossolalists man consists of a natural and a spiritual entity. The natural half is rational and uses natural language and cannot be in touch with God; it is the spiritual half that God communicates with and transforms. This is why there can be thought and language in a spiritual dimension. In glossolalia God bypasses rational man to deal with the inner or spiritual man. This view finds confirmation in passages such as the following: ". . . the Spirit also helpeth our infirmities: for we know not what we should pray for as we ought: but the Spirit itself maketh intercession for us with groanings which cannot be uttered [a description, glossolalists believe, of their unintelligible tongues]. And he that searcheth the hearts knoweth what is the mind of the Spirit, because he maketh intercession for the saints according to the will of God" (Romans 8:26–27).

That was Paul writing to the believers in Rome. This is what contemporary glossolalists say: "The Holy Spirit literally clothes Himself with us and in so doing uses us as an instrument" (J. Slay in W. Horton, p. 232, cf. 223); "If one prays through his intellect his mind creates the speech patterns and words. When one prays through his spirit, it is his spirit in cooperation with the Holy Spirit that forms the words of a new language"; "[a person's] intellect relinquishes active control of the speech centers for a moment" (Roberts, p. 22). And when two of my respondents write in a similar vein, they seem to imply that in glossolalic praying God is talking to himself (with emphasis added):

Speaking in tongues is a very important spiritual experience because it gives us a better way to pray—even about matters of which we know nothing. An individual for whom we are praying may have problems we are not acquainted with, nor do we need to know—*the Lord knows and intercedes for them and for us.* Also it lets us verbalize our feelings and get burdens off our unconscious mind.

An (unknown) tongue cannot communicate to man since if there is no understanding there is no communication. The *origin of the tongue is God* the Holy Spirit. It is logical then that *the communication is to the rest of the Godhead* (who understands all things).

It should be said parenthetically that some glossolalists are less "mechanistic" about the causality of tongues. Some insist that the Holy Spirit is not the one who speaks and the human is not merely a medium. The Holy Spirit inspires the utterance and the human is "fully active in will and thought and feeling" (Gee, p. 75, also 58, 116).

The belief that the Holy Spirit prays through a person, using his vocal organs to produce glossolalic speech, leads to several interesting views, some of which must be considered quite heterodox, if not heretical, from the Christian point of view. For example, since the Spirit prays in his own languages the Devil cannot understand what is being said.[3] Therefore a person who engages in glossolalic praying has, one respondent said, a "private line to God where the Devil cannot interfere." Moreover, since the prayer is uttered by the Spirit himself one has the assurance that he is praying for the right things. It follows from this that there can be no doubt about the prayer's being answered: what the Spirit prays for will be granted by God. This means that when a person is praying in tongues, God is going to do something wonderful, whether one hears of it later or not. Reduced to a formula it reads: "Prayer produces Miracles." Since rational prayers are not this efficacious, it is no wonder that glossolalists who hold these views can be sanguine about life.

Because of this peculiar power glossolalia is supposed to be especially effective in healing and in exorcising, even though there is no Biblical precedent for such a belief. Praying for someone with physical problems takes place in very much the same way it would in normal language: one can be in the presence of the needy person or far removed from him; one starts with the conscious desire that the person be healed, delivered from pain, etc. and then engages in glossolalic discourse. The object of concern

---

[3] But in a science-fiction story it is the Devil who uses this mechanism. Here he is speaking to a man who has made a pact with him: "As for colloquial English, when I enter your world I naturally adjust myself to it— or am adjusted. My own tongue cannot be heard here. I'm speaking it, but you hear the Earthly equivalent. It's automatically adjusted to your capabilities" (Henry Kuttner and C. L. Moore, "The Devil we know," quoted by Krueger, p. 72).

need not be a person, however. One of my respondents, a twenty-year-old practical nurse, has prayed for her pet cat! This she does by putting her hand on it: "He almost always purrs and is well or almost well within twenty-four hours."[4] Moreover, illness, as one would expect in the mid-twentieth century, is frequently conceived in psychological terms: one prays for release from tension, worry, frustration, guilt, etc. These are also seen as "spirits" (for example, the "spirit of worry") to be exorcised or prayed away.

The speaker naturally is not encoding any of the specific concepts that could be realized in normal language. Nothing is specified in the prayer about when the healing should take place, how much people would appreciate it, etc.—subjects that would be touched on in normal prayers. Sometimes, as has already been indicated, one discovers by an examination of "coincidences" that a glossolalic prayer was for someone's healing unbeknown to the speaker. It is, however, unfair to the praying glossolalist to say that his mind is empty as he prays. This is no more true of him than it is of a Catholic who recites his *Pater noster* in great sincerity. I can think pretty clearly myself while reciting One-two-three-four-five-six-seven-eight-nine-ten. And if I were a Sokka Gakkai Buddhist, I am sure that I could meditate while repeating the Daimoku, *Namu myo ho rengekyo* ("Glory to the lotus sutra of the mystical law"), although I might not want to apply myself to the solution of a difficult intellectual problem.

Exorcism in the traditional sense is driving an evil spirit out of a person. A common formula in Protestant circles for this purpose is "I command you in the name of Jesus, depart!" I witnessed such an exorcism at a regional meeting of the Full Gospel Business Men's Fellowship International where a man began to groan and scream uncontrollably during a speech. The command was in English although this was a charismatic meeting. Others might have used tongues in the belief that "exorcism in tongues is more efficient," to quote one of my respondents who gives no reason. Equally real for some charismatists are "evil spirits" of fear, jealousy, pride, and lying. (One would expect that the exorcist's gen-

---

[4] The "laying on of hands" in healing is not a specifically Christian practice. Among the Bushmen, for example, healing on the part of individuals in trance is effected by rubbing one's sweat on the body of the patient (Lee 1968:44).

eral behavior would be different with these "spirits," since they are not considered to be personal creatures.)

It is a short step from these functions of glossolalia to that of control. Not surprising therefore is the practice of one woman who, in addition to exorcising in tongues, also speaks to herself in tongues while conversing with someone to make them "say what God wants them to say"; glossolalia has the same effect, she says, as saying the name Jesus in silence.

In the light of these practices, almost all reported by female respondents, we are justified in suggesting that some glossolalists function as shamans (medicine men in pagan societies), because they see themselves performing a special role with special powers for the good of others. The word "power," indeed, is one that they employ to describe the efficacy of tongues. Oral Roberts, for example, says—in a lengthy italicized passage—that the baptism of the Spirit provides an "inner power" that is released by the giving of tongues (p. 15). One of my respondents, a Wesleyan Methodist, even said that when a person spoke in tongues "there is power released in the room" and "this would benefit anyone present." This is similar to the views of Pentecostals interviewed by Wood in a southeastern part of the United States who believe that the Holy Spirit is a supernatural force or flow of energy. One informant described it as working like electricity: "If it comes down upon one, and another is there, it might just run on through the first into the second" (p. 18). It appears that these people have reduced one of the "persons" of the Trinity to something impersonal at the level of folk religion. These are, however, undoubtedly trinitarian, not "Jesus only," Pentecostals as far as their official creed is concerned. The latter believe that true baptism must be only in the name of Jesus (taking Acts 2:38 literally). They deny the Trinity by asserting that the Godhead consists of three Beings but only one Person, Jesus, and that he is the source of all power (Nichol, pp. 89–91).[5] Even within Pentecostalism, however, they are considered heretical.

[5] A better understanding of the concepts of power and holiness in the teachings of Pentecostals would bring this use of glossolalia into sharper focus, but the necessary theological discussion would take us too far afield. It might be pointed out, however, that the quantification of spirituality is an important aspect of evangelical Protestantism and some circles within Roman Catholicism—not to speak of other branches of Christianity—and is not restricted to Pentecostalism.

Glossolalia then is used as an instrument. We infer this from our own observations, but it is explicit in the rhetoric of glossolalists. They call glossolalia a "tool of grace" or, to use the more traditional expression, a "means of grace." What this actually means will vary from group to group and between individuals although the differences certainly are not infinite. Another case of glossolalia being used instrumentally is that of the man who discovered that he was on a sinking ship, and, when he spoke a few words in tongues, "immediately all fear was gone" (*Voice,* May 1969, p. 28).

This use of glossolalia is almost magical, and it compares very closely with the use of "holy words" in the Church of the Lord, an African independent church. In this group, words that designate the names and attributes of God are uttered to bring some particular power of God to bear on a special situation, such as encountering a snake (Turner, p. 278). Some utterances, it should be noticed, remind one of glossolalic devices, such as *Ajuba, Kajuba, Sajuba* (p. 279). Other words are like *Hullah, Yieohor,* and *Ajjawworrakkabb* whose special power is represented by exotic spelling.

Tongues are specifically mentioned in connection with *obeah* men in Jamaica. These are believed to be agents of the Devil with power to cure and kill. In treating people, it was learned from interviewing Jamaicans in England, "Some read Biblical passages, while others may speak in 'tongues' with the 'duppy' (ghost) during an interview" (Kiev 1963:359). It is not strange, of course, that these non-Pentecostal healers should use a Christian term for their spells because of the way Christian beliefs, especially Pentecostal ones, have been integrated into traditional, even African-based, beliefs. Indeed, it is not at all improbable that this "tongue speech" uses some words that are not English in origin. Although this last is speculation, it is not necessary to assume that *obeah* "tongues" are glossolalia in our sense of the term.

Messages

Glossolalia is also used in addressing a group with the intent of passing on to them a message from God. Since the discourse is unintelligible by definition, it must be "interpreted." Biblical precedent for this use is found in passages like the following:

To sum up, my friends, when you meet for worship, each of you contributes a hymn, some instruction, a revelation, an ecstatic utterance [literally, "whoever has a glossa" or "language"], or the interpretation of such an utterance. All of these must aim at one thing: to build up the church. If it is a matter of ecstatic utterance, only two should speak, or at most three, one at a time, and someone must interpret (1 Corinthians 14:27–28, NEB).

As has already been indicated, many glossolalists identify this use of tongues as "the gift of tongues" in contrast with tongues as evidence of the baptism. It is therefore also known as an "anointing," meaning that a person is inspired by the Holy Spirit; the anointed discourse is called an "anointed tongue." For some people the expression "speak in tongues" refers only to the giving of messages, and it contrasts with "pray in tongues."

Because one gives a message by inspiration this phenomenon is also considered prophecy; in the theological lexicon this means any inspired utterance of special religious value and not simply one that foretells the future.[6] A prophetic message is distinguished from an ordinary one (like a sermon) by the evidence of "anointing." Such evidence, however, is not amenable to a set of criteria of identification. The speaker or audience senses the anointing. Hence for many people prophecy and glossolalic messages—both inspired and anointed—differ only in the absence or presence of tongues. While not denying divine inspiration in both cases, Gee, a traditional Pentecostalist, says that one can err in deciding which channel to use for its expression in a given situation (p. 92), and by taking this stand he makes way for the control of public glossolalia.[7]

[6] I have heard only once of glossolalic sermons. A sermon, by definition, at least in terms of ordinary language, is a somewhat long discourse that expounds a subject or Biblical text. It is also characterized as a special genre of discourse in terms of rhetorical devices, both linguistic (for example, having three points whose headings are alliterated—"Worship, Wealth, and Wisdom") and nonlinguistic. There is no reason why some of these features could not be duplicated with unintelligible speech if speakers chose to give "sermons." The single case is that of a minister who said that he "preached for an hour" in tongues, but that is all the information we have since the respondent was anonymous.

[7] Different from these prophetic pronouncements are the following uses of tongues. Hayes reported having observed a speaker who "would talk for a few minutes in English and then run off suddenly into the speaking with tongues. . . . It seemed to us that the speaker resorted to the tongue when he

Because the glossolalic message duplicates the function of prophecy and because the speaker is in potential conflict with the recognized source of spiritual guidance, the preacher or his equivalent, there is a great deal of ambiguity about the place of glossolalic messages in the corporate life of the church. This is why the apostle Paul counseled the Corinthian believers, without advising against the public use of tongues as Cutten (p. 26) and Christian antagonists of Pentecostalism seem to think. Modern charismatists continue to grapple with the problem.

Theoretically, anyone can utter a glossolalic discourse, although the evidence indicates that informal—and sometimes not so informal—forces lead to a selection of "qualified" people. In regulating the use of tongues, for example, Christenson cautions the Spirit-filled "not to speak out unless he receives a definite 'anointing' by the Spirit" (p. 18). Oral Roberts' advice is that the message-giving believer, "either man or woman, is one known to the group, a member in good standing and who exercises the gift in a responsible manner" (p. 86); this rules out strangers, he says (p. 65). According to Gee (p. 88) the correct use of the gift of tongues is "merely the application of ordinary principles of expediency and decency." By decency is meant taking one's turn, being in control of oneself, and knowing when and where to speak (Roberts, pp. 59–67). Some groups also insist that there be no more than three glossolalic messages in a single meeting, in applying a certain interpretation of the Pauline regulations, and that no one give a message unless an interpreter is present. Expediency would suggest, for example, de-emphasizing tongues in a meeting where "unbelievers" are present (H. Horton, p. 207).

In general one behaves in conformity with the rules implicit in the ethos of the given group. The person new to a group would presumably have difficulty at first. As one respondent put it, "Tongues in a service should always blend with the theme and tone of the meeting and add to it." However, when a person be-

---

could think of nothing else to say" (1913:88–89). This behavior has not been reported recently, but I witnessed it at a snake-handling meeting in West Virginia. One of my respondents, a Presbyterian minister in Canada, informs me that he preaches in tongues from time to time to an empty church while vividly imagining (but not in trance) a congregation. He adds that after such experiences his sermons to a real congregation "are often delivered with more emotion."

haves in an unacceptable way, he is dealt with by the preacher, deacon, or some other person with authority. Oral Roberts makes it clear that the tongue speaker is not entirely free to respond to the anointing, "he must submit himself to be judged" (p. 65). But Bartleman, the irascible leader of early Pentecostalism, would not abide such regulations; he would tolerate excesses so as not to "quench the Spirit" (pp. 37,44).

Since no meeting is overtly structured so as to leave room for glossolalic messages, the anointed person must choose appropriate places when he can break in. It is considered rude to interrupt a sermon, for example. The rule that applies here is the saying, "The Holy Spirit is a gentleman." The sensitive glossolalist therefore looks for openings very much in the way a conversationalist does. At FGBMFI meetings, for example, I was fairly successful in predicting when someone might burst forth in glossolalia. The main factor was an emotional one. The speaker arrived at a point where the audience was keyed up and intense, where it was "in his hands"; then at some longer-than-normal pause, before the "paragraph" was closed, someone in the audience would speak out in tongues. Since the message was given in a nice manner, the speaker was recognized and one of the officiating members seated on the dais interpreted. Recognition also depended, one assumes, on how the speaker viewed his own role vis-à-vis that of the tongue speaker. Kathryn Kuhlman, the publicized healer, did not yield to a man who broke into her two-hour discourse. She continued talking, only eventually lowering her voice, until the man had finished. There was no interpretation. Had this man spoken in a disagreeable way, I am quite sure that he would have been silenced by someone in the room. More is said below about control in a charismatic setting.

Interpretations

The interpretation of a glossolalic message—occasionally of a prayer—is a supplementary discourse in natural language that purports to reveal the meaning of the otherwise unintelligible one.[8]

---

[8] Mistakes do occur. One charismatic Lutheran minister in Germany informed me that a Czechoslovakian, speaking in his native language, had been "interpreted" in the belief that he was speaking in tongues!

Leaders in charismatic groups are careful to point out that this is more like a commentary or explanation than a translation, but the distinction is a moot one since it is based on no linguistic comparison. It only puts the phenomena beyond reach of critical assessment, and it effectively accounts for the obvious discrepancies between two supposedly paired discourses in length and style of delivery. Charismatic doctrine maintains that the interpreter is free to formulate the interpretation in any way he sees fit as long as he is faithful to his inspiration. He may "summarize" or "expound" as Pentecostals put it, and he may use a poetic style instead of prose (H. Horton, pp. 168ff). An interpretation follows (always immediately, so it seems) the entire glossolalic message and never articulates with it in a sort of sentence-by-sentence fashion.

Notwithstanding what has just been said, there are some people, perhaps the more naive, who view interpretation as translation. This is certainly what they mean when they give the meanings of short phrases or words in isolation. Lombard, for example, records that one Pentecostalist reported having been given a word-for-word translation of his own text in tongues (p. 182). For further examples see under Meaning in Chapter 4.

Since a glossolalic discourse is meaningless (except for affect or feeling) the "explanation" cannot be a reflection of it. The latter is given not in response to a message but to context, only part of which is glossolalic activity. That is, an interpreter may take some cues from the original speaker so that a pleading speech will be matched by a pleading speech. It is more common, as I have personally observed, for the two discourses to be very dissimilar in style. They should therefore be described as barely overlapping circles. Both have their origin in the immediate context. This might be described in terms of "expanded expectation," where the audience works hard to meet the speaker—especially if he is fully integrated in the group and if group harmony is at a high peak—by contributing meaning to the message. At best, therefore, an interpretation is like the sympathetic resonance of one violin string to another. This is why one or the other, message and interpretation, might be considered inconsonant with the feeling shared by members of a group.

The fact that an interpretation is contextually situated—that it responds, in other words, to the whole event in which people par-

ticipate—is supported by the nonexistence of written interpretations of glossolalic messages given on some earlier occasion. Nor is
there any record, to my knowledge, of written glossolalic texts
(about which more is said later) being interpreted. The cases of
Simon and Le Baron (pages 90f and 89f) are quite special.[9]
Some glossolalists do get self-interpretations for utterances made
in prayer (such as the example on page 169), but we are talking
here about messages in a group.

A few words must be allowed here to disabuse ourselves of the
notion that the members of a charismatic group are odd because
they are, as some have said, in tacit conspiracy to deceive themselves. We shall not argue about some measure of self-deception,
but we shall about its oddness. What we must remember is, as
Berger has made clear (1963:145), that "deception and self-
deception are at the very heart of social reality." By this he means
that we believe that the "institutions" of society are real: without
this commitment society, not merely *a* society, would be impossible. So the charismatic belief in interpretation is just another
manifestation of this phenomenon. We return to this subject in
Chapter 12.

That the meaning conveyed in a glossolalic utterance is emotional and social is clear in statements made by glossolalists. For
example, an interpretation may not even be necessary, for one person claims to have been "understood" without it, a phenomenon
she recognizes as strange to the Biblical pattern. (She would have
learned of another person's response, of course, only by being told
about it.) Others identify this response as feeling the "blessing but
not the meaning" of the utterance; there is "an answering Amen"
in one's heart. This is why others in a group feel that they would
have given just about the same interpretation. When "the general
essence of the message," as one respondent put it, is love, assurance, and "healing of the mind," it would not be difficult for another
person to respond with a harmonious chord. The interpreter in fact
might even do a better job of expressing the other's emotions. In
the immediate context, the latter knows that the interpretation
"was what I had longed to say but couldn't."

[9] So is the case in Mormon history of Joseph Smith's decipherment of
the gold plates he is supposed to have discovered. There is no evidence
whatsoever that the message was glossolalic in construction.

The appropriateness of an interpretation is like the predictability one finds in ritualized speech events, where communion between participants is more important than information. In this respect political speeches are often no different from religious sermons; one also finds similarities in the chatter that goes on among friends at a social gathering, where one of the functions of speech may be phatic communion, where ties of union are created by merely exchanging words. We can also look at the message-interpretation event from a sociological point of view, using Goffman's concept of the "situation." The interpretation is functional or "meaningful," because it "fits in" in an expectable way.

There would also be nonfunctional variables in the glossolalic discourse such as the actual sounds and kinds of syllables that are produced. However, a "harsh" discourse, as we have already seen, could have situational meaning. To this viewpoint could be added that of a philosopher like Ayer (p. 50) who seeks to distinguish private from public languages. One might say that a glossolalic message is public language in the sense that the speaker is experiencing and "referring to," if only expressively, an experience that is communal. This is true because in a religious event, as at a tragic accident or thrilling sports-event, people are "communally exposed" to the same experience. Therefore no matter what a person says (or "says") at that time is "understandable" and in a sense "verifiable" (Ayer, p. 51).

There are times when the interpretation is dissonant and is perceived as such either by the group or by the speaker. In such a case other people may offer an interpretation of the message, although some charismatic leaders deplore multiple interpretations (like H. Horton, p. 173). Interpretations may even be rejected, contrary to what some observers of glossolalia have said. Here is what one such leader wrote me:

After addressing a large crowd down at the [X] Hotel some time ago, I brought forth a message in tongues; and three people in succession started to interpret it, and in each case I stopped them. I sensed, in a way that I cannot describe, that they were speaking "off the top of their head." I do not insist that a person, in interpreting a message in tongues which I have brought, speak that which I may have felt at the time. . . . However, if someone is bringing forth a wrong interpretation, I feel grieved in my spirit and unsatisfied.

It should be observed that here also social stature gives the speaker in tongues the liberty to manage the speech event. A lesser personality would be presuming too much.

Although glossolalists generally take interpretations quite seriously, and in some circles do not even permit the public use of tongues unless there is an interpretation, this is not to say that they do not recognize the superficiality of many of them. One of my respondents said that they are very often "simple," and another one said that they do not make "heavy impressions" because they are for local situations. But influential leaders like Gee have also pointed out that interpretations were usually "only something which the preacher would have almost certainly said in the ordinary course of his sermon" (p. 94). Sherrill was bothered even before he became a charismatist by the stereotypic nature of messages (pp. 94–95). And Oral Roberts, the world-famous "faithhealer," felt obliged to advise would-be interpreters not to copy others (p. 89). I tested one obviously influential personage at a large meeting in the lobby of the hotel where it was held to see what impression his own interpretations had made on him. Although he had given them three times, more or less repeating himself in my opinion, he had considerable difficulty in remembering what it was he had said. And this was definitely not a case of post-trance amnesia!

If information, that is, unpredictable content, is so absent from messages, it is not surprising that the interpretation "just 'comes to you' almost as you say it," as one respondent put it. The interpreter's fluency is due not to any divine inspiration but to a familiarity with certain themes and linguistic material that verges on the rote, illustrated in the preceding paragraph.

It is not inconsistent, of course, for interpreting glossolalic messages to be taken seriously whereas little attention is paid to content. In other words, it might be more important *that* a message be interpreted than *what* it has to communicate. This is, admittedly, not part of the explicit beliefs of glossolalists, but it certainly is implicit in their experience. This is nothing unusual. Human beings engage in all kinds of speech events that have cultural value without being communicative in the linguistic sense, as we just noted.

Interpretations will, from time to time, of course, contain information that is significant to the group, the more so if the group expects glossolalic messages to be revelatory in nature (many are just worshipful or supplicatory in a general sort of way). It is not at all uncommon, therefore, to be told, "We prayed about [so-and-so], and God revealed to us in a message that was interpreted that we should [do so-and-so]." In The Overcomers' Church—small, independent, and not officially Pentecostal—this is the only recognized use of tongues (called specifically "the gift of tongues") apart from evidential tongues that accompanies the baptism in the Holy Spirit.

It should be noted, moreover, that information may come to a group outside the message/interpretation pattern. It is common, although not theologically recognized, for people to seek out the significance of "words" that are given by God. If, for example, a person were to use the glossolalic "word" /hizâk/ on several occasions, perhaps with great conviction, others might begin to discuss its significance, using what they knew about similar-sounding words in other languages and going to a Bible concordance for help. Often enough they find something that relates to their situation. This is obviously an oracular use of tongues.

Not all interpretations contribute directly to group harmony or the resolution of immediate problems. Some, whatever may have been the function of the glossolalist's discourse, verbalize personal or group animosity. Denouncements of a general or even specific nature are therefore found in some groups, especially those whose general approach to life is defensive and polemic. This is not surprising. People who have been religiously educated through fundamentalist fire-and-brimstone preaching from the pulpit can be expected to imitate their teachers when they have an opportunity to speak from the floor. Thus H. Horton, longtime leader of the Assemblies of God, laments being interrupted in a sermon "by eight or ten fragments of other tongues interpreted as fiery, cutting judgments of God" (p. 209). Oral Roberts therefore rules out correction and rebuke, along with guidance for the congregation, as functions of glossolalic messages; he understandably leaves these prerogatives to the authority he recognizes in the church, the preacher (p. 84).

The style of the interpretation reveals how much the speaker sees himself as an actor in a religious drama. It is as if he were on stage. This is why one school teacher should "feel more compelled" when interpreting but relaxed or happier when praying in tongues.

Another active laywoman, member of the Methodist church since childhood but glossolalist for only two years, also reported a difference in behavior: "When interpreting, there is a sense of awe, a quickened heartbeat, almost a pounding. . . . I am less aware of the people present. [The interpretation] always leaves me weak and very humbled that I have been in [God's] power and control. Usually I weep after these times."

Another reason, I suggest, for feeling "on the spot" (or is it "in the spotlight"?) in interpreting is that it is difficult to give form to the feeling of inspiration that stimulates a person to speak; there is no authenticating evidence of supernaturalness and one has to "carry it off" in behavior that everyone understands. This is certainly why one respondent wrote, "It takes practice to gain confidence that one is speaking via the Spirit when speaking one's own language." He is a layman, however; a professional has been established in his role in many other ways.

Delivery of a glossolalic message is confident if not authoritative. Sometimes it is introduced or closed with the formula "Thus saith the Lord." Authority is manifested in voice quality, intonational and stress patterns, volume, and speed of utterance. Interpretations, as far as I have been able to tell, are pronounced with great fluency, with no pauses to indicate a groping for words. (Since both the original message and interpretation differ in this respect from glossolalic prayers, which are very often said with more deliberateness, we must infer canons of appropriateness that govern charismatic speech activity.) The message is also tagged as religious by devices that are derived from the group's tradition, most of which can be traced to Hebraic prophetic style in the English translation of the Authorized Version. This is why messages strive for poetic construction or are, as one respondent put it, "usually in rather elegant prose." Repetitiousness, one of their striking features, is an obvious attempt at Hebraic poetic style.[10]

---

[10] The striving for a sacerdotal style is apparent to charismatists as well as outside observers. For example, Oral Roberts advised interpreters to speak in a normal voice and to avoid using Biblical language like *thee* (p. 89). Contradictory observations must be explained as ad hoc to a limited set of data. Motley, for example, says (p. 25) that interpretations are "neither simple nor plain" but are "somewhat complex and unpredictable." Compare his statement, "The interpretation is never questioned or challenged," with the contrary evidence above.

Here follow three samples of interpretations and one sample of religious prose written in apparent imitation of the Bible from *The Book of Mormon.* The interpretations are transcriptions of tape-recorded discourses. Samples 1 and 2 are of messages pronounced at the FGBMFI meeting already referred to. The first was in response to a glossolalic message uttered by a man in the lull immediately after a professional football player had been "prayed for" on the platform following his testimonial. The glossolalia was a good performance—distinct, deliberate, confident, with a very regular intonational and metrical pattern. The interpretation was declared by one of the many clergymen seated at the long table on the dais. The second interpretation was in response to a message uttered by a woman, and it was delivered in a nervous or excited, rapid, shrill manner. The interpretation takes its cue from the event that preceded the woman's discourse. A Canadian Roman Catholic priest had given a testimonial about his charismatic experience in halting English with a heavy French accent. The fact that a person from a different background and language shared the religious experience common to the group stirred the preacher who gave the interpretation with increasing speed and volume; the audience began to cry out and pray in a loud, excited way before he was finished. The third sample followed a prayer. It occurred in the recording of a prayer session by a group of neo-Pentecostals in an Episcopal church. The recording was made by the leader of the group at my request. I should imagine that it is the leader who gave the interpretation because it obviously is directed to me. The inconsistency of a prayer being interpreted as a message seems to escape many charismatists. The fourth sample of religious language is included to show the influence of a single tradition on two kinds of discourses produced under different circumstances.

I.

Heed ye the word of the Lord. Yea, hear ye my voice as I speak to you this day. Hear ye not in words, nor in voice, but hear ye in the hidden recess of your heart. Yea, I say unto you this morning, though you have not heard a voice, yea, ye have heard me speak to you already today. And this is the new thing that I do on the earth. Yea, of old ye have read that I make a new covenant. And yea, ye know that I have ratified the new covenant in my Son whom I have sent to take away the sin of the world. And yea, receive into your hearts this message of love that I make [unintelligible] the being that is within you and heal the wounds, yea, that have been since the Garden of Eden. And yea, I speak to that new heart, and new mind, and new spirit that is within you that is crying to be recognized. Yea, hear my voice today and yield to me as I speak to you in the tender voice of the Lord, your God.

2.

Oh, from the east and from the west, from the north and south, the Lord will call together his people. The Lord has chosen those that He hath called to impart His Spirit to them that they may magnify the name of the Lord. For the Lord hath many languages to praise Him. The Lord has not just called one race or one people or one segment of the great population, but the Lord said from every nation [. . .] there are those that He hath called. He will bring together and fill with His Spirit, for the Lord will do the work in these last days. From all over the universe, and all over this world, God is looking for those whose hearts are perfect toward Him, people that will open their eyes to him and receive his blessing and receive his anointing, for these *are* the last days and the Lord hath arisen to do a mighty work in the earth. He will break down the barriers. He will reach in past the barriers that man has lifted and [. . .] for hundreds of years. The Lord knows how to reach the hungry and to impart to them his blessing. [The rest is incomprehensible because of many voices.]

3.

Oh my children, I bid you to praise me in every tongue, not only with your tongues, but with your lives. Find the most creative way to go forth in my name, in my Spirit, in my power. Some people may not call it religious, or churchly, but where I am working, there is the power of God. Where I send you, there I am also, saith the Lord.

4.

19. For he will not suffer you that ye shall live in your iniquities, to destroy his people. I say unto you, Nay; he would rather suffer that the Lamanites might destroy all this people who are called the people of Nephi, if it were possible that they could fall into sins and transgressions, after having had so much light and so much knowledge given unto them of the Lord their God;

20. Yea, after having been such a highly favored people of the Lord; yea, after having been favored above every other nation, kindred, tongue, or people; after having had all things made known unto them, according to their desires, and their faith, and prayers, of that which has been, and which is, and which is to come. . . .

23. And now behold I say unto you, that if this people, who have

received so many blessings from the hand of the Lord, should trans-
gress contrary to the light and knowledge which they do have, I say
unto you that if this be the case, that if they should fall into trans-
gression, it would be far more tolerable for the Lamanites than for
them. (The Book of Mormon. Alma, 9.)

As there is control in the exercise of the gift of tongues, as we
saw above, so is there in the gift of interpretation. Although self-
interpretation is possible (and one of my respondents never interpreted anything but her own glossas), it is generally someone else
who does this. Perhaps the glossolalist recognizes that leadership
gained from habitual self-interpretation would be inauthentic; an
interpretation from someone else, however, validates one's role in
the group. Of the two roles, speaking in tongues and interpreting,
the latter has greater prestige. But this prestige is redundant, for
those who habitually interpret are already leaders in the group.
This is clear from the eighty-five answers to my question "How often do you interpret the tongues of others?" Of these, forty-one
(48%) said never, twenty-eight (33%) said rarely. Of the thirteen
who said fairly often and the three who said rather often, all (say,
19%), as one infers from their autobiographical data and the answers to other questions, seem to be group leaders. Most of these
are in fact clergymen. Compare these figures with those for the
question "How often are your tongues interpreted in a public
meeting?" Of eighty-five respondents, forty-two (48%) said never,
ten (12%) rarely, only five (6%) fairly often, and twenty-eight
(33%) always or almost always.

If today the interpreter seems to have more prestige than the
speaker in tongues, the case is not very different from that in the
early church. This is clear from the most thorough treatment of
tongues in the New Testament, in Paul's letter to the Corinthians
(I Corinthians 12–14). While insisting that all gifts are equally
from the Spirit (I Corinthians 12), he advises that one's religious aspirations should be directed to prophecy or interpretation, both of
which are intelligible speech:

When a man is using the language of ecstasy [a translation I deplore]
he is talking with God, not with men, for no man understands him;
he is no doubt inspired, but he speaks mysteries. On the other hand,
when a man prophesies, he is talking to men, and his words have
power to build; they stimulate and they encourage. The language of

ecstasy is good for the speaker himself, but it is prophecy that builds up a Christian community. I should be pleased for you all to use the tongues of ecstasy, but better pleased for you to prophesy. The prophet is worth more than the man of ecstatic speech—unless indeed he can explain its meaning, and so help to build up the community. . . . I say, then, that the man who falls into ecstatic utterance [a free rendition of "let the one who speaks in 'languages' "] should pray for the ability to interpret (14:2–4,13, NEB).

For the good of the group, the message giver and the interpreter (ordinarily a glossolalist) must work in concert even though their immediate goals might be different. The interpreter, because he makes sense and because he has the last word, can easily upstage the message giver. Therefore the group must control his activities as well as those of the glossolalist. This is surely the reason for Oral Roberts' saying that an interpreter must be willing to be judged "on the honest report of his character, his timing in utterance," and so forth (p. 89). This is the kind of person Gee calls "proved" (p. 61). However, because charismatists recognize the danger of restricting interpretation to a few individuals they generally frown on an ecclesiastical office of interpreter (Gee, pp. 61,74). A certain ambivalence, however, is seen in H. Horton's advice that "where there is a likelihood of some fanatical or selfish person misusing the Gift [of interpretation], the leader of the meeting or the assembly should take all the interpretations until he [the leader] is sure of his ground" (p. 174). What the last clause (that is, "until. . . .") means is not clear. It is possible, of course, for individuals to resist the domination of a group by setting up their own group—autonomous or satellite—where they can say what they want to in peace, that is, where messages could be given and interpreted (often denouncing the actions of individuals in another group) without restraint. Naturally H. Horton deplores such "little groups in private rooms" (p. 165).

It is easy to see that the use of the gifts of the Spirit is related to the exercise of authority in a group (as noted also by Wilson, p. 500). Over a period of time, as we shall see below, the change in authority structure can lead to significant differences.

We have now seen how glossolalia figures in two important aspects of the religious life of those involved in the Pentecostal movement. The approach was primarily descriptive. We tried to keep inferences and speculations to a minimum. We could have noted, for example, that although praying in tongues, as in ordinary language, can be a preeminently subjective experience, it plays an important function in developing mood—another dimension of religious experience—and group empathy. As for messages, we could have noted that these are obviously meant to be instrumental, as a literal meaning of the word would indicate. Without interpretations, however, they would hardly be messages. But such analyses on my part are reserved for Chapters 10 and 11. In the next chapter we are to look again at use, once more descriptively but from a general point of view.

8

SUNG AND WRITTEN

BECAUSE THERE ARE different uses for glossolalia, there are also different ways to speak in tongues, each one in some way appropriate to the context, for glossolalia is as much an artifact of culture as language is. In every society speech may be ironic, humorous, sarcastic, sententious, intimidating, or entreating as befits the person spoken to, the topic being discussed, and the place where language is being used. (There's a difference between how a lawyer talks to a client in a crowded elevator and from behind a desk in a plush office!) The characteristics of speech are culturally determined in the sense that they recur in a patterned way and that deviations from the pattern are noticed by the members of the society. (One doesn't introduce dinner guests to each other as one does a distinguished speaker at an annual banquet.) If we can call these different patterns styles of talking, we can also say that there are different styles of talking in tongues.

Even if glossolalia were a trance phenomenon, in which a person is supposed to be beside himself (a notion that we must reject), there would still be reason to expect a certain amount of cultural speech adaptation. The reason is that an altered state of consciousness rarely, if ever, deprives a person of a sense of cultural value.

Anthropologists Ralph Linton (p. 132) and Erika Bourguignon make this quite clear. The latter says the following in her world survey of trance and possession states:

In possession trance, we find a very clear expression of the influence of learning and expectation on the behavior of the trancer. From a cultural and psychological point of view, it is important to stress that there is great variation in the amount of leeway which is permitted for the direct or symbolic expression of personal motivations and psychological themes. The more ritualistic, stereotypic, and formalized the proceedings, and the more the trancer must follow a dramatic "script," the less room will there be for a satisfaction of idiosyncratic needs (p. 12). . . . When we are dealing with a belief in possession by spirits rather than powers, we find that the trancer acts out an impersonation of the spirit. The behavior will, therefore, vary in conformity with the concept of the spirit which is to be impersonated. It may vary from the chaotic behavior of participants in the Kentucky revival to the formal and orderly behavior of the Balinese child trance dancers. It may be stereotyped, as in Bali, or individuated, as in the case of the Haitian voodoo pantheon; it may be traditional and prescribed drama, as in Bali, or *commedia dell'arte* improvisation, as in Haiti. In both of these instances we find dramatic performances (p. 11).

Styles

The sociocultural determination of glossolalic speech seems to have escaped observers of the charismatic movement. Many have thought, for example, that speaking loudly was part of the very nature of glossolalia. Lombard explained that if glossolalists murmured, they were trying to suppress it (p. 16). It is more reasonable to suppose that volume correlates with the symbols and uses of glossolalia. For example, since power is a dominant theme of the charismatic movement, it is revealed in powerful physical activity.[1]

[1] Loudness among snake cultists is interpreted quite differently by La Barre. Using a psychoanalytic approach, he asserts that the psychopath's and the hysteric's God, like a human father, does not know everything and is not aware of every secret sin. Knowing that he is not really sincere in his faith, the snake cultist must therefore be loud so as to divert God (p. 170). But all of La Barre's interpretations must be evaluated in the light of his assumption that, among other things, these people are psychopathic with "tortured" and "twisted" egos, a bias that has been exposed by Gerrard's study (as we have already seen).

This correlation is quite clear in the words of Barratt: "In that way I could sometimes speak in a strange language, and my voice grew stronger and stronger under this mighty power, until thousands of people could have heard me" (quoted by Bloch-Hoell, p. 135). The same symbol is implied in the coupling of the phrases "*great volume* of *spiritual outpouring*" by one of my respondents. This is also seen in the delivery of sermons in an African quasi-Christian cult, described by J. Fernandez (1967).

Another particular style is whispered glossolalia. It is best observed in small group prayer meetings although there is reason to believe that individuals also whisper prayers in situations that tend to inhibit overt glossolalic utterances (for example, during a university examination). The following case observed by myself is probably typical in its main features.

Several couples, all intimate friends and all glossolalists from a non-Pentecostal main-line church, had spent the evening together at dinner and conversation. Toward the end of the evening someone suggested that we pray together. (I do not recall who it was, but it makes no difference, because in such gatherings such a suggestion need not be made by a leader.) It is understood among these people—as it indeed is among Protestant evangelicals in general—that one will pray "as the Spirit leads." That is, once the session of prayer has begun, individuals can pray in whatever order and for whatever purpose they choose. So it was on this occasion, but this is not to say that there was no structure or pattern to what happened. Even where the Spirit leads there is an opening, main event, and closing. During the brief opening, before the first person volunteered, one could hear exclamations like "Thank you, Jesus!" in a soft voice or short stretches of barely audible glossolalia that one took to be prayers. Then when one person after another prayed aloud in English (in this case taking turns around the circle in the living room), several others accompanied him in whispered glossolalia. The session closed with a tapering-off period in which the group waited to make certain that there were going to be no further prayers. During this moment several people continued with exclamations or whispered prayer.

It would appear that on such occasions glossolalia was being used to fill in silence or to help people get in the mood for prayer, but the more important function is to establish phatic communion —to help the individuals share their experience. It is an explicit desire on their part to participate fully in the whole event and with each individual as he prays. One wants to "pray with" the other person. In evangelical but nonglossolalist circles one keeps oneself involved by exclaiming "Yes!" or "That's right!" and so forth or by making little noises of approval or commiseration. Here the participation is more complete, because the person can pray along with another person, *feeling* his own prayerful attitude but *listening* to the other person. This function of glossolalia is recognized by many neo-Pentecostals.

Since meter and intonation are also part of speech styles, it is not surprising that these should figure in different varieties of glossolalia. Some manipulation of intonation is probably motivated (unconsciously, of course) only to distinguish glossolalia from ordinary language. Thus, one respondent thought that "monotony of inflection" was not a spiritual element (therefore something to avoid), a view that was seconded by another respondent who said that "the anointing of the Spirit gives a special cadence" to speech, and if most tongues were spoken in an ordinary manner, she would think that they were just foreign languages.

Other characteristics are implied by the expression "tone of voice" (nicely reviewed for natural language by D. Crystal). Thus, we would expect a message in tongues to be "prophetic" or "oracular" in style; it would certainly be different in delivery from a private prayer. Yet there is room for much variation even within each use: a message might be denunciatory, instructive, or assuring, for example. One of my respondents reported that on one occasion he "agonized a short message in tongues" that gave the impression to him and to others at the meeting that Jesus was praying through him. The message in fact was interpreted as follows:

> Your heartbreak is my heartbreak.
> Your heartthrob is my heartthrob.
> Have I not gone the way before you?
> Walk on in faith,
> For, lo, I am with you alway.

There is more to speech than just vocal activity: bodily activity, varying in amount and kind, may be less important than language, but it is nonetheless inextricably involved with it. Gestures, for example, are taken for granted until a person has to learn, at least in the west, that he cannot wave his hands around before a formal audience as he does in conversation. So there is plenty of physical activity with glossolalia, especially when it is public. This is certainly why a glossolalist's behavior strikes one as being somewhat theatrical at times: one of my respondents said that she "made gestures like an Indian dancer while chanting in a dialect." A less pronounced, but functionally equivalent "esoteric" gesture is closing one's eyes while speaking in tongues. (One of my matter-of-fact respondents objected to this practice on the grounds that the speakers did not have enough faith to keep their eyes open; that is, they were making glossolalia too exotic an event.)

Since speech styles with a normal use of language are socio-culturally determined, a fact that needs no documentation, we would expect differences between different cultural traditions. This is exactly what we find. It is quite clear that the speech style of Pentecostals is different (more demonstrative, for example) from that of Episcopalians. There also appears to be a higher incidence of altered states of consciousness with the acquisition of glossolalia among traditional Pentecostals, although statistics are lacking. Perhaps an ostentatious behavior is called for by the belief that the infilling of the Spirit is a powerful experience. Because the baptism among Pentecostals usually takes place in public meetings characterized by group activity, the candidate is always in competition, so to speak, with many others for demonstrating how much more wonderful his own experience is. This would be true for those seeking the experience for the first time or for those who sought "refills."[2]

Where loud and energetic glossolalia was common for an "evidential" function, it would be expected in messages also, particularly because glossolalic messages could be made by anyone. In an ethos where "freedom in the Spirit" is very much valued, there is plenty of opportunity for a person to be self-assertive, aggressive, and authoritative under the Spirit's cloak. Competition, or at least tension, would naturally develop within a group (as Bartleman's first-person account of early Pentecostalism unambiguously demonstrates); in this context the shy glossolalist loses out. But neo-Pentecostals bring a different set of values to the religious use of

[2] This is not a flippant metaphor. A Pentecostal preacher himself called the camp meeting "the filling station for ministers to be filled with the power of God" (Wood, p. 52).

language. Many of them are from "main-line" Protestant churches or Catholicism where emotionalism in religion is eschewed.

Song and Poetry

In apparent enhancement of religious experience, there is a tendency among glossolalists to use special genres of discourse. The two most commonly identified by the practitioners themselves are poetry and song.

Song is easy enough to identify by its characteristic use of pitch. Sometimes the melody of a song already known is used to carry along glossolalic "words." Often enough, however, the tune, or whatever there is of one, is improvised on the spot. This is indistinguishable, of course, from what many of us do under the inspiration of light-heartedness.[3]

What is interesting among glossolalists is that these "compositions" are taken seriously and that they also characterize group activity: someone starts a tune and others join in (the best they can, I would have to say), each one naturally using his own "words." The singers have no apparent difficulty in fitting the music to the "words" (or vice versa) because of the syllabic nature of glossolalia. The following is one observer's description of such an event:

It was more or less difficult to get the thing started, but when it once got to swinging it was a really remarkable exhibition of extemporized melody. It was a weird, unregulated chant, rising and falling, dying away and swelling out again unexpectedly, as though some heavenly musician were playing upon his human instruments at his own free-will (Hayes, pp. 91–92).

Although "spiritual songs" are mentioned in the New Testament (for example, Colossians 3:16), the only unusual aspect that gets mentioned is their incomprehensibility. This is implied in

---

[3] A good sample of this kind of singing was produced commercially: Scepter Records, Inc., Mace Record MCM 10040/MCS 10040, "The gift of tongues: glossolalia," with a single male voice. The recording is quasi-religious but not Pentecostal. Two other records were privately produced in Berkeley, California, by John W. Hopkins, entitled "Music in the spheres," in what he calls the "Celestial Language." The two samples given are from Wolfram, pp. 98–99.

Two samples of glossolalia in song

1. *To the tune of "Fairest Lord Jesus"*

1. ká ka ka chán ta la   kó ko lo fón to lo   ka lá sta
2. kí sha na mí re ta   ka ko ka mí fo na   pár hi ko

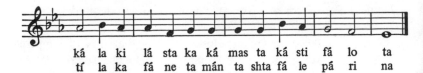

ká shti ni   pa lo   ma   ká la ki   chá ma ma
chán ti la   ma fi   ta   kí la ka   má de ka

ká la ki   lá sta ka ká mas ta ká sti   fá lo   ta
tí la ka   fá ne ta mán ta shta fá le   pá ri   na

2. *To an original melody*

kán ta va sta ká la ká ra pá sta ka ka ká   la

ká sta má na ka shta ká ká ko   la   ká shta ma vi

kó ne fá cha má le ta kó ná fa che má le ta

ko lá ka   lá ko chan te la fó na   ste ma   chi

Paul's discussion about interpretation: "If I pray in a tongue, my spirit prays but my mind is unfruitful. What am I to do? I will pray with the spirit and I will pray with the mind also; I will sing with the spirit and I will sing with the mind also" (1 Corinthians 14:14–15, RSV). Here too he apparently was trying to resolve the polarization of the congregation over the charisma by saying that it was not a question of glossolalia *or* natural language but a wise use of *both*.

If anything like poetry occurs in a glossolalic discourse, it is only in the sense that certain poetic devices are used. There are surely no poetic discourses in the sense of units of speech with a definite internal structure, but the use of meter, alliteration, and even rhyme might give short stretches of speech the appearance of poetry. Of course, if a person were to remember stretches of glossolalia, he could mold them poetically; the task, in fact, would be easier than in natural language, for he would not be constrained by lexicon and grammar. Perhaps the Shaker songs already cited are the result of this kind of artifice. So also must be the following "spiritual song." It is quoted by Cutten (p. 121), and there is no information about how it was originally obtained from the German Pentecostal who is supposed to have created it:

> *Shua, ea, shua ea*
> *O chi biro ti ra pea*
> *aki lungo tari fungo*
> *u li bara ra tungo*
> *lachi bungo ti tu ta*

(The spelling has been changed a little to follow English conventions.) One of my own respondents submitted the following poem. The original was lettered by hand, and it was difficult to decide in a couple of places if word division was intended. Her phonetic transcription has been slightly altered:

Kyupanami yata	"Who questions My words?
Kupanimi kuzha tima	Who looks into My Spirit?
Kupanipanashaiya	Who really needs to know?
Kyama tupaiya makuzhi	When do you want Me to bless you?
Typazhi namaka	I am Blessing ITself.

Pupanyaň mi pokanishi	With My presence within you
Pitamanka	You have eternity there.
Kwinakashinamakwiya	What more can you want?
Pumaiyakishiwa	Physical deliverance from discomfort
Pita pomakĭ mapanya	Can be and is overcome
	By an unbroken flow of My presence/power.
	Yes, unbroken.
	I have said this."

These attempts at glossolalic song and poetry give evidence to a universal tendency among men to use "noncasual" speech with those parts of experience that have high personal and cultural value. But special styles and special genres of discourse are used not only to "frame" certain kinds of experience but also because they are esthetically pleasing in their own right. This is a topic that we shall be coming back to in later chapters.

Written Glossolalia

Glossolalia is a spoken phenomenon, and this is so not because it resists transcription but because speech better suits its functions than writing does. Much to the surprise of laymen, and glossolalists for that matter, glossolalia can be written down by almost anyone if he is able to mimic an utterance and remember it; tape recordings only make the task easier. Slowing speech down helps one's memory, but glossolalists would ordinarily find this artificial in speech. However, one person who was not able to write down her own speech did succeed in transcribing, in shorthand, the "words" of her glossolalic songs. Special training in phonetics is necessary only when one encounters unfamiliar sounds. Glossolalists themselves have written down samples of their glossas for me. If they have any difficulties, it is primarily because they do not know how to represent the sounds. Thus, the following sample is undoubtedly an inaccurate transcription of actual speech: *play coon del ē cues pel suel proloque doos fundos en day den doos*. People appear inclined to make their task more difficult by writing exotically. Thus, although /sh/ is a common sound in the glossas of native speakers of English, as it is in their native language, they very often represent it by "sch," as in German!

It seems fair to conjecture that the reason why glossolalists should try to make a written sample of glossolalia look exotic is that it is supposed to be different from normal language. For many, in fact, it is sacred. This is why many of my respondents refused to write anything whatsoever, and the woman who wrote down *La Re Gu She a. Munde Ra, Munde Ra, Kulea, Kulea, Kumbisando, Kashia, Lagia, etc. etc.* added: "This seems almost too sacred to repeat."

It is the presumed strangeness of glossolalia, for one thing, that keeps it from being used religiously in written form, because this strangeness, which is conveyed as much by intonation and paralinguistic features (such as "tone of voice") as by consonants and vowels, cannot be fully portrayed in the common use of the Roman alphabet. The other reason is that it is impossible to translate into a series of consonants and vowels the totality of events that gives glossolalia its significance. It is experience, not speech as speech, that is religious.[4] Of course, this experience can be translated into sound, and when sound specifies experience it is meaningful: this is the function of language—normal language. Because glossolalia is meaningless, however, because it is not related to experience in a discrete, systematic way, there is no point in recording it; it wouldn't say anything. This is one possible explanation for the nonexistence of written glossolalia.

It is only when an utterance becomes a part of tradition, like a religious relic, that there is a desire to record glossolalia. There appear to be very few cases of this kind of traditionalized glossolalia. I know only of the following two. There are, of course, lots of examples of writing that has religious significance (cryptic, cabalistic, archaic, unintelligible, strangely written, etc.) in different

---

[4] By the use of the word "experience" here I do not intend to espouse an existential position that denies a "non-existential ultimate reality" to religion. Whether or not truth—religious truth—exists apart from what human beings experience is irrelevant to what I am talking about. I am only saying that religion, as recognized by different groups of human beings in different cultures and subcultures, involves the *meaning* that is attributed to the events that man goes through, not just the forms or the events themselves. The problem here is that "experience" has special meanings for Pentecostalists as well as some theologians (see, for example, McDonnell 1970).

parts of the world and in different religions. But we are talking here about something quite specific—glossolalia that is more or less accurately recorded and that has religious value.

The first is from the Russian Molokan sect, most of whose members immigrated to the United States early in the twentieth century, locating themselves on the west coast. It is heretical certainly from the point of view of Russian Orthodoxy and perhaps even marginally Christian when compared with traditional Christian beliefs and practices. It is, for example, Zionist (in believing that Molokans are the "chosen people"), and it practices neither baptism nor eucharist in any form. As already noted, the Molokans were tongue speaking long before there was anything like a world-wide Pentecostal movement.[5] (For further information see the works of Berokoff, Bolshakoff, Conybeare, and P. Young.)

Among the Molokans any person who feels inspired to speak to the congregation must first present himself to the priest and say *Parginal assurginal* (*yuzgoris*). If the priest responds with this same formula, the prophet may speak. Now the words are understood by the Molokans to be glossolalic, as is clear from one of the songs in which they appear (here in translation from Russian):

> Let us sing, Brothers and Sisters,
> This song of our King,
> According to the dictate of God's Spirit from above,
> In new fiery tongues:
> (Chorus)   God is alive and the Lord be blessed,
>   And we are their people in the Holy Spirit.
>   *Parginal Assurginal Yuzgoris.* Amen.[6]

---

[5] It should be noted that it was the Molokans, identified by historians of the Full Gospel Business Men's Fellowship International simply as "Russian Pentecostals," who were responsible for the conversion of the Shakarian family from Armenian Presbyterianism to charismatic religion. The Shakarians were "Pentecostal" when they immigrated to the United States and before they had come in contact with the new American Pentecostalism. (It was Demos Shakarian who was largely responsible for the establishment of the FGBMFI, about which see T. R. Nickel.) Among the Russian Molokans, however, their coreligionists are known simply as Armenian Molokans. There is no schism between them, but neither is there fellowship.

[6] *Sionskiy Pesennik* ("Songs of Zion"), 1958, Number 518. There are many other meaningless words in the *Dukh i Zhizn* ("Spirit and Life"), an anthology of sacred writings, but these appear to be the names for God, the Devil, angels, etc.: for example, *Admeil, Tavtan, Anga Ishmaga Shagmas, Alkhaim Fatmi, Alfeil Likhtamis, Tarifta Rafti Khental', Fel'fa Sal'ma*

We can assume that these words are preserved from some long-forgotten glossolalic event.

The Shakers, an "emotional" sect that broke off from the Friends (Quakers), was also tongue speaking, and glossolalia provided the "words" to many of its songs. These are from Andrews' *The Gift to be Simple* (pp. 117,76).

O san-nisk-a-na nisk-a-na, haw, haw, haw,
    fan-nick-a-na nisk-a-na, haw, haw, haw.
O san-nisk-a-na, nisk-a-na yea se-ne-aw, fan-a-na,
    nisk-a-na, haw, haw, haw.
O san-nisk-a-na-na, haw, haw, fan-nik-a-na-na, haw, haw,
O sen-a-go fan-a, nick-a-na-na na nick-a-na-na
O sen-a-go fan-a, nick-a-na-na na.

The following occurs with interpretation:

O sa ri anti va me	"O Saviour wilt thou hear me
O sa ri anti va me	O Saviour wilt thou hear me
I co lon se ve re	I am poor and needy
I con e lo se va ne	I'll come and bow before thee
I con e lo se va ne	I'll come and bow before thee
Se ran te lo me.	Thy cross I'll take upon me."

For written glossolalia to be exotic it must be both incomprehensible and orthographically unusual (we can call it *glossographia*), but such writing is not difficult to produce if one already knows a writing system. All that a person needs to do is abstract a few of the motions that make up the system and combine them in a more or less haphazard way. Children do this when they pretend to write; adult glossolalists do it rarely.

In Pentecostal literature there is no discussion of glossographia; the subject is not even mentioned as far as I know.[7] But observers of Pentecostalism have noted a couple of cases.

Khal'migar' Yul'khin Esvamil' Darmigal' Gindagu. Some of these look more like borrowings from a non-Slavic language than glossolalia.

[7] One would think that the well-known incident of the handwriting on the wall, interpreted by Daniel for Belshazzar, King of the Chaldeans, might have given rise to glossolalia, at least among poorly-educated Pentecostals. For the record, in any case, it should be noted that the problem that Daniel was called on to solve was to explain the meaning of *Mene, Mene, Tekel, Parsin,* not to decipher the handwriting. (See Daniel 5.)

Mary Campbell, whose glossolalia had some influence on the congregation of E. Irving's Presbyterian church in London, is reported by Miller to have transcribed her tongues in an unknown system which "had most likeness to those [characters] one sees on Chinese tea-chests" (so states Cutten, p. 109). Another interesting case is that of a certain "Simon" whose writing resembles shorthand (see above, page 90f). He was raised and confirmed in the German Lutheran church at the beginning of this century but had a Pentecostal experience when he was twenty years old at a meeting conducted by a Norwegian evangelist. Simon's glossographia (seen below), which Pfister calls "idiographie," is said to be related to concepts, not sounds. Since translations are provided by Simon, one also observes that some symbols are used for entirely different concepts, something that we also find when glossolalia is interpreted by the speakers. This inconsistency could pose no problem, however, because Simon seems to have indulged in glossographia only for writing out "sermons" for his own pleasure.

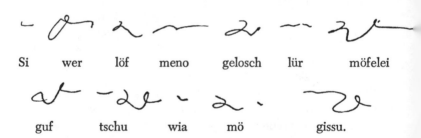

Si   wer   löf   meno   gelosch   lür   möfelei

guf   tschu   wia   mö   gissu.

Glossographia with German transcription (Pfister, p. 36).

The social use of glossographia is reported by J. A. Samarin, an eyewitness to an event that took place in a Molokan church about forty years ago. One of the prophets scribbled a message on a piece of paper and handed it to the priest during the church service. Neither the prophet, who was a glossolalist, nor anyone else could interpret the message that day; in fact, it was ridiculed by one of the elders as being nothing but squiggles. (The eyewitness reports that the writing resembled shorthand.) On the following day, however, another prophet under inspiration took the message which had been placed in the altar-Bible and gave its interpretation. The prophecy is supposed to have come true but the manuscript was long ago lost. Forty years after the incident, even the prophet, whose reputation was not enhanced by it, had forgotten this event.

It must be noted that in the Molokan case there is no evidence whatsoever that this was automatic writing in the technical sense, that is, in a state of dissociation. Nor am I convinced that Simon's was automatic. However, Helen Smith (mentioned earlier) did write in a state of trance as did the young man whose glossographia of a nonreligious sort is illustrated below. He is a member of the group that has become interested in parapsychological and occult phenomena mentioned earlier (page 138). It illustrates how a written pseudolanguage has its own ways of appearing exotic. It is also worth noting that it has some "Germanic" features, as does the spoken glossolalia of another member of the group (for which see Appendix C).

1. Automatic writing in a pseudolanguage while in trance: that is, "glossographia."

2. First two words of the third line of the above sample enlarged.

9

USE AND DISUSE

C HAPTER 8 dealt with two special uses of glossolalia, prayer and messages. Here we are concerned with more general, but not less important, uses of glossolalia.

Contexts, public and private

Glossolalia is best known in its public use and especially in connection with religious behavior that Ronald Knox calls "enthusiastic" and others "emotional." It was emotional Pentecostalism that attracted so much attention in the first three decades of this century and on which is based the characterizations of glossolalia found in dictionaries and encyclopedias. Excessive in many ways, even as charismatists today will admit, traditional Pentecostalism has been replaced in the public's eye by the neo-Pentecostal movement, but the older tradition has not died out, as the following account will demonstrate.

The last week of 1968 at a Puerto Rican Assemblies of God church in the Bronx was devoted to special meetings whose speaker was a guest evangelist from the island. I attended the evening service on Sunday. The church is a nicely remodeled movie-theater facing "the elevated." Its membership is around eight hundred, socially progressive and concerned with the needs of the young people, the new immigrants, the unemployed, and those addicted to drugs. The pastor is a member of a church-sponsored society for the rehabilitation of the addicted. He was in charge of the service until the evangelist came to the pulpit.

The service started at the appointed hour, 7:30 P.M., but a great deal of activity had been going on for an hour before: the young people's choir, about eighty strong, had been practicing and praying (in Spanish) on the platform; others in the auditorium had been praying in small groups or alone or had simply been listening to the music. So when the service started—with a full auditorium—there was already an atmosphere of involvement and expectancy. One or two people already were trembling in what must have been an altered state of consciousness. When four members of the choir gave their "testimonies," the audience responded enthusiastically with loud cries of "Halleluiah," stamping of feet, and clapping of hands.

The order of service up to the sermon consisted of testimonies, congregational singing, a solo, announcements, offering, reading of Scripture, etc. The evangelist did not come to the pulpit until nine o'clock. Instead of preaching, however, he simply spoke a few words in a matter-of-fact way and invited people to be converted. Four women came to the front of the church, and while these were being counseled by some other women, he continued with his remarks, asking all those who wanted to be baptized in the Spirit to come forward. A large group, some from the choir, went forward, females on one side and males on the other.

I had expected a long sermon that would build up to an emotional climax. Instead, the evangelist stepped down to the front and, as the pastor led the congregation in singing a chorus, began dealing with each secker. He placed a hand on top of the head and turned the person around, as if he were a top, and instructed him to repeat *Sella-me* ("Seal me," a prayer to God to be sealed with the Holy Spirit; cf. Ephesians 1:13). He was assisted in this work first by his wife and then, as more and more people began to get active or to lose control of themselves, by others from the congregation.

The pastor of the church stayed on the platform, in full control of himself, but walking or trotting up and down as he lustily sang. The song was a simple chorus that was repeated without interruption for almost an hour with the accompaniment of a piano, organ, marimba, drum, and trumpet, amplified with a loudspeaker to a deafening roar. Fewer and fewer people were left behind him on the platform as members of the choir took seats in the audience or sought the baptism with the others, but many were "stricken" while still on the platform. They twitched and jerked and appeared to have difficulty remaining on their chairs.

On the floor hilarity was mixed with anguish, stupor with uncontrollable shaking and dancing, girls leaped their way through the crowd, and one chubby girl walked about histrionically like a preacher with hand raised saying again and again, "My God! My God!" (in English). And through it all, soon left all by herself at the edge of the platform, sat a girl of three years in her Sunday-best, complacently pounding away at a tambourine.

In this din it would have been impossible for one to hear glossolalia without being right next to a person. Moving freely among the others, I was deceived more than once before I was satisfied. "Without the blessing, there's no tongues" someone in the congregation said to me, but tongues were scarce although blessings appeared to abound.

The other public uses of glossolalia are more fully integrated into a total event, appear to be better controlled by the group, and therefore appear to have more social significance. Prayers and messages were discussed in Chapter 7; glossolalic songs were discussed in Chapter 8.

Glossolalic "conversations" appear to be nonexistent in Pentecostal religious behavior. Such a dialogue would, of course, consist of at least two people talking to each other under the inspiration of the Holy Spirit. What the function of such an event would be—since neither would understand the dialogue and both would be speaking for God—is difficult to imagine. The participants could, of course, see themselves in combat, with each one seeing the other as a false prophet. Or they could conceive of themselves as speaking for heavenly beings. But this is just speculation.

Dialogue is reported to take place occasionally among the Molokans (about whom see page 184). Although I have never observed such behavior, knowing something about this sect, I would imagine that is was polemic in nature. It should also be noted in this connection that members of a certain Swazi sect indulge in telephone conversations when possessed by the Spirit (as they say, although dissociative symptoms are not always evident). These are carried on while people, usually men, stand or walk around together, their hands held to their ears as if listening to the telephone. It is reported that the speech seems to depend heavily on English, the words and phrases being those that men might learn in the mines.

Samples of tape recordings I have heard support the view that this is not glossolalia by our criteria.

It is nevertheless not unreasonable to suppose that religious glossolalists have found themselves in "conversation" from time to time in settings that do not have the approval of their religious tradition. Here is one such case. This happened after a meeting of neo-Pentecostals in a YMCA building when four people were chatting. As so often happens among these people, one of them had asked for prayer and the others had complied by doing so on the spot (in English). The report continues: "[In a lull the woman] began to speak in tongues. She stopped; I began [reports my friend], and I knew at that moment I was speaking to her. She responded. . . . As soon as I stopped, she replied." Both of the participants thought that they were carrying on a conversation, and the woman reported—my friend said—that she felt she had understood the other person without knowing what was said. What may have happened is that both persons had not pulled enough switches: they had switched on "Conversation" after having turned off "Prayer" but had failed to switch on "English" and turn "Glossolalia" off. This is the kind of thing that happens when a person goes from one language to another in a conversation with different people, as we have already noted (page 115). A. Carlson actually recorded a sample of this kind of switching. A speaker answered a question by saying that although glossolalia was much like language "quite often there's quite a bit more *mundarabudi-andara basa marakiarasa—Oops!*" A slightly different kind of lapse occurred in the speech of the medium Helen Smith (see page 135): after awakening from a trance she was interviewed by members of the group, one of whom asked her who were present at a recent meeting. She answered, using "Martian" *métiche, médache,* and *métaganiche* instead of the French *monsieur, madame,* and *mademoiselle.*

Part of the context of the public use of tongues is the people who take part in the total event: whether the participants are more or less equal or whether there is a strong or respected leader among them; whether the group is uniform in belief and commitment or whether there are skeptical or hostile nonbelievers present. Such factors as these affect whether or not glossolalia occurs, how much of it occurs, and to what use it is put. One respondent indicated the value of tongues in a group by saying, "If all present believe in the Power of the Holy Spirit, [tongues] seem to open up new realms of thought." Another one had been told that she "quenched the Spirit" (cf. 1 Thessalonians 5:19), that is, restricted the Spirit's freedom, because she was not comfortable in a noisy Pentecostal service. (This conception of the Spirit as some kind of impersonal Power—like Polynesian *mana*—is implicit in much of the language that is used about charismatic religion. See above, page 158.) Some charismatic leaders have gone so far as to give advice about how glossolalia is to be used when there are unbelievers present: for example, playing it down.[1]

Not all the factors that affect the public use of glossolalia are social, however; there are personal ones as well. For example, a better educated, middle-class glossolalist with a non-Pentecostalist background will be quite selective in his use of tongues. Typical of this kind of person is a forty-year-old minister of the Presbyterian Church in Canada. Although he still considers himself a charismatist, he has moved upward in church affiliation, previously being a member of the Pentecostal Holiness Church and then in the noncharismatic United Missionary Church. He finds it easier to speak in tongues in private, but he is somewhat less reserved with "sympathetic people."

The private use of glossolalia (much more common for some people as we have seen) is religious when its purpose is prayer, but there are some private uses that are more "secular" than religious. Pleasure may be part of the motivation (as we shall see in Chapter 10) for those who speak in tongues while washing dishes, walking, driving a car, or flying an airplane solo. It is not clear from my respondents' statements whether the person thinks of himself as praying; the one who said "I enjoy talking in tongues while driving my car" very probably was not praying.

It is certainly not irrelevant in this connection that these occurrences of glossolalia—that is, private and light-hearted—are associated with action and not contemplation. In these contexts, glossolalia may in fact take the form of song. It is also not irrelevant

---

[1] Since the very beginning, Christians have been concerned with the effect that glossolalia might have on outsiders. One of the reasons that Paul gave for controlling the use of tongues in a church service was that the nonbeliever would think that the believers were crazy (1 Corinthians 14:28ff).

that the people who reported this kind of behavior, like the people who are diffident about using tongues in public, are better educated or successful in some career: among my respondents one, for example, is a test pilot, another a general insurance agent, and another a hospital comptroller.

When glossolalia takes the form of "inner speech," it always seems to be associated with prayer. At least this is how the glossolalist interprets it, because it sometimes arises unconsciously and a person only becomes aware of it "after a while." There are people, as we have seen, who wake up at night "praying in the Spirit" as they say and others who pray internally when they are unable to do so audibly, for example, while engaged in conversation. The absence of an interpreter may also be a cause for unverbalized speech, as we see from the apostle's injunction: "If there is no interpreter, the speaker had better not address the meeting at all, but speak to himself and to God" (1 Corinthians 14:28, NEB).

Nonuse and Disuse

Although normal people and normal societies do not manifest marked tendencies to increasing or decreasing speech activity over a period of time, this is not the case with glossolalic speech. Here there appear to be first an increase and then, in most cases, a decrease; but the movement may not be simply up and down, for there are many factors that might induce a new upsurge of activity, which would then be followed by a falling off again. This evolution might be considered a part of the adaptive processes that go on in the histories of individuals and groups briefly reviewed in the preceding section.

A falling off in the use of glossolalia is documented several times. The Russian Molokan Spiritual Jumpers, for example, see far less glossolalia in their church services than they did about forty years ago, but prophecy continues to flourish. Bloch-Hoell found the same to be true in interviews with Pentecostal leaders (pp. 146,163). People like Donald Gee lament the disuse into which glossolalia has fallen, pointing out that some congregations do not hear glossolalia for as much as two years (see Bloch-Hoell, p. 146). In some churches only the preacher speaks in tongues, as one of my Foursquare Gospel respondents reported. But it is wrong to assert, as Lombard did, that in any group glossolalists *always*—even over a period of time—represent a small proportion of that group (p. 111). The number of glossolalists in a group depends on the characteristics of the group itself: its size, its uniformity, its implicit or explicit reason(s) for existence, and so forth. Obviously, not everyone in a Catholic church will talk in tongues, but practically everyone in a charismatic group of Catholics—at, for example, a youth center—can be expected to practice glossolalia.

In response to my question "How often do you speak in tongues now?" (that is, since the baptism experience), sixty-seven out of eighty-five respondents (or 81%) said every day, with many adding "every few hours," "throughout the day," "many times a day," etc. Only two indicated several times a week, one said once in a while, and one said rarely. The latter two should be considered "inactive" glossolalists of which there are, in spite of the above figures, probably more than "active," that is, practicing ones. My respondents, it must be remembered, are for the most part rather new recruits to the Pentecostal movement, but there are scores of thousands who have been in it all their lives.

A more precise description of the frequency of usage among glossolalists is found in the study by Gerlach and Hine (1970). On the basis of 239 responses to a questionnaire they found that second-generation Pentecostals speak in tongues less frequently than adult converts (at the .05 level of significance). By "frequent" they mean daily or weekly and "non-frequently" monthly, a few times a year, or at the initial experience only. Complementing this difference between traditional and "new" Pentecostals is the fact that people from liberal backgrounds use glossolalia more frequently (the significance being at the .001 level) than people from fundamentalist or Pentecostal backgrounds.

There surely must be many reasons for inactive glossolalia where one has not repudiated it. Some of these are personal and others cultural. As one finds less private, extemporaneous prayer in the Congregational than in the Methodist church for cultural reasons and a great disparity between members of even the same Methodist church for personal reasons, so even Pentecostal churches as a whole and members of Pentecostal churches will

probably differ in this respect. About thirty years of personal observation would suggest this.

One other factor that may lead to inactivity is time. It is reasonable to suppose that unless glossolalia is periodically revali-
dated in terms of personal or social value, disuse will set in. It is
not surprising therefore that the two inactive glossolalists among
my respondents are middle-aged and had had their first experience
twenty-seven and twenty-three years ago. It should also be noted
that both belong to interdenominational churches and list only
Sunday school teacher under "Offices or duties in church, past or
present" in their autobiographical sketch, so they may have "back-
slidden," as it would be put in holiness rhetoric, with respect to
their original Pentecostal convictions.

Explanations given by glossolalists themselves for disuse naturally ignore sociological factors. The personal ones are dominant. The usual explanation is that there is some kind of breakdown in communion with God as there would be if one gave up
reading the Bible and praying in natural language. This can result
from sin, "spiritual dryness," as one described it, or unwillingness
to be fully dedicated to God. One Presbyterian minister said that
failure to pray in tongues for a while usually occurred when he was
mad at God. However, many people are quite tolerant about
glossolalic inactivity, saying that it might result from seeing tongues
misused or that it is simply due to inadequate understanding of the
importance of tongues. Among the latter, according to one leader,
are people who say, " 'When I speak in tongues, it's got to be all
of God and nothing of me.' They expect their human personality
to be shunted aside and the Holy Spirit to speak through them."
In other words, they want a peak experience every time they speak
in tongues. This tolerance is exhibited in answers to my question
"Does a failure to speak in tongues for a long time indicate a bad
relationship with God?" Out of eighty-five respondents fifty-six
(66%) said no or not necessarily, and only seventeen (20%) said
yes or something that tended to be affirmative. The rest of the
answers were ambiguous. Categorical answers in the affirmative
tended to come from people of the older Pentecostal tradition in
which either/or categories figure importantly in doctrine. One
sees here, then, further evidence for the evolution toward personalism and pluralism in modern western religion (as described, for

example, by Stark and Glock). Glossolalic activity is presented as something useful, not necessarily obligatory. One respondent actually stated that the amount of use depended on a person's need.

It should be added that disuse, according to some Pentecostals (for example, H. Horton, p. 159), leads to loss. But this is surely only a manner of speaking. There are many reasons for no longer speaking in tongues, as there are for no longer going to church, but a skill as easy as this one cannot really be "lost."

10

PLEASING AND SYMBOLIC

WE RETURN NOW, after having looked rather closely at what glossolalia is as a linguistic phenomenon and how Pentecostalists fit it into the patterns of their religious life, to a more general examination of its functions. The point of view in this chapter is somewhat psychological and that in the next sociological. The distinction, however, does not pretend to any special validity, being one of convenience more than anything else. A few of the inferences made in these chapters were suggested earlier in one connection or another.[1] They are here enlarged on and related to other observations under three principal headings: the symbolic, pleasureful, and expressive values of glossolalia.

Symbolic

The most interesting, and most complex, personal uses of glossolalia are symbolic: complex not only because glossolalia means

[1] These chapters will be brief and—for those who specialize in the sociology and psychology of religion—inadequate in their treatment of the functions of glossolalia. Getting into this subject more seriously would have required the introduction of considerably more technical discussion, of which there is undoubtedly already enough for the nonspecialist reader.

different things to different people and to the same people at different times, but also because the meanings are intricately interrelated. Some of the elements in this network of meanings are change, proof, submission, and self-assertion.

Change. For all those people who become involved with middle-class Pentecostal experience, whether they come into religious life for the first time or move into this particular one from another, the acquisition of glossolalia both signals and symbolizes the transition. The exact point in time during this transition (or conversion experience, as it can be called) need not be important.[2] Although it can accompany this experience of fulfillment, it can also precede or follow it (for example, Kelsey, pp. 109,164–167). Like an initiation or transition rite, it symbolizes a fundamental break with the past. It sets the believer apart; in effect, he burns his bridges. It is, in other words, a commitment act dedicated to and demanding change in one's life. So suggest Gerlach and Hine, social anthropologists who seek to describe the structure and growth of social movements of various types. They hypothesize that in other movements there will be commitment acts equally dramatic although not necessarily linguistic in nature.

Useful as it is, the hypothesis itself is not startling. This function of glossolalia is easily inferred from statements made by people converted to the charismatic movement. Viewed in this way, moreover, glossolalia has the same function that "standing up" or "going forward" do in some Protestant, for example, Methodist, traditions. (In fact, at a time when revival meetings—with their public rites of commitment—are in decline, the charismatic movement can be considered a revival of this tradition.) On the other hand, the Gerlach and Hine hypothesis has value in explaining why people join movements. The reason is not social or individual preconditions, they say, but the characteristics of the movement itself. Thus, it ought to be found that one of the reasons why so

---

[2] The evangelical Protestant would hardly use the word conversion in this way, even metaphorically, because the term applies to being "saved" by placing one's faith in Jesus. Yet the testimonies of converts to the charismatic movement indicate that there is frequently more change in life-style and orientation after being filled with the Holy Spirit than when they first became Christians. But the same kinds of changes are among others reported for the evangelical type of conversion without the Pentecostal experience.

many Hindu East Indians in Surinam have recently been converted to Christianity through the Pentecostal movement, in spite of the more or less futile attempts of the long-established Moravian church, is the demands that the movement makes on the converts, one of which, of course, is speaking in tongues. On the other hand, the attraction of Pentecostalism might be its stress on personal devotion and its corporate religious activity that appear to resemble similar features in Hindu Bhakti movements. Such speculation must be checked by facts about India itself, of course. A Jesuit missionary to India feels that Pentecostal results in that nation are not at all spectacular. He feels, moreover, that "Indian Pentecostals have shown contemplative and mystical tendencies in their approach to prayer. Tongues-speaking is not prominent" (Damboriena, p. 144).

Glossolalia can hardly have this symbolic value for people who have been born into a charismatic way of life. They will go through the rites prescribed by the group, but these will probably not be as psychologically satisfying or meaningful as for the true convert (that is, new Pentecostal). Life commitment, in fact, may be an antithetical act. Young people, for example, may dramatize their conversion to secularism by flagrant violations of the group's ethical standards. In any case, the "native-born" or "first generation" Pentecostalist will, we assume, have a different set of functions for glossolalia. (We have already noted, for example, that he seems to use glossolalia less frequently than a new convert does.)

Proof. The value of glossolalia in symbolizing change is not simply in its newness. Although this is important, its supernaturalness is what gives it its significance. This is why it validates the baptism experience. And for many people every occurrence of glossolalia, whether spoken by oneself or heard from others, is "palpable proof of God's influence on man" as the Pentecostal leader Barratt once wrote (quoted in Bloch-Hoell, p. 101), or as an Appalachian preacher more directly put it: "If Jesus is *in* you, he'll talk *out* of you." It therefore confirms and strengthens belief, as William James long ago observed about experiences that are supposedly induced by powers beyond one's will (p. 362); one of these is possession (R. Prince, p. 164).

Glossolalia can even arouse expectancy and thereby determine the nature of belief and behavior. This is seen in the statement that glossolalia "makes me expect a miracle." Charismatic religious discourse is consequently replete with reports of unusual experiences whose origin is supernatural and whose significance religious. Glossolalia is not always directly associated with the experiences, but there seems to be a correlation between the degree to which one supernaturalizes glossolalia in particular and the way one interprets life in general: for many Pentecostals of one variety or another, religion is excitingly experiential rather than rational or contemplative. For these people glossolalia has value as a supernatural linguistic "happening."

Submission. In many religions a person is possessed by a spirit without his foreknowledge and even against his will. This is true, for example, of the *zar* cult that is found among Jews, Christians, Muslims, and pagans of Ethiopia (see Leslau) and the Chipunha cult among the Shona-speaking peoples of Rhodesia (see Blakney). But in some glossolalist sects, at least in their contemporary form, God "takes over" only when a person deliberately yields to him. As one person put it, one is "filled, possessed, monopolized, and utilized" by God only by "being emptied of self." Bartleman wrote, "In the experience of 'speaking in tongues' I had reached the climax in abandonment" (p. 45). And Oral Roberts teaches that "you have to bend your intellect and submit your tongue to Christ, because your tongue speaks from out of your total being" (p. 39). This is why, as we have seen (page 49), one must be willing to "risk all," and why the religious struggle can be so violent.[3] One man wanted the Spirit but nevertheless fought against it: "I didn't want [God] to control my entire being. He could work through my hands or my feet, flatten my ears, or make my nostrils flare, but I didn't want God to tamper with my tongue" (*Voice,* Jan./Feb., 1969, p. 13). This is also why the symbol is so real. Every time a person speaks in tongues, performing an act that is

---

[3] It is easy to suppose, as Oman has (p. 50), that because a person is willing to be a fool, he thus relieves himself of guilt feelings for not being the kind of Christian he means to be; but it is another thing to prove the existence of "guilt feelings." Guilt is obviously different from a general psychological disorientation.

cognitively meaningless, he is reminded that he is being used by God.

The pneumatology (doctrine of the Holy Spirit) that makes blessing conditional on submission is, however, only one Pentecostal view, although it appears to be the dominant one at this time. (It certainly pervades the rhetoric of neo-Pentecostals of all stripes.) But in the southern sections of the United States, especially where hyper-Calvinism has long been established, it would not be surprising at all for Pentecostalists, who tend to be Arminian (therefore, free-will), to be influenced by the doctrine of "irresistible grace," that is, the predestinating power of God. How this difference in theology might correlate with differences in the total glossolalic experience (psychological and linguistic) and with statements about it is not at all clear.

Correlated with submission is an acknowledgement of one's helplessness and fallibility. Glossolalists talk about the inadequacies of their understanding and the limitation of their knowledge. For them glossolalia is a symbol of this circumscribed humanity in the face of incomprehensible fate. This is why one of the effects of the experience is peace. But since the gift makes up for one's limitations, one can, as we have seen, look on it instrumentally.

Self-assertion. In yielding to the supernatural, one rejects the natural; one takes sides with God and opposes man. This is why it is not surprising that there is an anti-rational stance among so many tongue speakers. Language and thought with which it is associated are seen as human phenomena, and they are considered less an instinctive activity than one fabricated by man. Implicit in all kinds of statements, it is explicit in a snake handler's explanation to me that what man did at the Tower of Babel was to reject God's language and make his own. For him and many other glossolalists, therefore, speaking in tongues is returning to original divine speech.

The ideas and feelings of many a glossolalist are therefore ambiguous in their content and meanings. Whereas his ego is lost in the supernatural when he considers the antithesis between the supernatural and the natural, his ego is asserted when he denies society's authority over him. For this reason glossolalia is a mechanism for and a symbol of self-assertion in a social setting as well as in private.[4] I have seen people with little status in a public meeting break forth in glossolalia during an accidental pause in someone else's discourse. It is as if he were saying, "I'm somebody too." In those Pentecostal meetings, however, where self-expression is institutionalized, where one "does his thing" in the Spirit, there is, of course, no such need. This is a reminder that the functions of glossolalia vary importantly from one kind of microsociety to another.

More will be said on this topic in the next chapter, but we might add at this point that many speakers in tongues derive pleasure from having people hang on their words. One middle-aged respondent, for example, spoke appreciatively of the "tremendous response" to what she had said (in interpretation) to a group of 150 people.

Pleasureful

Glossolalia is also indulged in, because speakers appear to derive pleasure from the experience. They enjoy doing something they once considered impossible; they like the way their discourses sound; and they enjoy both the fantasy and "ecstasy" that are associated with the use of this pseudolanguage.

Mastery. Many a person has reported the fun he has in talking, even experimenting with, glossolalia. Early in one's experience the pleasure is partly derived from becoming proficient in a newly acquired skill. The speaker learns to "say more"—by talking longer or using more "words"—and to do more things with his language. (We have already talked about this improvement in facility, page 68ff.) Many people also pray for "different lan-

[4] There is an interesting parallel to this phenomenon in social-psychology as it is linguistically manifested. In multi-ethnic societies, like Nigeria, where a national ethos has not yet emerged, language suppression is seen as ethnic and individual suppression. As a group's self-awareness develops, it is translated into linguistic and political terms: thus, a tribe insists that its own language be used instead of the standard one (see, for example, Wolff). This is why linguistic homogeneity characterizes the political states in which, among other things, "Primordial ties and passions are more likely to be under control" (Fishman, p. 24).

guages." The pleasure is sweeter, perhaps, because the language was once out of reach, as a supernatural gift, or beyond desire, as something to be despised.

Fantasy. There may be a bit of fantasy—and maybe on occasion even quite a bit—in the experience of some glossolalists, caught up as they are in talking a spiritual language that is private, secret, esoteric, or hallowed. (One woman had a sacred glossolalic name for Jesus she would not disclose to me, or, she said, to anyone else.) It is surely not improbable that a glossolalist's private reveries while using tongues are similar to what a linguistic colleague indulged in when she was a child in Canada:

When I was of school age, up until nine or ten at least, I regularly talked to myself in a pseudolanguage. This was during day-dreaming sessions alone, and it gave a great sense of power and pleasure. As I look back on it now [after thirty-some years], the sociocultural conditioning for this is obvious. My sister and I were the only English monolinguals in a school full of Polish, Russian, Ukrainian, and German kids, all of whom spoke, in addition to their own native language and English, somebody else's language. The language of the playground was Ukrainian, and we never had more than a marginally receptive control of this, while everyone else seemed to have productive control. I remember feeling distinctly deprived and "left out" at times when everyone laughed at a joke that I didn't get or when I was the butt of ridicule that I only partially understood. In private, then, I had some of the skill and power that my peers had and that I envied in them.

It would be wrong, however, to label the private experience of a tongue speaker pejoratively "childish" because of this similarity. Fantasy is akin to imagination, and there is undoubtedly a great deal of "adult" reflection at these times. But this is just speculation. I have no information about what glossolalists really think about when their vocal organs produce linguistically meaningless speech.

Ecstasy. Fantasy is not far from ecstasy. This, for our immediate purpose, is defined simply as a pleasurable state of intense emotion whether natural or linked with an altered state of consciousness. Sometimes, of course, it might be difficult for one to determine if the state were natural or altered. It is probably possible for a rapturous feeling to be induced, as a person prays, through changes in the breathing pattern that affects body chemistry.

The sanguine emotional states with which glossolalia is associated are described by many of my respondents. The following is what one middle-aged lady wrote in answer to the question "Do you feel better in any way after having spoken in tongues?"

It's like being out in my boat with the lake breeze blowing in my face —only better. It's being lifted out of myself into a world that is all wonder and light. It's new life and love and joy bubbling through the whole of me. It's Jesus, and I like to lie flat on my back within the circlement of His Being, and feel all these things mingled together.

It should be added, however, that glossolalia does not necessarily lead to such a state; and although a person does not need to be in a mood to indulge in glossolalia (as I learned in a specific question on this point), what one gets out of the experience depends on what one brings to it. But this is no different from every emotional experience a human being can have.

Other writers have a different definition or characterization of ecstasy. If they include dissociation as one of its features, then their expressions "language of ecstasy" or "ecstatic speech" as referring to glossolalia would be entirely misleading. The reasons should by now be fairly clear. Glossolalia is not simply a product of some altered state of consciousness, whether it be a pleasureful one (as in "ecstasy") or not. There is absolutely no doubt in my mind that many of the "ecstatic" experiences of glossolalists are the same as those of nonglossolalist but pious Protestants and Catholics. Some of these are what evangelicals refer to when they speak about having had a "real blessing" in prayer, Bible study and meditation, conversation of a religious nature, or public meeting.[5]

It is therefore worth noting that in a thorough examination of ecstatic experience, Laski makes no mention of pseudolanguage or even anomalous speech. What does characterize the "language of ecstasy" is a certain kind of rhetoric (p. 226). There appears to be a recurrence of certain kinds of metaphors and similes, for example. Some of these rhetorical devices are associated with certain

[5] If this is an accurate statement, it would contradict M. Laski's observation that it seems that "communal worship is not likely to induce individual ecstasy" (p. 197). But perhaps we are talking about different things—always the trouble with the subject of "ecstasy."

kinds of ecstasies. An example of this kind of language is the following from C. S. Lewis' novel *That Hideous Strength* (pp. 318–319). In my interpretation of the story, the passage describes a religious conversion.

There was no form nor sound. The mould under the bushes, the moss on the path, and the little brick border, were not visibly changed. But they were changed. A boundary had been crossed. She had come into a world, or into a Person, or into the presence of a Person. Something expectant, patient, inexorable, met her with no veil or protection between. . . . There was nothing, and never had been anything, like this. And now there was nothing except this. Yet also, everything had been like this; only by being like this had anything existed. In this height and depth and breadth the little idea of herself which she had hitherto called *me* drooped down and vanished, unfluttering, into bottomless distance, like a bird in a space without air. . . .

Words take too long. To be aware of all this and to know that it had already gone made one single experience. It was revealed only in its departure.

It is quite possible—indeed, quite probable—that the tongue speaker enjoys his speech at times for its formal esthetic value. This would be true especially of prayer, when a person is engaged in relaxed meditation. In a happy frame of mind, producing something that sounds to him religious, he will delight in the melody and rhythm of his discourse. Even without song, then, such speech can function as background music to a person's meditations. It is no wonder that in such pleasant contexts praying goes on, as glossolalists say, for hours.

Expressive

According to the explicit statements of middle-class speakers, glossolalia is used to express emotion or feeling. It is compared to instrumental music, "expressionistic" poetry, or impressionism in art.

This function of glossolalia, as we have already seen (page 154), is associated with prayers. It would seem, in fact, that tongue speakers do not think of messages as having the same emotional value for themselves personally. If they get "assurance," for example, from messages, it is not from the initial glossolalic event, but from the subsequent interpretation. And it should also be added that the effect can be in the opposite direction. Praying in tongues can induce the feelings that are otherwise said to come from the experience. Thus, Rev. Larry Christenson says that glossolalic praying has a "profound effect on the deep feelings and attitude which the mind cannot always directly control" (p. 23).

The feelings expressed by glossolalia are—roughly speaking—anxiety, joy, and anger. The expression of anxiety or concern leads to a person's being "edified." This is a common word in the religious vocabulary of evangelical Protestants, taken from the Authorized Version of the Bible, but for the Pentecostalist it has an additional meaning, at least when it is associated with tongues. As Oral Roberts puts it, being edified in tongues means being relieved of things that are hidden but are troubling one; it means expressing "the heights and depths" of what one feels. This is why praying in tongues "seems to help restore vitality" (pp. 46,49,50). (This last statement, like the one made by Christenson, may have a special meaning for leaders in the charismatic movement. In large public meetings they are treated like celebrities and many demands are made of them—such as prayer and healing. At one very large Pentecostalist conference, I followed one such leader with whom I was trying to get an interview, and he was almost beside himself from being pulled this way and that. If these people are at all sincere in their calling, they would certainly want to be in a proper mood for some of their religious work. It is possible, therefore, that glossolalic praying helps them to get their equilibrium.)

Anger is certainly the least talked about emotion associated with glossolalia. My questionnaire regrettably did not elicit information about it, so the few statements made by respondents were accidental. However, I was told by one psychiatrist about two ministers (presumably neo-Pentecostal) who gave up glossolalia, because in their own experience it was associated with anger. It is not known if this anger was directed to God or to people.

Judgments about another person's emotions based on our own observations can be misleading. It is very common, for example, for people to think that someone is speaking angrily if the speech is completely unintelligible. If this is true for ordinary language, it would also be true of glossolalia. Therefore we need to be critical of an observation made by an outsider who is not familiar with all the nuances of communication in a Pentecostal meeting. Parsons, for example, says that some of the glossolalia of an American Pentecostalist church made up of South Italian immigrants consisted of "aggressively-toned words and phrases . . . not quite distinguishable as to content, but which sounded suspiciously like either curse words or like everyday derogatory expressions such as 'shut up.' Here it was as if the aggression which is so freely expressed in South Italian culture had somehow to return, even within the framework of the religious service" (pp. 258–259).[6] This speech seems to have been addressed to God in the "prayer-period," but on those apparently uncommon occasions where glossolalia is used competitively, between speakers, as in West Indian Pentecostalist sects (see below), anger may be directed to another human being.

It would appear, generally speaking, that glossolalia is not used in the Pentecostal society to express anger and hostility. Individual cases most certainly exist, but contrary to early notions about glossolalia this pseudolanguage is not simply the product of anger (as we saw in Chapter 2). It is possible, of course, that the Pentecostal might use tongues to camouflage his anger by eliminating intelligibility. This appears to be the explanation for some people who use glossolalia nonreligiously (see pages 141–142) as it is for the use of nonsensical strings of another language (as among certain "Pennsylvania Dutch"-speaking religious communities that eschew all forms of profanity in English). It is more reasonable to suppose that if the glossolalist switches to tongues, he does so because he feels that in that speech he has divine sanction for his own wrath.

There is a certain kind of praying, regardless of the emotion associated with it, that is figuratively referred to as the "groanings of the Spirit." Glossolalists do not, of course, mean that they really groan, only that they have an intense emotion that is expressed with difficulty in ordinary language. The phrase, in fact, comes

---

[6] This was not confirmed in my visits to Italian Pentecostal services in Italy and Canada. I was, in fact, struck by the decorum that characterized them. We are reminded again how cautiously one must make generalizations about Pentecostals. The minister of the Canadian congregation, for example, far from being a marginal person in his society, was working on a B.A. and was currently taking a university course in philosophy!

from a passage in the Bible (Romans 8:26) that is interpreted by glossolalists as referring to praying in tongues.

It has been seriously suggested by at least one psychologist, however, that the vocalizations of Pentecostalists, including interjections as well as real glossolalia, were manifestations of painful sensations produced by thoughts about personal guilt. This "groan"-hypothesis is interesting, but it has never been researched. If it were to be tested, one would have a difficult time isolating elements of guilt-thought and then correlating them with vocalizations.

One of the principal arguments against the "groan"-hypothesis, in any case, is the significant absence of interjectional material (not ejaculations, discussed on page 117 above) in fully developed glossolalia. By interjectional here is meant the use of short utterances that are frequently made up of sounds that are not in the phonemic (that is, linguistically systematic and fundamental sound) systems of the natural languages known by the speaker. This is a remarkable fact when one remembers that "sound gestures, which tend to form a layer apart even in the language of the adult, appear to seek out those sounds which are inadmissible in a given language" (Jakobson 1968:25–26). One notes, for example, that the North American English sign of disgust *yugh,* pronounced /yăx/, contains a strongly articulated back velar fricative /x/ which is not used in the make-up of the ordinary vocabulary of the language. There are, of course, exotic sounds in some glossolalic speech, but these are usually borrowed from other languages, and they appear to be used as normal sounds. It would, however, be presumptuous to deny the possibility that some exotic sounds are sometimes used interjectionally.

The expression of emotion is seen by tongue speakers as definitely nonrational; the mind in fact is excluded as an interference. The "cord of transmittance" between the mind and the tongue, as one man puts it, is blocked while that between the heart and tongue is established. Glossolalic prayer is everything prayer is, another says, "minus what is contributed by the mind." Speakers say that with glossolalia there is an "opening and releasing of the deep centers of life." (Many of the metaphors are liquid ones, like glossolalia being a means of "drawing off" tensions or "pouring out your soul and mind to God.") One respondent wrote that "speaking and singing in the Spirit releases the intellect from vocabulary concentration, thus permitting great mental agility in covering many praise and prayer subjects." In explaining what it means to talk "not unto men, but unto God" (1 Corinthians 14:2), another respondent said that a person "is not trying to impress man but has dropped the façade of logical flesh and is on a plateau of privacy with our Father beyond the subtle influences of accepted social niceties." This person has been released from the restrictions of man's language and is pouring out his "unspeakable praise" to God.[7]

But the intellect is also said to be stimulated by tongues. This appears in two comments on a Biblical passage just following the one mentioned above: "He that speaketh in an (unknown) tongue edifieth himself" (verse 4). One person said, "As I pray to God in a tongue I receive back from Him a clarifying of many things in the conscious mind"; and another person, "This has happened to me often. I can be very upset about something I feel I need to know. I pray in tongues and often the answer will come into my mind as if it had been there all the time—when I did *not* know the answer." Similarly, Oral Roberts says: "I often feel a blossoming of my intellect when I have finished praying or praising God in tongues" (p. 31).

It is obvious that the expressive function of glossolalia, whether in prayer or in message-giving, is not purely personal and subjective. There are also social aspects. Glossolalic prayer might be interpreted, for example, as a means to help the speaker identify with another person. He needs to have an audience, someone with whom he can talk out his problems, so he addresses himself to God. Interesting as this conjecture is, we must not let it lead to too

---

[7] Note how far this experience is from that of a person who uses language as an object of contemplation while under the influence of hemp (hashish): "Even grammar, dry-as-dust grammar, becomes something like a sorcerer's conjuration. The words are resurrected in flesh and bone: the noun, in its substantial majesty; the adjective, the transparent robe that clothes and colors the noun like a glorious burnish; the verb, angel of motion, that gives a sentence its impetus." This person selected different material from his linguistic experience partly, one supposes, because he was a poet. The drug enhanced a practice that was already familiar to him (Charles Baudelaire, quoted in Ebin 1961:32). I would speculate that a drugged glossolalist, if he dwelt at all on his speech, would be struck by its "musical" features: melody, rhythm, and accent.

broad generalizations, for example, that most glossolalists are—by
personality or because of social or emotional problems—alienated.
The charismatic movement is, in fact, characterized by a great deal
of "sharing" as the members call it. They become intimate friends
and discuss all kinds of matters, even those they would admit are
somewhat trivial. It is possible, of course, for the more socially
withdrawn to use glossolalia in talking with God rather than or
more often than in talking with their human peers. But we have no
information about such differences.

Therapeutic

For millions of people, both in and outside the church, it is almost inconceivable that a religious event of a social nature could
be pleasureful and exhilarating. Yet this is exactly what it is for
those who stress the feeling component of religious experience, and
any account of "emotional" sectarianism that omits this sanguine
and therapeutic part of the total picture is doing the movement a
disfavor. Even an objective but empathetic social scientist cannot
help but be caught up by the "sacred hilarity" of something like an
Appalachian meeting. Here is how one preacher I heard exhorted
the congregation: "Get in the service and obey the Lord"; "Feel
your freedom and enter into the Spirit of the Lord"; "God wants
his people to be happy"; "You gotta *feel* God every day"; "If you
got something you can't feel, there's something wrong with you";
"Preach the way you feel"; "I feel good tonight"; "I gotta be jus'
what I am"; "You gotta get *out* of the flesh and *into* the Spirit before you can please God."

The therapeutic effects of charismatic religion are not simply
inferred from observations of what has happened to people or
from statements about these changes. Neo-Pentecostals in particular are frequently quite explicit about how they have been helped
in resolving emotional problems. It is not at all clear, however,
what contribution, if any, glossolalia in particular made in the
therapy.

Several functions of glossolalia for individual tongue speakers
have been reviewed in this chapter. Some of them are already
part of glossolalist "doctrine"; others are inferred from both their

behavior and statements about themselves. Not all of these explain *why* a person takes up tongue speaking. That, I have tried to make clear from the very beginning of this book, is required by the movement (as a religious subculture) he converts to or identifies himself with. And it has already been established that no special power needs to take over a person's vocal organs; all of us are equipped with everything we need to produce glossolalia. But once it is acquired, glossolalic speech can achieve different psychological ends, some more and others less consciously manipulated.

If nothing has been said to indicate the ways in which glossolalia, as anomalous speech, is psycholinguistically unique, it is because this has already been said. Its special features are only two: (a) it consists of strings of generally simple syllables (b) that are not matched systematically with a semantic system. The most important fact, psychologically or sociologically viewed, is that glossolalia is used at all.

Seen from a psychological perspective, therefore, glossolalia appears to be much less aberrant than one might suspect it to be. This conclusion will emerge again in the next chapter where it is examined in more social terms.

11

PARTICIPATION
AND POLITICS

I N THE PRECEDING CHAPTER we saw that glossolalia serves the
individual psychologically in several different ways. Yet these
are mostly unknown to the tongue speaker, and it is doubtful
indeed that he took up speaking in tongues for all these purposes.
A similar conclusion must be reached when we examine the use
of glossolalia by a group and by an individual as he participates in
a group. Once again we see that the functions of glossolalia are
more numerous than would be suggested by a casual posing of the
question: "*Why* do people talk in tongues?"

Only half of this chapter is taken up with a description of some
social functions of glossolalia. The rest is devoted to two related
topics: change in use and factors influencing the use of tongues.

Participation

What is a validating experience for the individual, as we saw in
the preceding chapter, is a demarcating one for the group: it symbolizes the group's difference from others. In this respect glossolalia serves the same function that any form of speech may have,
like the in-group languages of students (slang) or secret societies.
The latter, of course, also have communicative functions in the

strict sense of the term. Thus, in Melanesia the cargo cultists not only broke with the past by abolishing many important taboos, clan exogamy, and bridewealth, for example, but emphasized their solidarity by adopting a new "language" that symbolized linguistic unity in an area that was very diversified linguistically (Worsley, pp. 150–151,249). As with glossolalia for Pentecostalists, this speech may have served an instrumental function as well. Some of these people believed that their backwardness, by contrast with the wealth of the industrialized peoples, was due to their ignorance of other languages. For them the millennium was to be a time when gifted leaders would teach them Dutch, English, and Chinese (Worsley, p. 141). Although these new languages are called glossolalia (and it is not clear who is responsible—the cultists or the observers), they appear to be concoctions of words and phrases borrowed from other languages rather than the linguistic phenomenon described in this book.[1]

Symbols can become frozen, but when a movement is new, they are especially significant. Thus, the demarcating function of glossolalia is more important for neo-Pentecostal groups than it is for the established Pentecostalist ones which perpetuate themselves biologically (where children are born into Pentecostal homes) rather than sociologically. (However, where Pentecostalism is spreading rapidly, as in Brazil, we can expect glossolalia to retain its symbolic demarcating function, unless other symbols have superseded it.) In these groups, then, it is not enough for a newcomer to identify himself as a Christian. The members will want to know if he has had "the experience." One of the best answers is simply "Yes, I have spoken in tongues." This marks solidarity with the group. Indeed, reliable reports indicate that some groups will not integrate a person unless he gives evidence of being a tongue speaker. The expression is not theirs, but this is their "requirement for membership."

[1] Although places like Papua and New Guinea are extremely multilingual, there already are contact or trade languages that are used by people who do not understand each other's native languages. Pidgin English (also called Neo-Melanesian) and Police Motu are two of them. One would have thought that Pidgin, for example, would have been used to symbolize a new unity. Perhaps this rejection (if that is what it is) of Pidgin is an indication of its lowly status by comparison with the other foreign languages at the time when conditions are being described.

This is not one of the functions of glossolalia that all neo-Pentecostals would themselves recognize, yet it is unquestionably suggested by the way they talk about tongues and the way they treat the interested participant in their meetings. It is not enough to take part by singing, praying (in ordinary language), and "sharing." Any deeply involved Christian can do these. The real test for full acceptance into these groups (not necessarily by individuals) is the use of glossolalia in some context. The testimony of one established member of the group is sufficient witness, but apparently some people feel that others are holding back if they do not use glossolalia, at least in prayer, from time to time in group meetings. (Perhaps equally important in setting off the charismatic group is *what* it talks about and *how* it talks, that is, the content and rhetoric of formal and informal speech. It would include special terms like "sharing" and expressions like "The Lord gave me . . ." A different style of speech will set off the observer as an outsider. Learning to use this language is part of the process of becoming integrated into the movement.)

This unifying function of glossolalia is, of course, seen from the point of view of the group itself. Seen from outside, the rise of a charismatic group within a traditional church very often leads to divisions, and the reasons are very often what they were when Paul dealt with them at Corinth (page 15 above): a feeling of superiority on the part of the tongue speakers and the disorder that the practice of glossolalia introduces into corporate worship.

If glossolalia is symbolic externally, it is also symbolic internally. That is, it helps the members to reaffirm their difference as often as they will.

In some groups, according to Pentecostal writers, there are people who feel that a meeting of a particular kind is not complete without an occurrence of glossolalia. By introducing a glossolalic pronouncement or ejaculation they "sanctify" (as I would put it) the meeting somewhat in the way the close friends of a night-club entertainer will affirm solidarity with him (and "bless" him) by leading the audience to applause. At poorly attended meetings, as Calley has documented in his study of West Indian sects, almost every nuclear member of a church contributes in some way (p. 101). It is as if the group proclaimed solidarity at the threat of disharmony. Since a well-attended meeting is a sufficient sign of integration and solidarity, nuclear members can relax; it is then, observes Calley (p. 80), that many nonnuclear members speak in tongues, as if to declare their solidarity with the group.

What the preceding paragraph only suggests must be made explicit, namely, that as a symbol for a group, glossolalia can be manipulated by its members. Among some groups glossolalia indicates a person's favorable response to his own or someone else's participation in the religious event; he indicates his approval or pleasure, for example. Calley noted this in the West Indian meetings he participated in (p. 91), and I saw it among Appalachian snake handlers. This behavior must be compared with the verbal participation in some forms of folk Christianity in the western hemisphere, not to exclude other areas. At Camp Creek, for example, speakers expected (for example, "You believe that?") and got response from the audience: "Shine on!" "Speak out!" "I believe that!" "Lookee here!" "That's what I want to hear!" "Come on, now!" and so forth. The same kind of behavior was witnessed at a Jamaican pocomania service.

Even while glossolalia serves its symbolic role for the group, it achieves a pragmatic purpose. A Christmas tree is an instructive analogy because it represents a holiday and contributes at the same time to its enjoyment. Glossolalia, as a manifestation of the divine, contributes a sacred note to a meeting, something it does much less frequently and to a lesser degree in private experiences. Glossolalists describe the feeling that pervades a meeting as one of awe or keen awareness of the divine presence. By some people, as we saw above, it is felt as a power that "electrifies the whole building."

Another practical function of glossolalia is to contribute to the spontaneity of a meeting. Because a discourse or utterance in tongues can come unexpectedly at almost any point, it reminds the participants that this is an open meeting: anything can be done by anybody. This principle—sacred serendipity it might be called —is a dominant one in the charismatic ethos, without which the culture of these groups cannot be understood. A liturgy is abhorrent to many of them, and even an "order of service," a kind of religious agenda, is too much like a strait jacket. What these people want is "freedom in the Spirit."[2]

[2] The individual and social benefits of this existential, "be yourself" religion have not been fully appreciated by observers in spite of the value that it places on just this kind of self-assertiveness (Gerrard, Gerlach, and Wood —sociologist, anthropologist, and psychologist respectively—are exceptions.)

From Appalachian sects, where almost "anything goes" in the name of freedom, to neo-Pentecostal ones where Anglicans and Catholics participate, there is a great difference in cultural tradition, but all share the same value; it is only manifested differently. Thus, although the middle- and upper-middle-class groups might have an order of service, there is constant improvisation. It would seem that the more overtly the meeting is supervised by leaders, the more overt are the improvisations. The leader can rearrange or modify the program in all kinds of ways and call on people to perform some deed or make some speech unexpectedly. The speaker may announce that he will not talk on what he had planned, because the Spirit has just given him a new message. Whether it be an ecumenical breakfast meeting at a Howard Johnson's restaurant or a snake-handling Saturday-night meeting in Scrabble Creek, it is always the same: "Now Brother (So-and-so) didn't know I was going to ask him to do this right now . . ."[3]

This use of glossolalia clearly illustrates how speech not only helps realize the ethos or way of life of a society but also the ethos of a social occasion. Goffman spoke to this point when he wrote that some social occasions, like funerals, possess "a distinctive ethos, a spirit, an emotional structure, that must be properly created, sustained, and laid to rest, the participant finding that he is obliged to become caught up in the occasion, whatever his personal feelings" (p. 19). But he said too little about what the role of speech was on such occasions. We must understand that there are different ways of talking that are appropriate to different realms of human experience, but we must also understand that different forms of speech (seen in their totality) contribute to *making* an event. A formal dinner party in some social circles, for example, would be somewhat of a failure without a certain kind of conversation. It is in this sense that glossolalia contributes to the making of

---

The explanation for this failure must certainly be a particular kind of bias in our society.

[3] We do not, of course, have to believe that all of this is genuinely spontaneous, no more so than it was when a Quaker introduced his talk to the assembly with the words "In the silence, it came to me that . . ." What a colleague of mine had observed, however, was that this prominent visitor had sneaked a manuscript from his pocket and had slipped it on to the pulpit. But a few such lapses do not negate the aim of a group to be spontaneous, and a belief in freedom can be expected to have effect on the general behavior of those participating in a religious event.

a religious event. It does not merely "add" something, like a bit of spice. Without it the meeting would be significantly different. It is not at all from insincerity, therefore, that a fully participating Pentecostal bursts forth in the Spirit's language.

Politics

If the individual can use glossolalia within a group to achieve its goals and support its values, he can use it for his own good as a participant in that group. He may, in fact, consider that what is good for him is good for the others. This is clear with leadership and authority; both are enhanced or validated by the use of glossolalia in religious meetings. But the ways in which this is achieved are different from group to group. The following discussion only suggests the possibilities.

In those circles where leadership is informal and there is yet no organizational structure, as in some neo-Pentecostal ones, almost everyone uses glossolalia. But as the size of the group increases, its membership becomes less uniform and a kind of political structure (that is, recognized leadership) emerges to govern its activities. The result is that the use of glossolalia is largely monopolized by its leaders. Accompanying this development is increased control of glossolalic activity in public meetings. (Compare what was said above about messages and interpretations.) This is clearly seen in the history of the Pentecostal movement (see, for example, what was said in Chapter 7). Similarly a minister of the independent Church of the Lord (Aladura) in West Africa is a speaker in tongues, "for he is a man of spiritual power set apart for the special work of God" (Turner, p. 33). But a lower degree of power may be manifest in a layman who is a good "visioner" or speaker in tongues. Whatever the latter may refer to linguistically, it is obviously something considered anomalous and spiritual by the adherents of this sect.

If both leaders and members of a developing group appreciate the status marking of glossolalia and use it instrumentally to guide the congregation by means of glossolalic prophecies, competition would obviously result between the leaders and the led. Although this freedom of use could be institutionalized as a form of check-and-balance, it is much more likely that authority would finally be focused in one part of the leadership and either that part would monopolize the use of glossolalia or else its use would disappear.

A slight variation of this use is found among the West Indian sects in London, if Calley's analysis is correct. There it is not so much a narrowing down of the users of tongues as of the uses: everybody has recourse to glossolalia in competition with others, to assert, for example, one's holiness and authority. Thus, one woman leader mixed a long spate of glossolalia into her speech when she was rebuking her congregation for not having fasted as she had instructed them to. In another group, when a member challenged the authority of its leader, the latter answered him by beginning to speak in tongues; not to be outdone, the church-member came back with his own glossolalic answer, and for a while both of them were "speaking to each other" in tongues (see Calley, pp. 46,48,78,79).

In these West Indian sects Calley observed very little interpretation, and he explains its absence by the suggestion that members may be unwilling to back another person up by authenticating his message. This explanation may have some validity where the level of hostility is high, for it is rather unlikely that one would interpret someone else's speech if there were hostility between them, unless he intended to subvert his influence with a damaging interpretation. (Such subversion is only hypothetical; I know of no such case.) A low incidence of messages-with-interpretation, however, should not always be explained in these terms.

We infer similar struggles from every Pentecostal discussion, like Gee's, that deals with specific problems. Such competition is to be noticed in connection with Paul's advice to the Corinthians. He taught that all the gifts, including glossolalia, had equal status for the individual, but that for the congregation "tongues" was the least of them. For the group, to put it strongly, understanding (Paul's *nous*) became more important than inspiration—by apostolic decree. And the history of each new tongue-speaking movement within the Christian tradition is the same; Mormonism and Pentecostalism are just two instances.

Change and Adaptation

We have just seen that an evolution in the functions of glossolalia accompanies changes in a Pentecostal organization whether it be just a small group, a sect, or even the whole movement.

This change in functions can also be biographical. In private use, praise seems to precede intercession. There is a possibility, however, that the glossolalist only interprets the function of his glossolalic activity as praise to God because of the tradition of the group he is identified with; his first emotions may in fact be too vague or unfocused for joy and adoration to be correlated with speech. But as the individual is resocialized—as he becomes an intelligently interacting member of a new society—his relationship to the other members is manifested in concern for them and for people outside the group and this concern would be verbalized pseudolinguistically. In this view a person who does not advance to intercession is one who is not fully resocialized.

And in public use, especially in some groups (contrary to what was observed above), a person's rise in status is correlated with a decrease in the use of glossolalia, on the one hand, and, on the other, an increase in the use of other "gifts," like interpretation, healing, discernment (in its more vulgar forms being nothing more than rebuking other members of the group for irregular attendance or other evidence of lukewarmness), and prophecy. In other words, if there are more effective instruments for leadership in a group, an aggressive member will graduate to their use. Prophecy is often one of these. It is through prophecy that one announces that unless the group does such-and-such it will suffer the consequences ("thus saith the Lord"). However, unless prophecy issues from the established authority, it can be dysfunctional and it would be considered a usurpation of authority. This is why the highly structured Methodist Pentecostal Church of Chile ignores prophecy (Willems, p. 257) and the leaders of West Indian sects in London do not rule by prophecy (Calley, p. 91).

Glossolalia has also been adapted to contemporary beliefs and practices, as we have already had occasion to see. This is why greater emphasis is laid on the use of glossolalia in prayer, whether private or public, and why the kinds of things that are of concern to neo-Pentecostals are expressed in psychological rather than physical terms.

One of the most interesting cases of adaptation is that of Roman Catholic Pentecostalism. Since the Catholic is believed to receive the Holy Spirit at baptism (for most people while still infants), a fact that is later "confirmed" at his first communion, the Catholic theology of the charisma would have to be different from a Baptist one, for example. And since Catholic religious practices are controlled by a completely different tradition, some of the more radical, even anti-authoritarian, uses of glossolalia are unlikely. In fact, at the present time the opposite is true. This is what one Catholic observer reports:

The Roman Catholic Pentecostals have, if anything, found themselves more attached to the structural church than before their involvement in the movement. . . . While many of them remain critical [that is, of the church, the bishops, and ecclesiastical structures], their attitudes after the experience tend rather toward compassion for those in positions of authority and understanding for structural processes (McDonnell 1970:50).

Adaptation occurs not only in the uses to which glossolalia is put but also generally in the behavior that is associated with it. There appears to be, for example, a correlation between the occurrence of symptoms of dissociation (that is, altered states of consciousness) and one's identification with traditional Pentecostalism. Although neo-Pentecostalism has contact with this older form of the movement, it appears to exhibit less of these trance experiences.[4] (My data are admittedly scanty, but they do point in this direction.) On the other hand, neo-Pentecostals have taken over some of the other "cultural baggage" of traditional Pentecostalism (like hand clapping and hand raising), much to the distaste or disappointment of their sympathetic co-religionists. Some Catholics, for example, while appreciating the contribution that the charismatic movement makes to religious life, would like to see it filtered free of its lower-class Protestant characteristics.

Social Factors Influencing Use

Other variations in the use of glossolalia that respond to social variables are contemporary, not evolutionary. We have observed several of them in our discussion to this point: for example,

[4] I imply, of course, that some aspects of trance behavior are learned, but this is generally understood by social scientists. That is, whether or not a person uses dissociation socially and how he uses it are conditioned by his own culture. For one example of how possession is acquired and controlled through practice see Lee's description of healing among the !Kung Bushmen of South Africa (p. 48).

social class, amount of education, and length of involvement in the charismatic movement. Two more are mentioned here: nature of the religious meeting and beliefs about language. Also added are some comments about age and sex.

For any group, the nature of the meeting itself—such as size, membership, general purpose, and organization—influences the amount of glossolalia that occurs at any given time. In some groups, for example, we see that the incidence of glossolalia drops when nonbelievers or outsiders are present; in other groups the reverse is true (Cutten, p. 94, citing Oliphant). Obviously then, glossolalia is an in-group phenomenon in the one group; in the other it is a means to demonstrate the presence of supernatural power to convince the unbeliever.[5] Likewise, special meetings (special because of the emphasis put on attending them, for example) would have more glossolalia than in similar but regular meetings, because they require a glossolalic seal of approval, a "sign of blessing." Gee, a Pentecostal leader, implies such functions when he criticizes the belief that a message in tongues has more authority than didactic preaching (p. 118).

In considering how beliefs about language affect the form and use of glossolalia, we might include other forms of anomalous speech. Three factors are worth mentioning. The first is the amount of information a society has about other languages. I would expect people who were aware of language differences and who valued the knowledge of other languages to produce glossolalia that was different in significant ways. Freed from the necessity of having to produce a foreign language that met the demands of a teacher or of native speakers (even in one's imagination), a glossolalist would be free to produce what was pleasantly exotic. There is as yet, however, no empirical data to prove such influence.

The next factor is the function of a pseudolanguage. We have already seen that there are differences in the ways glossolalia is delivered, depending on whether one is praying or giving a message and what one imagines himself to be talking about, and so forth.

[5] Compare the statements found in 1 Corinthians 14:13,16,22: "Therefore, he who speaks in a tongue should pray for the power to interpret. . . . Otherwise, if you bless with the spirit, how can any one in the position of an outsider say the 'Amen' to your thanksgiving when he does not know what you are saying? . . . Thus, tongues are a sign not for believers but for unbelievers, while prophecy is not for unbelievers but for believers" (RSV).

In this connection, it is worth comparing Pentecostal glossolalia with "spirit language" of non-Christian societies. In Christianity, where the Holy Spirit transcends human spirits, the inspired language is "unknown" in spite of belief in xenoglossia. For if every glossa were identified as such-and-such a normal language, its mystery would vanish. On the other hand, where spirits from another "tribe" are supposed to speak through a person, as in southeastern Bantuland (see Aquina and Blakney), a fairly good approximation of that language is to be expected, because it will be more convincing. (There are spirit languages among non-Christians, of course, that are unintelligible when subjected to any analysis. But they are, we would say, meant to be so, because only the shaman or medium is supposed to understand what the spirit says; the others just listen.)

We are reminded once again that what observers call glossolalia is not always the kind of speech we are concerned with in this book. Thus, when Fernandez explains the evolution of the Bwiti cult among the Fang people in the Gabon Republic, he says that the original visionary leaders may find themselves unable to deal organizationally with their followers. More powerful leaders take their place, and the "prophet may be exalted at the expense of his effective political power and reduced to talking in tongues" (1966: 44). By this he only means that the mark of the upstaged prophet is metaphorical and recondite speech.

I would like to make the strong hypothesis that artificial, human-like languages—in other words, glossolalia as I use the term—are rarely found in societies that have had no contact with Christianity. This claim would reject other ones to the contrary, on the grounds that what is unintelligible or unlike human language to an observer is not to be automatically designated "glossolalia." Eliade's thorough study of shamanism is often referred to in this connection, although it is based on many sources differing—at least linguistically—in reliability. But there is no authentic case of glossolalia in the whole work: exotic "languages" are invariably very unlike human language indeed.

Finally, glossolalia is influenced by what a society or individuals within a society think sounds good or bad, or, if indifferent to these qualities, appropriate to a certain kind of behavior.

Other features, like age and sex, are less important to the use of glossolalia even though they may be significant in explaining the movement as a whole.

Although children as young as six are reported to have spoken in tongues, there is no institutionalization of juvenile glossolalia in our western society in a way that is comparable, say, with ritualized possession among Balinese girl dancers. Protestants seem to have less place for children as religious innovators than Catholicism does: Protestant children much less commonly see visions, for example. (Or maybe they are just taken less seriously.) It is a fact, on the other hand, that the average middle-class neo-Pentecostal is in his thirties and forties, at an age, that is to say, when he can still redirect his life by a new commitment. This maturity will naturally have an influence on glossolalia in all kinds of ways.

One of the things that glossolalia does for women, on the other hand, is to give them a greater share in an institution that is dominated traditionally by men. Religious activities that are marginal are allowed society's, as it were, "marginal" members. Enthusiasm is only one of these. Sometimes, of course, a given religious body cannot tolerate innovating female activities, and a new body is created, like Eve from Adam. It is not surprising, therefore, that women have figured importantly in several Protestant sects; all of them, however, are not "emotional" by any means (for example, Mary Baker Eddy and Christian Science). Aimee Semple McPherson is a well-known American example, but many others of less notoriety could be cited. (Analogies will certainly be found for Catholicism.)

It would be possible for me to demonstrate that one female "faith healer" whom I heard at a Full Gospel Business Men's conference was definitely "feminist" in her stance. Surrounded by about twenty leaders of the movement on the dais, she made explicit statements in her sermon that glorified women and implicitly demeaned men. After the sermon, when she was returning from the floor of the auditorium where she had laid her hands on people for healing, she touched—on her own volition—several of these leaders. Some fell to the floor as if struck; others swooned and laid their heads on the table. By the time she had returned to her place, the stage appeared to be a mass of swarming bodies.

Even in non-Christian societies, religions of enthusiasm provide women with more involvement and more status than they tradi-

tionally had. In Kenya, for example, "there was nothing in traditional Tiriki culture comparable to the group spirit possession so
common today among the Pentecostal congregations and several
other independent sects. . . . Tiriki all agreed that trances among
women were most unusual, never socially condoned, and that a
Tiriki woman was never granted the status of seer or prophetess"
(Sangree, p. 183). But in the local separatist Christian sect *Dini Ya
Roho* (also known as the African Church of the Holy Spirit)
women's behavior is different from the traditional one. And in
Rhodesia, "glossolalia" (or so it is considered by the observer) is
mostly restricted to women and newcomers of the Church of the
Apostles; only the higher-ranking members, mostly men, are gifted
for prophecy, healing, and exorcizing demons (Aquina, pp. 209–
210).

These generalizations are obviously valid to the degree that they
represent the facts, and there is admittedly a great deal that must
be known about the place of women in religion from society to
society and culture to culture. Even within Pentecostalism there are
some sects and, presumably, congregations that are more female-
dominated than others. In the Puerto Rican assembly observed by
me in the Bronx (page 188) women were certainly less an active
force than in the Jamaican pocomania group witnessed in Savanna-
la-Mar. In the latter, overt leadership was given by the "shepherd,"
but women actually did most of the testifying and dancing. But
Jamaican society, especially rural and traditional, is matriarchal in
a significant sense (notice the high number of female property-
owners). Therefore the function of women in the Rhodesian case,
mentioned above, must also be interpreted in the context of in-
digenous societies that are matrilineal, of which there are many in
that part of Africa.

By contrast with these groups neo-Pentecostalism seems to have
a fairly even balance of men and women. Other observers confirm
my own impressions. Wolfram's descriptions of two kinds of meetings—one for prayer and discussion and the other a campaign
meeting of the Full Gospel Business Men's Fellowship—show that
only in the latter were women in the majority. But this difference
might be explained by the time of the meeting. Plog's sample was
larger (see above, page 5), and the balance even closer. My own
explanation for this male-female participation in the neo-Pente-

costal movement is that converts are reached intimately, by friends, and as couples. This is confirmed by testimonies submitted by my respondents: many of them volunteered the statement that their experience had changed if not revolutionized their marriages. But there is little information at the present time on how glossolalia, in whatever function, differs significantly among men and women.

The conclusion we must come to again—this time having looked at glossolalia sociolinguistically—is that it is not at all aberrant behavior. Like any human language, it is accommodated in function to the institutions of the society in which it is found. Religious glossolalia is identified with a religious community, but its functions are not all "religious."

We see, therefore, that the social value of glossolalia is that it identifies membership (a social factor) as much as it identifies religious (in some respects a psychological) experience. Ordinary language does this too, like Russian for the Molokan community in Los Angeles. In addition to making explicit where one "belongs" vis-à-vis the "outside" world, glossolalia also makes explicit where one belongs within the charismatic society, sometimes only a group of intimate friends. That is, the use of glossolalia says something about the social structure of a group and a person's place in it. This function also is shared with language, for we all talk differently (*systematically* differently) with people, depending on their relationship to us.

Furthermore, like ordinary language, glossolalia changes the nature of a social event. It makes it, among other things, more "religious" for the Pentecostal. Because charismatists can choose to use or not use glossolalia in a given context, its *absence* makes a significant difference. In a similar way choosing to use one's native language instead of English—say, among Italian immigrants in North America—makes a difference how participants interpret a given event like a first-communion banquet or borrowing money from a relative. In the charismatist religious community, various kinds of speech are appropriate or expected in different situations. But this is true of all of us; these people just have a different set of choices than nonglossolalists have.

Finally, glossolalia responds to social factors. Speech is not uniform. It varies according to its uses, a fact that should have been obvious in discussions above about the nature of glossolalia as a linguistic event.

In short, glossolalic behavior—speech and use—is highly codified for interpersonal relations. This is further evidence, if we still needed any, that glossolalia is not simply a product of dissociative states, like trance.

12

SACRED AND PROFANE

T HERE IS NO mystery about glossolalia. Tape-recorded samples are easy to obtain and to analyze. They always turn out to be the same thing: *strings of syllables, made up of sounds taken from among all those that the speaker knows, put together more or less haphazardly but which nevertheless emerge as word-like and sentence-like units because of realistic, language-like rhythm and melody.* Glossolalia is indeed like language in some ways, but this is only because the speaker (unconsciously) wants it to be like language. Yet in spite of superficial similarities, glossolalia is fundamentally *not* language. All specimens of glossolalia that have ever been studied have produced no features that would even suggest that they reflect some kind of communicative system. This would also mean that contrary to common belief, it has never been scientifically demonstrated that xenoglossia occurs among Pentecostals: people just do not talk languages they are unfamiliar with.

Glossolalia is not a supernatural phenomenon. It is, in fact, a very natural phenomenon. It is similar to many other kinds of speech humans produce in more or less normal circumstances, in more or less normal psychological states. In fact, anybody can produce glossolalia if he is uninhibited and if he discovers what the "trick" is. Both the commonplace nature of glossolalia and experiments have proven this fact. (After writing that, I had no difficulty at all in producing /tríshata kunamínu, karabánki minamínu/, and I am no Pentecostal.)

Therefore there is no need to explain what *causes* a person to produce this form of speech. Nothing "comes over his vocal chords." Speech as people imagine does not originate there anyway. It starts in the brain. That is where the instructions to the vocal organs come from. And when someone speaks in tongues, he is only using instructions that have lain dormant since childhood. "Finding" them and then being willing to follow them are the difficult things. So the only *causes* that need to be found are those that explain why a person should *want* to use these rules again and how he becomes *willing* to do so. The rest is easy.

Glossolalia is therefore not aberrant behavior, only anomalous. It is anomalous, because it departs from run-of-the-mill speech, not because tongue speakers are in any way abnormal.

Tongues are indeed anomalous but not extraordinary. Producing tongues is not strange; it is belief about this pseudolanguage that is. Strange, that is, from the point of view of society in general. It is this dominant society that decides what is normal—in speech or anything else. And it has judged glossolalic behavior abnormal because of the belief by certain Christians that this comes from God. Society has therefore judged a *belief,* not behavior or people. Yet both the speakers and the speech are condemned.

Glossolalists are therefore not necessarily abnormal beings; it is only their belief that is not common. They are not abnormal, but they can be. There are healthy glossolalists, and there are sick ones. Being sick is not what leads to glossolalia. Nor is personality at the bottom of this belief in the supernaturalness of glossolalia. There is, in fact, no evidence whatsoever to suggest—let alone prove—that glossolalists are all of a single psychological type and that this personality of theirs predisposes (some would say *causes*) them to speak in tongues.

One does not have to be abnormal or of a certain psychological type to speak in tongues, but perhaps people of a certain type are *attracted* to the kind of religion that uses tongues. Let us not doubt the possibility of identifying such people from either a psychological or sociological point of view. This is as reasonable as it is to suppose that by-and-large a certain kind of woman becomes involved in the Women's Liberation Movement. Knowing someone, we could say, "Yeah, I would have expected him [or her] to get involved in that." Some things are not so obvious without rigorous analysis, of course. In any case, this does not mean that we therefore know what (inner) "force" led him to talk in tongues. The Pentecostal movement just gave him the chance to do something anybody can do.

Glossolalia is normal, not supernatural as the Pentecostal believes; it is normal, not abnormal as the man-in-the-street believes. Two sets of belief are thus exposed for what they are—bias on the one hand and prejudice on the other. Of these two errors, the greater, in my opinion, is the latter. Both beliefs prevented us from understanding what glossolalia *really* was, and this was never of merely an academic interest. Some would blame the tongue speakers themselves for this attitude, because they insisted that this meaningless speech of theirs came from God. But prejudice is worse, because it never gave them a chance. Christians should at least have been kinder, and social scientists more open-minded. Both groups of people were prevented by prejudice from being what we expected them to be. Now with the understanding that we have of tongues we can hope that we shall begin to understand glossolalists better.

If glossolalia is no mystery, what can be said of it? What does it teach about religion and the place of language in religion? And what are the consequences for those who believe in this phenomenon and even for some who do not? The first question first.

Glossolalia is made of common human stuff. It is, in itself, profane. But this should come as no surprise. All religion is incarnated in man. Its dimensions are those of *homo sapiens*. (Although the believer adds another dimension, the supernatural, he cannot escape the fact that even that is mediated through the carnal. The supernatural is perceived and manifested through a physically- and culturally-bound creature.)

The material of religion is human: bread and buildings, wine and water, crosses and colors, liturgy and language. They all figure in man's being religious and experiencing religion. They constitute the monuments to and the edifice of religion.

All the artifacts of religion—whether they be a Methodist

mourner's bench or a Catholic's confession box—say something about what humans experience internally as "religion." All religion expresses this experience. It is itself, in a sense, a language. Religion as language has its own "sounds" and "syllables"; its own "phrases" and "sentences"; its own "rhythm" and "melody." And behind them is the real stuff, the "semantics," the meaning. Without this the rest is just "nonsense."

Religion, then, is a "sacred language" (and not the only one some would say). But it is sacred, because it expresses the sacred, not because it is sacred in itself. What sacral glow it has is reflected from its source. In itself it is of very ordinary stuff.

Language, then, is part of "sacred language." It too is ordinary human material. Like candles and incense, pulpits and pews, it figures in all of religious experience: in sermons, prayers, spells, and song.

And like the rest of what goes into religion, language is modeled according to various needs. Like the changes of colors in a Lutheran religious year, language varies according to what a given event "says." There is one way for praying, and another for preaching. And both of these—as well as others for different kinds of religions—are different from ordinary speech. They do not *have to* be different; religion *could* be expressed in the language of the street, but it never is.

Shamans oftentimes introduce a language of the animal spirits in their conjuring or healing ceremonies. Buddhist healers in Ceylon use different languages—Sanskrit, Pali, Malayalam, etc.—depending on whether they are addressing the demons or the audience and depending on what they are talking about. The language of Islam is Arabic and that of traditional Roman Catholicism Latin regardless of the native languages of the adherents. The Coptic religion in Ethiopia uses an archaic Semitic language, Ge'ez, that has to be learned. These are examples of using different languages for religious purposes, but one can switch to different contemporary varieties. The language Jamaicans give their testimonies in at a pocomania service is not the ordinary Creole they speak but an approximation of elegant literary language. Pronunciation is also changed to mark the religious use of language. In one independent Christian church among the Zulu, "angel's speech" is made different by having all the *l* sounds changed to *r*. And in North America, when one woman faith healer preaches, she trills her *r*'s (*rule, road, wrote, there*) in the Spanish fashion. This does not alter the content of her sermon, but she changes a "talk" into a "sermon."

These are examples of religious language, not an analysis of what religious language is. But these are enough to illustrate that religious discourse is "uncommon." And it is uncommon in very similar ways throughout the world in religions of very different kinds. In spite of these superficial differences, furthermore, it always says the same thing: "This experience is special. It's sacred."

Glossolalia is part of this world-wide inventory of varieties of religious language. It shares the same linguistic feature (being different from ordinary discourse) and the same cultural function (setting apart a religious event). It just goes farther in one direction by changing its form to destroy practically all similarity to language in its systematic, arbitrary shape. It therefore goes beyond Latin and Ge'ez which may also be unintelligible for a participant in a religious event.

Therefore glossolalia speaks. A person does say something in tongues. He is saying that he is involved in something—at a given moment in time or as part of a pattern of life—that transcends the ordinary.

In short, glossolalia is a linguistic symbol of the sacred. So it is understandable that for the charismatic movement it is a sacred symbol, a precious possession, a divine gift.

Any anthropologist will understand what has just been said, because he is practiced—as a psychologist is—in getting behind what people *say* to find out what they really *mean*. It is his business to try to find out what a particular culture means for its participants. But the glossolalist is probably unaware of this level of the meaning of tongues.

The glossolalist is more conscious of something else that tongues say. He knows in some fashion or other that they represent the presence of God. Glossolalia *says,* "God is here." (Just as a Gothic cathedral says, "Behold, God is majestic.") This is why a glossolalist declares that praying in tongues leads to a "heightened awareness of God's presence."

This is not to be denied outright. Whatever it may mean to feel the presence of God, we must accept that the believer senses something that is different, something extraordinary. And glossolalia has something to do with it. The Pentecostal believes that God is there because of the linguistic miracle. *We* believe that it is no miracle, but we can also believe that it *symbolizes* God's presence. (Or, if one wants, it symbolizes the *belief* in the presence of God.)

Viewed in this way glossolalia is symbolic in the very way that the eucharist is symbolic. The eucharist (bread and wine for the Catholic, boiled manioc and lemonade for "Brethren" in the Central African Republic), of course, has different traditional meanings for different kinds of Christians. Disregard these for the moment. Whether the Lord's Supper is a "sacrament" for the Catholic or an "ordinance" for a Baptist, it represents the fellowship believers have with God.

In this instance—in somehow experiencing the presence of God —the glossolalist shares in a universal religious experience of one type. It is probably found in all religions in some form, but not all believers take part in everything that is comprehended by their religion. Some are satisfied with allegiance to a system, others are oriented by its explanation of life, still others enjoy most its ritual and ceremonies. But there are always at least a few for whom real religion involves personally encountering the "supernatural" in some form. It is "felt" and one is affected by this encounter. At the given moment one is not "normal" (that is, secular) but nonetheless fully normal (even without some "ecstatic" experience), and one's subsequent hours, days, or weeks are affected by this encounter. Reliving this experience becomes for many people an important goal, and religious practices are valued only if they induce and enhance it. This is what the Pentecostal calls "living in the power of God" or "being filled with the Spirit of God." It means being constantly "in touch with God."

Glossolalia therefore is an important component of personal, affective religion. Whenever a person prays in tongues, he is reminded of how close to him God really is, and he desires (consciously or unconsciously) that God will touch him to make his life different.

From all this we see that the mystery of religion is symbolized, represented, and induced by glossolalia. Like other parts of religion it marks the discontinuity between the sacred and the profane, but at the same time it functions most importantly in the feeling dimension of religion. On these two counts alone we should recognize the legitimacy and value of glossolalia, for it accomplishes two important functions in religion. And it does this without being itself any sort of mystery.

From glossolalia we get a new perspective on the nature of religion and of the place of language in it. This is what the curious but uninvolved observer of Pentecostal religion learns from this book. But what is its consequence for the glossolalist and for his non- or anti-glossolalist brethren in the Christian tradition? For them, a humanistic appreciation is a luxury, because, except for tongues, they are committed to the same religion.

For some glossolalists there will be no consequence, just incredulity. They will not believe that a linguistic scientist can demonstrate the nonlinguistic, noncommunicative nature of tongues. Some will say that since glossolalia is spiritual or divine communication; since its source and cause is God the Holy Spirit, it is not possible for a linguist, Christian or not, to understand this phenomenon in purely human terms. But the conclusion does not follow from the premise. Surely there is much to see without paying any attention to where glossolalia is supposed to come from. Once the speaker opens his mouth, the sounds are public property. The linguist is therefore as competent to describe this speech as a gourmet or a chemist would be to describe the *mana* the Children of Israel subsisted on in the wilderness and the wine Jesus made for the wedding banquet. One could at least say whether or not the wine the wedding guests drank was good.

It is no argument to say that glossolalia is divine communication, because the Pentecostal has no more idea what this is than he does of divine wine. But communication and wine are both from human experience, and we can tell—if our palates and our ears are good—if this is the real stuff. Many people are fooled by ersatz wines (even Italians who ought to know better!), just as many people are fooled by ersatz language. But belief no more changes pseudolanguage into divine language than it changes water (or ersatz wine) into wine. Belief is a powerful force; it changes many things. But among the things it cannot do is make a supernatural creation of something that is a poor imitation.

The glossolalist's incredulity challenges the linguist's competence, because this competence probes where he is most sensitive. But the encounter is an uneven match. We know more about language than the glossolalist does. We know enough to declare what is and what is not language. We know as much as a mathematician, who can tell the difference between a real formula and a pseudo-formula—one that *looks* like mathematical language but does not *say* anything. We do not know everything, of course. We do not know exactly what is the neurological basis for language, but we know that it is systematic and that this system is reflected in systematic arrangements in speech. The glossolalist must grant this, because one of his proofs for the existence of God is orderliness in creation. A hodge-podge of DNA produces biological nonsense as much as a hodge-podge of syllables produces linguistic nonsense.

Another response of glossolalists will be defiance. They will reject every rational description and explanation of glossolalia, not only my own, because these cannot account for the tremendous changes that take place in their lives in connection with this "gift." There is no need to document these changes. Although psychologists and sociologists would like qualitative and quantitative measurements of the effects of charismatic religion, we will—waiting for this kind of information—accept testimonials as proof of the *reality* of some change. Not all of it is measurable, in any case, for some of it is religious in a subjective sense. One does not measure a "deeper prayer life" in any scientific way, but devoutly religious people accept its reality as much as all of us accept the reality of happiness.

A charismatist's religious experience can be real, revolutionary, reconstitutive. A glossolalist accepts this transformation as supernatural, that is, *caused* by God. If it is a dramatic change—taking place where one did not expect it or more quickly than one expected—it takes on all the more appearance of the supernatural. But none of this proves that glossolalia is supernatural. No number of "miraculous" transformations will make of glossolalia what it is not.

People with this antirational approach to religion will therefore be unaffected by my exposé of glossolalia. They are like believers in the existence of Unidentified Foreign Objects that invade this planet from outer space. Because they have turned off rational argumentation, there is no talking with them.

Other Christians who are more tolerant of a scientific approach will, however, have their own questions and problems. In view of the fact that contemporary glossolalia is a simplified form of extemporaneous pseudolanguage, they will, for example, have to re-examine the Biblical texts that clearly refer to anomalous verbal behavior. For instance, did the Corinthian Christians talk "nonsense"? That depends. If we had a sample of a Corinthian's "language" that went something like

Θύρυνι θάνυμα ρίρανα θιμί.
Νύ, ρύθυνυ νάνινι ράριθαμα μιθί.
Μαμιθί, ράρυ θάνυμα ρίρυθυ θινιμιθά μυμαναράθα.
Μαμίνα.

we would have to answer, "Yes, it is linguistically meaningless." The reason is simple: *I* produced that bit of glossolalia myself by recording twelve syllables on slips of paper, throwing them up in the air, and then putting them together randomly, dividing into words according to how I felt they would sound best. (The syllables are as much those of English as they are—or could have been—of Greek or some other Mediterranean language.) This is not, of course, saying what the Corinthians really did. I do not know, nor does anybody, for sure. I do know, however, that this sample of "Greek" glossolalia is typical of tongues as we know them.

Others will wonder if this verbal phenomenon is "of God." If they mean by that "miraculous," then the answer is categorically no. Glossolalia is a perfectly human, perfectly normal (albeit anomalous) phenomenon. However, if it is charismatic religion that they question, then the answer will depend on what kinds of things they believe God does today. If God works only through people who interpret the Bible the way they do, then they already have their only possible answer. And I will not engage them in argument over whatever position they take.

Even without condemning glossolalists, still other Christians would like an explanation as to why intelligent, sincere, deeply committed fellow believers would talk nonsense. If glossolalia is what *I* say it is, what causes them to do this? So we end the book where we started it.

People talk in tongues, because it is part of a movement that offers them the fulfillment of aspirations that their previous religious experience created in them. They too want to believe in

God passionately, to know the delight of communion with him, and to see him at work in life. They see evidence of all this in members of the charismatic movement. It is intellectually satisfying, and belief is nurtured by intimate personal relations. This is why they accept the beliefs and practices of the movement. They accept tongues, too, because everything else is so attractive.

If they believe that tongues are real human languages, this is not the worst of human errors. The similarity between tongues and natural language is what misleads them. They are not victims of self-deception.

That accounts for the past. What of the future? If tongue speakers believe what I have written, they can no longer trust appearances. They will have to admit that in one instance at least Pentecostal doctrine is wrong. But this may be no tragedy, and the charismatic movement ought to be able to survive this realization, for glossolalia is only an artifact of religion, not its cause.

Many will not be convinced, but they will have my respect nonetheless. I will not be distracted by what I hear from Anglicans and Roman Catholics, Puerto Ricans and Appalachians, traditional Pentecostals and neo-Pentecostals. What I *hear* is nonsense; the sounds make no sense to me. But I know that what lies beyond is what counts, and that is sacred ground.

So I take off my shoes.

That too is "nonsense."

Appendixes

The following appendixes include (A) a description of the questionnaire that I used in studying glossolalia among Christians, (B) a published testimonial about the conversion of one of these Christians, and (C) samples of different types of glossolalia. The latter include one sample of "literary" glossolalia, several more samples of Christian glossolalia, two sets of samples from occultic or spiritistic glossolalia, and one of nonsense swearing.

Appendix A
QUESTIONS ABOUT TONGUES:
A LINGUISTIC INQUIRY

THE QUESTIONNAIRE referred to in this study was preceded by two tape-recorded interviews with glossolalists, one a store-front Pentecostal preacher from Texas and the other a Presbyterian minister with a B.D. from Princeton Theological Seminary. These interviews guided the preparation of the questionnaire. (Many others were held subsequently.) Its purpose was to elicit general information to supplement what had been learned from reading, observation, and personal interviews. With it I hoped to reach a fairly representative sample of tongue speakers even though it might not be a "random sample" in the sociologist's sense.

The questionnaire was distributed personally or by friends to known tongue speakers. Contacts were made in New England by myself at regional meetings of the Full Gospel Business Men's Fellowship, at a week-end charismatic retreat held at a Presbyterian church, and by mail. Addresses were obtained by placing an advertisement in the bimonthly journal *Christianity Today* (November 24, 1967) that read in part: "Past and present tongue-speakers are invited to participate in a sympathetic and unbiased investigation of glossolalia." About 200 copies of the questionnaire were also made available by an influential charismatist following an announcement in his personal news-letter of January-February 1968 in which he said, "I would highly recommend that ministers and laymen offer assistance in answering 70 [sic] good sensible questions." People were usually supplied as many copies as requested. Of the 300 that were mimeographed, 84 (or 28%) were completed and returned. (A late-arriving 85th is not included in the following tabulations.) There is evidence that some people thought that the booklet was a gift and that others thought the questions too difficult to answer. (It was a mistake on my part not to request the return of the questionnaires if not completed for any reason.)

The respondents are now grouped according to different categories.

There were 43 male and 41 female glossolalists who cooperated. In age they are classified as follows: 10–20 (3 respondents), 21–30 (7), 31–40 (26), 41–50 (25), 51–60 (13), 61–80 (5); the ages of 5 are unknown. In other words, 60.7% of the respondents were in the 31–50 age range.

Most of the respondents were rather young in the charismatic experience: 63 (or 75%) began to speak in tongues around 1956 or later. (This is about the time when the neo-Pentecostal movement began to gain momentum.) Thirty-five had been glossolalists for 1–2 years, 18 for 3–6 years, and 10 for 7–12 years. The others ranged from 15 to 43 years; for 5 there is no information.

There were 57 respondents from 19 states in the USA, 5 from Canada, 2 from England, and one each from the Netherlands and Germany. For 18 there is no information about residence.

The education of the respondents was very diversified. Whereas 44 went beyond high school, 5 had less than a high school education. There were 5 with doctorates and 29 with some other postgraduate degree, of which 13 had a Bachelor of Divinity; however, 7 had an M.A. In addition to the 28 who had a B.A., there were 4 with a B.S., 4 with a Bachelor of Theology (a Bible college degree), one with an LL.B., and so forth.

As the level of education might suggest, the occupations were decidedly not lower class: 26 people might be said to have "unskilled" occupations, but 23 of these are housewives. (There were 2 students and one truckdriver.) The "skilled" occupations (business, civil service, engineer, secretary, lay church worker, etc.) were represented by 21 individuals. The "professional" occupations included medicine (3 respondents), education (8), and the clergy (23, with one Roman Catholic priest), a total of 34. The occupations of 3 are unknown.

All of the respondents identified themselves with the Christian religion although 10 recorded that at the time of writing they were members of no congregation. This is significant in view of the fact that 18 (21.4%) of the respondents left the church of which they were members when they were "baptized" to become members of another one that was apparently more hospitable to the charismatic experience. Nevertheless, 48 of the 63 Protestants were members of "churches" in the technical sociological sense (e.g. Baptist [5], Presbyterian [14], Episcopal [8], United Church of Christ [7], etc.), and 15 were members of what sociologists call "sects." Of these, 11 were from the established Pentecostal groups. The Roman Catholic "Pentecostal" movement is represented by 4 respondents, but for 7 individuals there is no information.

The religious backgrounds of the respondents can also be pictured by listing the names of churches given under the heading "Previous church membership(s)." Several varieties of a common group are marked by an asterisk, but different kinds of "independent" groups are not distinguished. The word "church" is omitted from the names given here: Anglican/Episcopal, Assembly of God, Baptist*, Bible, Christian and Missionary Alliance, Community, Congregational, Elim, Evangelical Free, Evangelical Lutheran, Evangelical Reformed, Evangelical United, Brethren, Foursquare, Independent, Interdenominational, Lutheran*, Methodist*, Pentecostal Holiness, Roman Catholic, Presbyterian*, and United Missionary.

In summary, most of my respondents were middle-class Protestant members of the neo-Pentecostal movement rather than members of the established Pentecostal groups.

The questionnaire was presented in booklet form (5½" x 8") with each right-hand page devoted to four questions and spaces for the answers. More space was available on the backs (that is, left-hand pages). The last page (back cover) requested personal information and provided space in which to write: "Name (optional). Address (optional). Sex. Age. Occupation. Present church membership. Since when. Previous church membership(s). Date of first church membership. Approximate date of Spirit baptism.

Offices or duties in church, past or present. Languages that you speak and understand. Languages studied in school. Languages other than English spoken at home. Amount of education [to check off]: High school graduate. College graduate (B.A. or B.S.). Postgraduate degrees. Other schools."

A 500-word preface introduced the questionnaire which included statements like the following: "The purpose of this questionnaire is to gather information about the linguistic aspects of glossolalia (speaking in tongues). . . . The investigation is being carried on as one does any serious linguistic study—by collecting data in an objective way. . . . This is a personal research. No institution or individuals sponsor or support it. But many Spirit-baptized people have encouraged me in it. . . . This questionnaire is being sent out to as many people as possible. Some have volunteered to answer it; others may learn of this investigation only by receiving this booklet in the mail. I hope that everyone will answer the questions as fully as possible. . . . As is quite common in scientific investigations, some of these questions might seem irrelevant. They are not; all of them are included to obtain information which is of importance to the study." The questions are here given in full:

1. Do you consider speaking in tongues an important or necessary spiritual experience? Why?
2. What do tongues contribute to the spiritual life of other Christians present when they are spoken?
3. What is the meaning of the statement: "He that speaketh in an (unknown) tongue speaketh not unto men, but unto God" (1 Corinthians 14:2)?
4. What is the meaning of the statement "He that speaketh in an (unknown) tongue edifieth himself" (1 Corinthians 14:4)?
5. When did you first begin to speak in tongues? Give approximate date.
6. Describe the circumstances when you began to speak in tongues.
7. Did you speak with tongues at the time you were baptized in the Holy Spirit?
8. Did you expect to speak in tongues on being baptized in the Holy Spirit?
9. Did you want to speak in tongues? Why?

10. How many of your friends or relatives spoke in tongues at the time you began?
11. What kind of encouragement, exhortation, or persuasion did people give you to speak in tongues?
12. Did anybody talk to you about what you should do or what would happen when you began to speak in tongues?
13. Did you have any difficulties when you began to speak in tongues? Describe them.
14. Was your first experience in speaking in tongues easier than you had expected?
15. Did your ability to speak in tongues improve as time passed?
16. How much time passed between the time you first heard tongues and when you began to speak yourself?
17. How soon after the first experience in tongues did you speak again? In what circumstances?
18. Have you spoken in tongues since the baptism? How often do you speak in tongues now?
19. What does speaking in tongues do for you personally? In what way is it good for you?
20. Do you feel better in any way after having spoken in tongues? In what way?
21. Relate any unusual or memorable experiences that you have had in connection with speaking in tongues.
22. Have you ever felt unusual sensations in the vocal organs while speaking in tongues? Describe them.
23. Do your tongues sound different from English? In what ways?
24. What languages have your tongues resembled?
25. Has one of your tongues ever been identified as a known human language? What language was it? Who identified it?
26. Do you recall any words from your tongues or from the tongues of other people? Write them down as best you can.
27. Is there any special reason why you remember these words from tongues spoken by yourself or others?
28. Do you have the feeling that certain words from your tongues have meaning? List the words and their meanings.
29. What similarities—either in sounds or words—do you notice in the tongues you speak from time to time?
30. Do your tongue messages (or those of other people) begin or end in more or less similar ways? If so, describe them.

31. Do some of your tongues sound better to you than others?

32. What differences, if any, do you notice in the tongues spoken by men, women and children?

33. In what different situations have you spoken in tongues?

34. Is it easier for you to speak in tongues in a gathering than in private, or vice versa?

35. Do you speak in tongues more often in a group than in private, or vice versa?

36. Are you able to speak in tongues at any time?

37. Can you speak in tongues at will? If not, why not?

38. Do you have to be in a certain mood or spiritual state to speak in tongues? What kind?

39. Do you feel tense before, during, or after you have spoken in tongues?

40. Do you tend to be timid or reserved when talking among or to a group of people?

41. Do you find it easier or harder to speak in tongues than in your own language?

42. Did you ever have problems like stuttering or stammering as a child?

43. Do you ever have to grope for words while speaking in tongues or does speaking always come easily?

44. What is the longest period of time that you have spoken in tongues?

45. How much are you conscious of what is happening around you while you talk in tongues? Give an example.

46. Have you ever felt that you were really talking to someone while speaking in tongues?

47. What different kinds of uses do your tongues have? For example, instruction, exhortation, command, praise, etc.

48. How often are your tongues interpreted in public meetings? Almost always _____ Rather often _____ Fairly often _____ Rarely _____ Never _____.

49. Have you ever felt that somebody's interpretation of your tongues expressed what you truly felt? Describe one such instance.

50. Have you ever felt that someone misinterpreted your message in tongues? If so, how did you account for it at that time?

51. How often do you interpret the tongues of others? Rather often _____ Fairly often _____ Rarely _____ Never _____.

52. Do you feel the same when interpreting as you do when speaking in tongues?
53. Here is a sample of tongues from one speaker. What is usual or unusual about it? "tiyshawariy tatasa tiyvariy shtuwari tutusutariyshti tiysupowriy tutusatey viytiyshtiytuwariy tutuvatusatariysti" (*iy* as in *beet, u* as in *but, i* as in *bit, ow* as in *boat, ey* as in *bait, sh* as in *shoe*).
54. Would you be willing to record a sample of your own tongues?
55. Do you think that your tongues are languages? If so, why?
56. Can you tell the difference between tongues and a foreign language in a public meeting?
57. Have you personally heard someone speak a human language that he did not previously know? What language was it? Did you identify it yourself?
58. What do people do while speaking in tongues that is like normal language use? For example, close their eyes, gesture with their hands, lift their heads, etc.
59. What different styles of speaking (like prose and poetry) occur in tongues?
60. Is there anything whatsoever in normal speech that reminds you of (or resembles) tongues? What, for example?
61. Do you think that anyone can show that tongues are *not* like human language?
62. If someone can show that tongues are not like human language, what would he have to consider them to be?
63. Can a person distinguish genuine from "fake" tongues? How?
64. Is there anything like demonic tongues? How does it differ from real tongues?
65. Does a failure to speak in tongues for a long time indicate a bad relationship with God? Why?
66. Have you ever been present in a meeting when you felt that speaking in tongues was carried too far? Describe what happened.
67. What do you think Paul was talking about when he warned of excesses in tongues?
68. How might tongues spoil a church service?
69. What do tongues benefit non-Christian seekers present in the meeting where they are spoken?
70. Have you ever heard a person speak somewhat boastfully of his tongues? (For example, that he spoke many different ones,

that they were especially beautiful, etc.) Describe the statements.

71. Do you believe that there is a difference between (a) tongues as evidence of Spirit baptism and (b) tongues as a gift for the edification of believers? If so, what linguistic differences, if any, are there between these two kinds of tongues?

Appendix B
A TONGUE SPEAKER'S TESTIMONIAL

THE FOLLOWING testimonial was selected mostly for its human interest, but it is typical of the hundreds that are available in published form and of the thousands that could be obtained from tongue speakers. This one appeared in *Voice* (Robert Ashkettle, "Saved from 'Soho' Club," Vol. 16, No. 9, pp. 16–18, November 1968). Familiarity with this periodical and the Full Gospel Business Men's Fellowship which publishes it leads me to believe that this is an edited (and perhaps rewritten) version of an extemporaneous testimonial given at an FGBMF public meeting.

"My home was in London's East End. When 13 years of age I ran away—principally because scarcely a day passed that my father didn't give me a 'bashing' with his big broad belt, or a kick from his heavy army boots.

"That first night I slept in Trafalgar Square. To me it was a very large, rather lovely place, with all the lights and the crowds of people. I swore never to return home. But a 13-year-old boy must eat, and I soon learned to steal from cafe doorways, where the deliverymen left the bread and rolls outside with the milk.

"It was not long before I learned how to steal money by going into a Public House and asking for a glass of water. As soon as the barmaid or barman turned to get the water, I would pick up a charity box. Sometimes there would be as much as four or five shillings—other times just a few coppers. By this time I had rented a furnished room for the princely sum of six shillings a week.

"One grows up rapidly in that kind of existence, and soon I began to run with thieves, stealing from cars, stores, and elsewhere. During this time I met a chap who was on the run from Borstal (a school for delinquent boys), and took him to my room for a night's sleep. He told me while he was 'inside' he had heard much about a chap called Billy Hill, a gang leader. Not long after that I met Billy Hill and he offered me a job in one of his 'clubs' in Soho, working from 3:00 to 11:00 P.M. with a one-hour break in between. In the mornings, from 11:00 until 2:00 I and another chap, or sometimes a woman, went shoplifting. In the Club I kept my eyes and ears open and learned many things, for most of the people who frequented it were thieves, prostitutes, fences, touts, bookmakers and pickpockets.

"By this time, with the money I made at the Club and profit from the shoplifting project, I had a bank balance large enough to open up my own club. Right from the first everything went exceedingly well. I started a new 'craze' of putting on 'Drag' shows (men dressed as women). It became an immediate success in the club world of Soho. I was making money hand over fist but by that time had also become considerable of a drinker, and there were always friends willing to buy 'Bobbie' a drink. By 1960 I had five drinking clubs and one coffee bar. The coffee bar didn't open until 10:00 P.M., and by 11:00 o'clock it was full of all types of undesirables.

"From quite an early age, and up until 1960, I was in and out of prison, having received sentences totaling 31 years. Of course, all that time was not served, because of remissions for good behavior.

"In November, 1965, while walking around the streets of Soho looking for empty premises that might be made into another coffee bar, I found a small group of people singing on a street corner, and listened for perhaps ten minutes (for it was good singing), until I realized they had begun talking about religion and Jesus Christ the Son of God. Telling myself 'this is not for me,' I walked away. However, about a hundred yards down the street I felt compelled to go back and talk to members of the group. They were quite nice to me and invited me to a place of worship the following Saturday evening. After evading, refusing, and insisting I was not really interested, eventually I agreed to go. Immediately I regretted it, because I had made a promise—and my promises I have always kept.

"Saturday evening I determined to go late and sit in the back row near the door. At the appointed time for the meeting to start, I walked in. Someone handed me a hymn book and murmured some number the congregation was already singing—a song about walking with Jesus. I took one look around, muttered an imprecation under my breath, and walked out.

"But something had happened to me—something I didn't realize or understand. Going straight to a Pub, I ordered a drink, took a quick swallow and roared at the barman that this was not the drink I had ordered. It tasted terrible. I walked out, leaving it on the bar. Saturday night, Sunday, Monday, Tuesday and Wednesday it was the same—wherever I went to buy a drink I had a row with the barman, insisting he was serving me bad gin.

"Wednesday the group was not holding its usual street meeting (I went to that corner to find out), but Saturday evening found me at the place of worship again. The only other person sitting on the bench in the back row was an elderly lady, and she was at the other end. As the meeting progressed people began to stand up here and there. Some praised the Lord, others clapped their hands. I thought to myself, 'What in the world have I let myself in for? These people are mad!' However, it seemed impossible for me to move out that door as I had done before.

"Gradually I became interested in what a tall man on the platform was saying. He was asking people who wanted salvation to raise their hands and come down to the front. Then something occurred, the memory of which will remain with me all my life. A voice from behind me said very clearly, 'Go down to the front.' Slowly I turned my head to look, although I knew there was no one there, because I was sitting in the last row. I turned back toward the tall man on the platform. The voice came again, clearly saying, 'Go down to the front.' This time I snapped my head around smartly to try to catch the speaker, but saw no one.

"That was too much for me! I went down front! The tall man came down from the platform and placed his hand on my forehead; and then it happened—Jesus Christ came into my life! I felt myself being turned inside out. All the black, evil, sin-stained life was stripped away and I was reborn, a child of God!

"The following Wednesday I went to the Westminster Chapel where the Full Gospel Businessmen's Fellowship from America was holding a meeting. Derek Prince invited those who wanted the baptism in the Holy Spirit to come forward. Tony Holloway and I went forward and God *did* give to me His precious gift of the Baptism.

"Immediately I knew what must be done. Early the next morning I went around to my clubs and coffee bars, not taking anything from any of them—just locking them up, one after another. Then I walked to the nearest street drain and dropped the keys down the drain. . . ."

Appendix C
SAMPLES OF GLOSSOLALIA

1. *Literary glossolalia.* There are features in the following sample of glossolalia that resemble the extemporaneous kind discussed in this book, but this text undoubtedly was affected by the literary process (as well, I should imagine, as the writer's inexperience with glossolalia). This is taken from the chapter entitled "Glossolalia" in John Barth's *Lost in the Funhouse. (Fiction for Print, Tape, Live Voice)* (Garden City, N.Y., Doubleday and Company, 1968, pp. 114–115), with italics added by myself.

Sweet Sheba, beloved highness: Solomon craves your throne! Beware his craft; he mistranslates my pain into cunning counsel. Hear what he claims your hoopoe sang: that its mistress the Queen no longer worships Allah! He bids you come now to his palace, to be punished for your error. . . . But mine was a love song: how I'd hymn you, if his tongue weren't beyond me—and yours.

> *Ed' pélut', kondó nedóde, ímba imbá imbá. Singé erú. Orúmo ímbo ímpe ruté sceléte. Ímpe re scéle lee lutó. Ombo té scele té, beré te kúre kúre. Sinté te lúté sinte kúru, te ruméte tau ruméte. Onkó keere scéte, tere lúte, ilee léte leel' lúto. Scélé.*

2. *Religious glossolalia.* Texts (a) and (b) are fragments taken

from Jaquith (pp. 3–4), the orthography changed to be consistent with the one adopted in this book. The first is from a song, the second from speech. Texts (c) and (d) are from a different man uttered during a neo-Pentecostal testimony-and-prayer session whose participants knew that their speech was being recorded for persons interested in studying glossolalia. No nonglossolalists were present. These two glossas (43 and 38 seconds in duration) are believed by the speaker to be different languages. The second prayer was introduced by the following statement:

God has given me different manifestations of the Spirit at different times. . . . I'm going to ask the Lord to give me another language that's entirely different from the language I just spoke which will also be recorded. "Father, we ask you now, that you will grant this manifestation of thy Holy Spirit in an entirely different language."

The two texts sound more unlike than they look, because (c) tends to be stress-timed whereas (d) tends to be syllable-timed. They are different also in their use of musical pitch: (c) has gradual up and down curves like ordinary English praying, whereas the pitch of (d) bounces around over single syllables (as in tone languages, like Chinese) or over small groups of syllables. In (d) the vowels are less diphthongized and the voiceless consonants /p t k/ are less aspirated than in (c). In other words, the consonants and vowels of (d) are slightly more like Spanish than they are in (c). Text (e) is also a complete prayer tape-recorded during a small prayer session of a neo-Pentecostal group. It is interesting because of the high degree of repetitiousness and the great frequency of the vowel /ă/ as in English *but* and the second vowel of *sofă;* the consonant /t/ also tends to be unaspirated, as in Spanish. The samples in (f) were supplied by my respondents at my request ("Do you recall any words from your tongues or from the tongues of other people? Write them down as best you can.") The spelling has not been altered. In (8) "sj," following the practice of Dutch, probably represents /sh/ and "mj" /my/ as in English *music*.

(a)

kelalaiyanano. kelalaiyenayeno. kelalayeyino. kelalaiyanakelaya-ano.   kelakelahŏrayanayelalaiyelayaanaiyo.   kelalaiyenanayano. kelalayeyina. . . .

(b)

kohĭnayakayowana. palaĭnyanokoyiyălalainakayuwara. halayo-
nĭnhĭrakăyaĭnyiyakatŏdŏĭnna. payanapoyananĕkiyalaluwănnă-
kăyĕraraynaykiyalalaya. haloyĕnapapayĕnakiyalalionoyanapay-
ĕra. . . .

(c)

kolama siándo, laboka tohoríămasí, lamo siándo, laboka tahando-
ria, lamo siando kolămasí, labo siándo, lakatándori, lamo siam-
băbă kătándo, lamá fia, lama fiandoriăkó, labokan doriasandó,
lamo siándoriako, labo siá, lamo siandó, labăkán doria, lama fiá,
lama fiandolokolămăbăbăsí, lăbo siandó, lama fiatándoria, lamo-
káyămasi, labo siandó.

(d)

mabasándo, kotándăhokătambasí, lamáhka kandăhŏndo, laham-
bakahiamasí, măhama kăttăhándo, kŏhómasi, makătahándo,
kahámbasi, mósiahanto, kohomba, mahápăkăhandohăi, lambosi-
hando, kohómba, lahambakati, yahamăsí, mópăsiyando, kotá-
hando, lamasi, papakando, lámasia, lashohóndo, kotamba, ba-
basi, lamasapŏnmotiakó, labasandó, másiando, kătandorí.

(e)

(1) sharisí tivătăshátaw vwarisítivĭrisi. (2) varasáta varashíta
wătí săvarăshătăporáti sítivĕrisĭ. (3) varasatalavári shítă situvă-
rayăti tuvălisítălĭshĭ. (4) warisi tăkălasha talisí tăwăray tatăvată-
sáy shătăvărísiti. (5) wătăsayi satá vilishítăvărăwa rĭsá tísătătă-
varăshi. (6) warăsatatatăvasí talăshí tavuwí sătálăvatăsi. (7)
sári shităwătisi títovăwări tatarăsáysi. (8) witătarihín tăwănay-
hínta watăsáy shătativishĕntí. (9) vwarítahita moritătăvătăshí
tătăvatasáy shĕtăvwa. (10) tatăshătatătí sătí sătăvorí tătăvătăsháy
sătá.

(f)

1. Ama conda amus. Keamo deamo no ma diamos. Aako mala
   amos ceamakaamos boraonba.
2. ki ladia sphona sa nania shuh ka lana moba deseen vi ladia
   so boda shan za she lava kadia nonamakaia pico dada shan
   veria dada ko camana.

3. "La Re Gu She a" Munde Ra, Munde Ra, Kulea, Kulea, Kumbisando, Kashia, Lagia, etc. etc.

4. Cánum achéniko holiconápay ofonamáchi lénia amakáynu políchinia séniay

5. kē a na ma na, la ghee - a va ta. Kē a ma na, tā a ka le a dvā da. Bo va dee v'a vo ghza - ma nē ka.

6. play coon del ē cues pel suel proloque doss fundos en day den doos

7. yo kay ti-ássa-mo keeta ke-ana say so ya ka-nása-towrea may mōsa-arie-te-enna

8. Uliamba magashami andjesta mengorio miliamba. Grakimi andjalu. Sjikambi guadialu amjesta. Gamalioumou, o kwanti kambiaru.

9. Lo holo manata hileato ka hola lama nati leato ala manata liaelo la hola manata . . .

10. eenanah malata hasha mow lotohoya alanaya latahaya teelonomo tahasho eetanama.

3. *Occultic glossolalia.* Samples from two different speakers are given. The first two extracts are from a single discourse produced in trance by a young woman (a member of the group discussed on page 51). Portion (a) is taken from the beginning of the discourse and (b) toward its end. The second is definitely poetic in style (for example, being in trochaic tetrameter). After the first four lines (as represented here, not in the discourse), the speaker changes the rhyme for two lines, but then she reverts to a nonpoetic structure, more like that in the first part of the discourse where there are only suggestions of the emerging poetic structure. Some new symbols have to be introduced here, because the pronunciation is quite exotic, more so than the spelling indicates: /x/ represents the sound of German "ch," /œ/ the sound of the vowel in French *seul,* and /dh/ as in English *the.* In the first set /r/ represents the sound in English *run* and /ř/ the sound in Spanish *pero* which is everywhere else represented by simple /r/, as in the second set of samples. Here and in samples (c) through (f) a comma marks the end of some kind of breath-group. One or more of these breath-groups are also marked by different kinds of sentence-melodies. The intonation in the second set (c–f) strikes me as being more artificial: everything is said as if a person were reciting in class.

As a matter of fact, the speaker claims to be learning the "language of Jakosta" from a black-skinned man she sees in visions and who is teaching her about her previous lives. Samples (c–f) are extracted from a tape recording made in Turkey by the speaker, a Turkish actress of the stage and screen, made available to me by Dr. Ian Stevenson, Director of the Division of Parapsychology of the Department of Psychiatry at the University of Virginia School of Medicine, who has been studying reported cases of xenoglossia. The recording was originally obtained by Mr. Resat Bayer, the President of the Turkish Society for Parapsychological Research. The speaker appears to be recording from memory rather than speaking in trance. In some respects this case resembles that of Helen Smith mentioned elsewhere in this book. This sample is extremely valuable, because it is one of the very few published texts of glossolalia uttered by a speaker whose native language is not related to the Indo-European ones (like English, French, Russian). It does not, however, reveal any of the features that are characteristic of the Turkish language, and it is different from the tongues of English speakers mostly in the vowels, which are not diphthongized, being "pure" as they are, for example, in French or Spanish.

(a)

ípf grŏvĕnk, íxs glŏzĕnk vŏdĭsta, glúx fŏrst vŏnkyĕk, ó vrĕk bĭlĕst, ŏx láyn dĭfrŏylĕnk sovánk, byóxlef olkáynt, stĭx, byóxlest vŏntyáp, pilóf, lípf shtrŏng sefŏr, lŏf vyastikŏn, gŏlk livifyo, vyorĕsgonk flâlĭshtŏnk, ifgœrn tĭfĕrs gĭhŏlaf, nojó stărĕndék, úrlĭx yăvăn vistár. . . .

(b)

ívřĕ stó, vĭyón kĕdyú,
lĭfston byĕl, lakárx fyorú.
byúdhĕd stón, tĭvyól gĕmbyú,
ník ho lĕs, to vyŏlâs tyú.
vídrâ vyónk devwál âvwá
pŏkyan dé ste láxya fwá. . . .

(c)

kárik "one," múta "two," ŏra "three," vínat "four," búka "five," ŏrat "six," múwa "seven," vúda "eight," búta "nine," wúna "ten," hóra "fish," kanúvŏ "I love," nuvótka "music," túwa lúra "Look at that," húndat túwa "What do you want?" hĕrvádho "at sea," kácha "to eat," kirimúla "he loves," túra múwa "egg."

(d)

kamaláya niyamŏya,
ŏhára, yahazŏwa, hĕrmadhŏya míya,
lámi dŏvára ŏmádŏ,
lástŏ dŏra, kamádo, nelásto, nelásto.

(e)

fínda fínda ŏva ŏva [two syllables unintelligible], turavúma, muvŏmŏya, salvatúra, zhakostíka, varánda, ŏya ŏya, ŏha ŏha [. . .] aláma, láma, láma.

(f)

mŏho veránda, yahóda, fida tran[. . .]cháts mázata "I am Princess Mazata, daughter of Judas"; zhakósta dŏra, shárako dŏra "Zhakosta Dora has been drowned at sea"; mŏra ĕzĕkĕríya kĕdha fastahŏa "My mother was a beautiful woman from the village of Zekeriya."

4. *"Nonsense swearing."* The speaker of this final sample is Santa Claus—on a television commercial. In this episode he emerges from the chimney and begins to take out the gifts for the children of the house, naming each one in turn. When he reaches in his sack for the final gift, he can't find it. In exasperation he looks deeper into the sack, and ends up disappearing into it. While the sack convulses with Santa Claus inside, we hear these "dirty words." That's what they sound like to me, because they are said with strong articulation and accent, as if one were saying *Dirty rat!* Each of the following words is said in isolation, followed by very brief pause. There is, in other words, no sentence-like melody for the whole discourse. The letter "r" here represents the first syllable of *dirty: dŕti blãkin dãkă rãkă flãsă fŕkĭt pĭkă rĭkĭp bakăp săfik.* An idea of their pronunciation is given by the following English "words" in their normal spelling: *dirty blacken dacka racka flassa frickit picka rickip backup suffick.*

Bibliography

THE FOLLOWING LIST provides documentation for references made in the text: included are only published works or those that are available at some libraries in Europe or North America. Excluded (with a few exceptions) are unpublished studies, talks given at conferences, and so forth. Many more works have been consulted than have been included here. This is therefore no bibliographer's guide to Pentecostalism, because the concern of this book is primarily with glossolalia. (Useful, although frequently inaccurate, bibliographies are found in many of the religious works cited.) However, several titles have been included even though they were not used, and some even though they are of questionable value. They enter the list because glossolalia is their purported topic.

The briefest possible reference is given in the text, sometimes only the author's name and the page number. The word "page" always refers to the present book and the abbreviation "p." to a different work. The date of publication is added wherever necessary to distinguish the works of a single author: thus (Berger 1958:45) and (Berger 1963:10) refer to pages 45 and 10 of the respective publications.

258   BIBLIOGRAPHY

Adair, Peter, *Holy Ghost People* [sound film]. Produced by Blair Boyd. Thistle Films.

Andrews, Edward D., 1940, *The Gift to be Simple: Songs, Dances and Rituals of the American Shakers.* New York: J. J. Augustin Publisher. 170 pp.

Aquina, Sister Mary, 1967, The People of the Spirit: an independent church in Rhodesia. *Africa* 37.203–219.

Ayer, A. J. (ed.), 1963, *The Concept of a Person.* New York: St. Martin's Press.

Bach, Marcus, 1970, *The Inner Ecstasy: the Power and the Glory of Speaking in Tongues.* New York: The World Publishing Co. 206 pp.

Barrett, David B., 1968, *Schism and Renewal in Africa.* Nairobi, Addis Ababa, Lusaka: Oxford University Press. 363 pp.

Barth, John, 1968, *Lost in the Funhouse. (Fiction for Print, Tape, Live Voice).* Garden City, N.Y.: Doubleday and Co. 201 pp.

Bartleman, Frank (edited by John Walker), 1962, *What Really Happened at 'Azusa Street.'* Northridge, Calif.: Voice Christian Publications. 96 pp. [Abridged version of *How Pentecost Came to Los Angeles* (1925).]

Bascom, William R., 1953, Yoruba acculturation in Cuba. In *Les Afro-Américains* (Mémoires de l'Institut Français [now, Fondamental] d'Afrique Noire, No. 27). Dakar. Pp. 163–167.

Bastide, Roger, 1967, *Les Amériques Noires: les Civilisations africaines dans le Nouveau Monde.* Paris: Payot. 236 pp.

Berger, Peter L., 1958, Sectarianism and religious sociation. *The American Journal of Sociology* 64.41–44.

————, 1963, *Invitation to Sociology: a Humanistic Perspective.* Garden City, N.Y.: Doubleday and Co. [Anchor Books]. 191 pp.

Berokoff, John K., 1969, *Molokans in America.* (Privately published.) Whittier, Calif.: Stockton-Doty Trade Press, Inc. 208 pp.

Blakney, Charles P., 1969, Chipunha, a Rhodesian cult. *Practical Anthropology* 16.98–108.

Bloch-Hoell, Nils, 1964, *The Pentecostal Movement: Its Origin, Development, and Distinctive Character.* London: Allen and Unwin, Ltd. and Universitets-forlaget (Scandinavian University Books). 256 pp.

Bloom, L., 1968, *Language Development: Form and Function in Emerging Grammars.* Unpublished Ph.D. dissertation. New York, N.Y.: Columbia University.

Boas, Franz, 1955, *Primitive Art.* New York: Dover Publications, Inc. (Originally published in 1927.) 372 pp.

Bolshakoff, Serge, 1950, *Russian Nonconformity: the Story of 'Unofficial' Religion in Russia.* Philadelphia: Westminster Press. 192 pp.

Bourguignon, Erika, 1968, World distribution and patterns of possession states. In Raymond Prince (ed.) [see below]. Pp. 3–34.

Brown, L. B., 1966, The structure of religious belief. *Journal of the Scientific Study of Religion* 5.259–272.

——, 1967, Some attitudes surrounding glossolalia. *Colloquium* 2.221–228.

Buley, R. Carlyle, 1951, *The Old Northwest Pioneer Period, 1815–1840, Vol. 2.* Bloomington: Indiana University Press. 686 pp.

Burdick, Donald W., 1969, *Tongues: to Speak or not to Speak.* Chicago: Moody Press. 94 pp.

Burling, Robbins, 1966, The metrics of children's verse: a cross-linguistic study. *American Anthropologist* 68.1418–1441.

Calley, Malcolm J. C., 1965, *God's People: West Indian Pentecostal Sects in England.* London: Oxford University Press. 182 pp.

Christenson, Larry, 1963, *Speaking in Tongues: a Gift for the Body of Christ.* London: The Fountain Trust. 32 pp.

Coe, George Albert, 1916, *The Psychology of Religion.* Chicago: The University of Chicago Press. 365 pp.

Cohn, Werner, 1967, A movie of experimentally-produced glossolalia. *Journal for the Scientific Study of Religion* 6.278.

——, Werner, 1968, Personality, Pentecostalism, and glossolalia: a research note on some unsuccessful research. *The Canadian Review of Sociology and Anthropology* 5.36–39.

Collinder, Björn, 1949, *The Lapps.* Princeton: Princeton University Press (for the American Scandinavian Foundation). 252 pp.

Conybeare, Frederick C., 1962, *Russian Dissenters.* (Harvard Theological Studies, 10.) New York: Russell and Russell. (Originally published in 1921.) 370 pp.

Courlander, Harold, 1960, *The Drum and the Hoe: Life and Lore of the Haitian People.* Berkeley and Los Angeles: University of California Press. 371 pp.

Crystal, David, 1971, Prosodic and paralinguistic correlates of social categories. In *Social Anthropology and Language,* ed. by E. Ardener (Association of Social Anthropologists, Monograph No. 10). United Kingdom: Tavistock Press; New York: Barnes and Noble. Pp. 185–206.

Cutten, George B., 1927, *Speaking with Tongues.* New Haven: Yale University Press.

Damboriena, Prudencio, 1969, *Tongues as of Fire: Pentecostalism in Contemporary Christianity.* Washington, D.C., and Cleveland: Corpus Books. 256 pp.

Drever, James, 1958, *Dictionary of Psychology.* Harmondsworth, Mixdlesex, England: Penguin Books.

Drummond, Andrew L., 1934, *Edward Irving and his Circle. Including some Consideration of the 'Tongues' Movement in the Light of Modern Psychology*. London: James Clarke and Co. 305 pp.

Du Plessis, David, 1963, *The Spirit Bade me Go*. Oakland, Calif.: Published by the author. 122 pp.

Ebin, David (ed.), 1965, *The Drug Experience*. New York: Grove Press, Inc. 385 pp.

Eliade, Mircea (translated from the French by W. R. Trask), 1964, *Shamanism, Archaic Techniques of Ecstasy*. New York: Random House [Pantheon Books] (for Bollingen Foundation). 610 pp.

Ervin, Howard M., 1968, *"These are not Drunken, as ye Suppose."* Plainfield, New Jersey: Logos International. 241 pp.

Fauset, Arthur H., 1944, *Black Gods of the Metropolis*. (Philadelphia Anthropological Society, Vol. 3.) Philadelphia: University of Pennsylvania Press.

Fernandez, James W., 1966, Unbelievably subtle words: representation and integration in the sermons of an African reformative cult. *History of Religions* 6.43–69.

————, 1967, Revitalized words from "The parrot's egg" and "The bull that crashes in the Kraal": African cult sermons. In *Essays on the Verbal and Visual Arts* (Proceedings of the 1966 Annual Spring Meeting of the American Ethnological Society). Seattle, Wash.: University of Washington Press. Pp. 45–63.

Fishman, Joshua A., 1967, Some contrasts between linguistically homogeneous and linguistically heterogeneous polities. In *Explorations in Sociolinguistics*, ed. by Stanley Lieberson (Indiana University Research Center in Anthropology, Folklore, and Linguistics, Publication 44). Bloomington, Ind. Pp. 18–30.

Flournoy, Thomas, 1900, *From India to the Planet Mars: a Study of a Case of Somnambulism with Glossolalia* (translated from the French by D. B. Vermilye). New York: Harper. [Third edition in French was used: *Des Indes à la Planète Mars*.]

Frodsham, Stanley H., 1946 rev. ed., *With Signs Following: the Story of the Pentecostal Revival in the Twentieth Century*. Springfield, Missouri: Gospel Publishing House. 279 pp.

Frost, Robert C., 1965, *Aglow with the Spirit*. Northridge, Calif.: Voice Christian Publications, Inc. 105 pp.

Gasson, Raphael, 1966, *The Challenging Counterfeit*. Plainfield, N.J.: Logos International. 92 pp.

Gee, Donald, no date, *Concerning Spiritual Gifts*. Springfield, Missouri: The Gospel Publishing House. 119 pp.

Gerlach, Luther P. and Virginia H. Hine, 1968, Five factors crucial to the growth and spread of a modern religious movement. *Journal for the Scientific Study of Religion* 7.23–40.

——, 1970, *People, Power, Change*. New York: Bobbs Merrill.

Gerrard, Nathan L., 1968, The serpent-handling religions of West Virginia. Trans-*action* [St. Louis: Washington University], May, pp. 22–28.

Gilmore, Susan K., 1969, Personality differences between high and low dogmatism groups of Pentecostal believers. *Journal for the Scientific Study of Religion* 8.161–164.

Glock, Charles Y. and Rodney Stark, 1965, *Religion and Society in Tension*. Chicago: Rand McNally.

Goffman, Erving, 1963, *Behavior in Public Places*. New York: The Free Press. 248 pp.

Goodman, Felicitas D., 1969a, Phonetic analysis of glossolalia in four cultural settings. *Journal for the Scientific Study of Religion* 8.227–239.

——, 1969b, Glossolalia: speaking in tongues in four cultural settings. *Confinia Psychiatrica* [Basel, Switzerland] 12.113–129.

Green, E., 1969, Phonological and grammatical aspects of jargon in an aphasic patient: a case study. *Language and Speech* 12.103–113.

Green, Hannah, 1964, *I Never Promised You a Rose Garden*. New York: The New American Library, Inc. (Signet Book). 256 pp.

Greenberg, Joseph H., 1957, *Essays in Linguistics*. Chicago: The University of Chicago Press.

Haas, Mary R., 1957, Interlingual word taboo. *American Anthropologist* 53.338–341.

Hall, Robert B., 1971, *An International Directory of Charismatic Groups*. Miami, Florida: The Agape Foundation.

Hall, Thor, 1967, A new syntax for religious language. *Theology Today* 14.172–184.

Halliday, M. A. K., 1964, The users and uses of language. In *The Linguistic Sciences and Language Teaching*, M. A. K. Halliday, A. McIntosh, and P. Strevens. London: Longmans. Pp. 75–110.

Harper, Michael, 1965, *As at the Beginning: the Twentieth Century Pentecostal Revival*. London: Hodder and Stoughton. 128 pp.

Hayes, D. A., 1913, *The Gift of Tongues*. New York and Cincinnati: The Methodist Book Concern. 119 pp.

Henry, Jules and Zunia Henry, 1940, Speech disturbances in Pilagá Indian children. *American Journal of Orthopsychiatry* 10.362–369.

Hine, Virginia H., 1969, Non-pathological Pentecostal glossolalia: a summary of relevant psychological literature. *Journal for the Scientific Study of Religion* 8.211–226.

Hockett, Charles F., 1958, *A Course in Modern Linguistics*. New York: The Macmillan Co. 621 pp.

Hollenweger, Walter J., 1969, *Enthusiastisches Christentum: die Pfings-*

bewegung in Geschichte und Gegenwart. Wuppertal: Theologischer Verlag Rolf Brockhaus; Zurich: Zwingli Verlag.

Horton, Harold, 1966, *The Gifts of the Spirit*. London: Assemblies of God Publishing House. 228 pp. (First published in 1934.)

Horton, Wade H. (ed.), 1966, *The Glossolalia Phenomenon*. Cleveland, Tenn.: The Pathway Press [Church of God]. 304 pp.

Hull, J. H. E., 1967, *The Holy Spirit in the Acts of the Apostles*. Cleveland and New York: World Publishing Co. 202 pp.

Jakobson, Roman, 1962, *Selected Writings, Vol. 4*. The Hague: Mouton and Co.

——, 1968, *Child Language, Aphasia and Phonological Universals* (translated by Allan R. Keiler). (Janua Linguarum, Series Minor, 72) The Hague: Mouton and Co.

James, William, 1958, *The Varieties of Religious Experience*. New York: The New American Library. 406 pp. (First published in 1902.)

Jaquith, James R., 1967, Toward a typology of formal communicative behavior: glossolalia. *Anthropological Linguistics* 9(8).1–8.

Jespersen, Otto, 1921, *Language: its Nature, Development and Origin*. New York: Henry Holt and Co. 448 pp.

——, 1964, *Mankind, Nation and Individual from a Linguistic Point of View*. Bloomington: Indiana University Press. 198 pp. (First published in 1946.)

Jung, Carl G., 1958, *Collected Works, Vol. II: Psychology and Religion: West and East*. New York: Pantheon Books, Inc.

Kelsey, Morton T., 1964, *Tongue Speaking: an Experiment in Spiritual Experience*. Garden City, New York: Doubleday and Co., Inc. 252 pp.

Kiev, Ari, 1963, Beliefs and delusions among West Indian immigrants to London. *British Journal of Psychiatry* 109.356–363.

Kiev, Ari (ed.), 1964, *Magic, Faith, and Healing: Studies in Primitive Psychiatry Today*. New York: Free Press. 475 pp.

Knox, Ronald A., 1950, *Enthusiasm: a Chapter in the History of Religion, with Special Reference to the XVII and XVIII Centuries*. Oxford: Clarendon Press. 622 pp.

Krueger, John R., 1968, Languages and techniques of communication as theme or tool in science-fiction. *Linguistics* 39.68–86.

La Barre, Weston, 1962, *They Shall Take Up Serpents: Psychology of the Southern Snake-handling Cult*. Minneapolis: University of Minnesota Press. 208 pp.

Labov, William, 1966, *The Social Stratification of English in New York City*. Washington, D.C.: Center for Applied Linguistics. 655 pp.

Laffal, Julius, 1965, *Pathological and Normal Language*. New York: Atherton Press. 249 pp.

——, 1967, Language, consciousness, and experience. *The Psycho-analytic Quarterly* 36.61–66.

Laird, Charlton G., 1968, Seen but not heard: language learning and language teaching. In *The Range of English: 1968 NCTE Distinguished Lectures.* Champaign, Ill.: National Council of Teachers of English. Pp. 75–103.

Lapsley, James N. and J. H. Simpson, 1965, Speaking in Tongues. *The Princeton Seminary Bulletin* 58(2).3–18.

——, 1964, Speaking in tongues. *Pastoral Psychology* 15(No. 144). 48–55; 15(No. 146).16–24.

Laski, Marghanita, 1961, *Ecstasy: a Study of some Secular and Religious Experiences.* London: The Cresset Press. 544 pp.

Le Baron, Albert, 1896–1897, A case of psychic automatism, including "speaking with tongues." *Proceedings of the Society for Psychical Research* [London] 12.277–297.

Lee, Richard B., 1968, The sociology of !Kung Bushman trance performances. In Raymond Prince (ed.) [see below]. Pp. 35–54.

Leslau, Wolf, 1949, An Ethiopian argot of people possessed by a spirit. *Africa* 19.204–212. [Reprinted in Leslau 1964, pp. 31–43.]

——, 1964, *Ethiopian Argots.* The Hague: Mouton and Co. 68 pp.

Lewis, C. S., 1965, *That Hideous Strength.* New York: The Macmillan Co. [Paperback edition; originally published in 1946.]

Linton, Ralph (edited by George Devereux), 1956, *Culture and Mental Disorders.* Springfield, Illinois: Charles C. Thomas, Pub. 139 pp.

Lombard, Émile, 1910, *De la Glossolalie chez les Premiers Chrétiens et des Phénomènes Similaires: Étude d'Exégèse et de Psychologie.* Lausanne: Imprimeries Réunies. 252 pp.

Luchsinger, Richard and G. E. Arnold, 1965, *Voice-Speech-Language, Clinical Communicology: its Physiology and Pathology.* Belmont, Calif.: Wadsworth Publishing Co. 812 pp.

Ludwig, Arnold M., 1968, Altered states of consciousness. In Raymond Prince (ed.) [see below]. Pp. 69–95.

Mackie, Alexander, 1921, *The Gift of Tongues: a Study in Pathological Aspects of Christianity.* New York: George H. Doran Co.

Mandelbaum, David G., 1966, Transcendental and pragmatic aspects of religion. *American Anthropologist* 68.1174–1191.

Martin, Ira Jay, 3rd., 1950, *Glossolalia in the Apostolic Church.* Berea, Ky.: Berea College Press. 100 pp.

May, L. Carlyle, 1956, A survey of glossolalia and related phenomena in non-Christian religions. *American Anthropologist* 58.75–96.

McDonnell, Kilian, 1966, The ecumenical significance of the Pentecostal movement. *Worship* [Collegeville, Minnesota] 40.608–629.

264   BIBLIOGRAPHY

——, 1970, Catholic Pentecostalism: problems in evaluation. *Dialog* [Montreal, Quebec], Winter, pp. 35–54.

Metz, Donald S., 1964, *Speaking in Tongues*. Kansas City, Mo.: Nazarene Publishing House. 109 pp.

Mezzrow, Mezz and Bernard Wolfe, 1946, *Really the Blues*. New York: Random House, Inc. [Quoted from David Ebin, ed. See above.]

Motley, Michael, 1967, *Glossolalia: Analyses of Selected Aspects of Phonology and Morphology*. Unpublished M.A. thesis. Austin: The University of Texas. 129 pp.

Needham, Rodney, 1967, Percussion and transition. *Man* (N.S.) 2.606–614.

Neher, Andrew, 1962, A physiological explanation of unusual behavior in ceremonies involving drums. *Human Biology* 34.151–160.

Nettl, Bruno, 1953, Observations on meaningless Peyote song texts. *Journal of American Folklore* 66.161–164.

——, 1956, *Music in Primitive Culture*. Cambridge, Mass.: Harvard University Press.

Nichol, John Thomas, 1966, *Pentecostalism*. New York: Harper and Row. 264 pp.

Nickel, Thomas R., 1964, *The Shakarian Story*. Los Angeles: Full Gospel Businessmen's Fellowship International. 32 pp.

Oates, Wayne E., 1967, A socio-psychological study of glossolalia. In Stagg, Hinson, and Oates (eds.) [see below]. Pp. 76–99.

——, 1968, *The Holy Spirit in Five Worlds*. New York: Association Press. 123 pp.

O'Connor, Edward, 1967a, Pentecost at Notre Dame. *Voice*, July/August, pp. 25–29.

——, 1967b, Baptism of the Spirit: emotional therapy? *Ave Maria* [South Bend, Indiana] 106.11–14.

——, 1968, Pentecost and Catholicism. *The Ecumenist* 6.161–164.

Oliphant, M. O., no date, *The Life of Edward Irving*. London: Hurst and Blacketts.

Olmsted, David L., 1953, Comparative notes on Yoruba and Lucumí. *Language* 29.156–164.

Oman, John B., 1963, On "speaking in tongues": a psychological analysis. *Pastoral Psychology* 14 (No. 139).48–51.

Opie, Iona and Peter, 1959, *The Lore and Language of Schoolchildren*. Oxford: Clarendon Press. [Paperback, 1967.]

Parsons, Anne, 1965, The Pentecostal immigrants: a study of an ethnic central city church. *Journal for the Scientific Study of Religion* 4.183–197. [Reprinted in *Practical Anthropology* 6.249–266 (1967).]

Pattison, E. Mansell, 1964, Speaking in tongues and about tongues. *Christian Standard* [Cincinnati, Ohio] 99.3–5.

Pattison, E. Mansell and Robert L. Casey, 1968, Glossolalia: a contemporary mystical experience. In *Clinical Psychiatry and Religion,* ed. by E. Mansell Pattison. (International Psychiatry Clinics, Vol. 5, No. 4.). Boston: Little, Brown and Company. Pp. 133–148.

Pfister, Oskar, 1912, *Die psychologische Enträtselung der religiösen Glossolalie und der automatischen Kryptographie* (Sonderabdruck aus dem Jahrbuch für Psychoanalytische und psychopathologische Forschungen, Band II). Leipzig and Vienna: Franz Deuticke. 107 pp.

Plog, Stanley C., 1964, UCLA conducts research on glossolalia. *Trinity Whitsuntide.* Pp. 38–39.

Prince, Raymond (ed.), 1968, *Trance and Possession States* (Proceedings of the Second Annual Conference of the R. M. Bucke Memorial Society, 1966). Montreal: R. M. Bucke Memorial Society. 200 pp.

Radford, Edwin and Mona A. (revised ed. by Christina Hole), 1961, *Encyclopaedia of Superstitions.* London: Hutchinson and Co.

Ranaghan, Kevin and Dorothy, 1969, *Catholic Pentecostals.* New York: Paulist Press Deus Books. 266 pp.

Read, Allen Walker, 1962, Family words in English. *American Speech* 37.5–12.

Roberts, Oral, 1964, *The Baptism with the Holy Spirit and the Value of Speaking in Tongues Today.* Tulsa, Okla.: Published by the author. 96 pp.

Sachs, Curt, 1962, *The Wellsprings of Music.* The Hague: Martinus Nijhoff.

Saintyves [= Janet], Pierre, 1912, *La Simulation du Merveilleux.* Paris: Ernest Flammarion, Éditeur. 382 pp.

Samarin, William J., 1968, The linguisticality of glossolalia. *The Hartford Quarterly* [Hartford Seminary Foundation] 8(4).49–75.

———, 1969a, Glossolalia as learned behavior. *Canadian Journal of Theology* 15.60–64.

———, 1969b, The forms and functions of nonsense language. *Linguistics* 50.70–74.

———, 1970a, Glossolalia as regressive speech. Paper given at the Summer Meeting of the Linguistic Society of America, Columbus, Ohio. (To appear in *Language and Speech.*)

———, 1970b, Language in resocialization. *Practical Anthropology* 17.269–279.

———, 1971a, Evolution in glossolalic private language. *Anthropological Linguistics* 13(2).55–67.

———, 1971b, Salient and substantive pidginization. In *Pidginization and Creolization of Language,* ed. by Dell Hymes. Cambridge University Press.

———, 1971c, The language of religion. Paper given at the Annual Meeting of the Society for the Scientific Study of Religion, Chicago, Illinois.

———, 1971d, Theory of order with disorderly data. Paper given at the Symposium on the Relation of Anthropology to Linguistics at the Annual Meeting of the American Anthropological Association, New York City.

———, 1972, Variation and variables in religious glossolalia. *Language in Society* [Cambridge University Press] (in press).

Sangree, Walter H., 1966, *Age, Prayer and Politics in Tiriki, Kenya.* London: Oxford University Press (for the East African Institute of Social Research). 312 pp.

Sargant, William W., 1961, *Battle for the Mind: a Physiology of Conversion and Brainwashing.* Baltimore: Penguin Books.

Saxman, John H., 1965, *Schizophrenic Speech: Selected Fundamental and Rate Characteristics.* Unpublished Ph.D. dissertation. Lafayette, Indiana: Purdue University. 138 pp.

Sherrill, John L., 1964, *They Speak with Other Tongues.* New York: McGraw-Hill, Inc. 165 pp.

Shor, Ronald E., 1959, Hypnosis and the concept of the generalized reality-orientation. *American Journal of Psychotherapy* 13.582–602.

Spoerl, Heinrich, 1933, *Die Feuerzangenbowle (Eine Lausbüberei in der Kleinstadt).* Düsseldorf: Mittag-Bücherei.

Stagg, Frank, E. Glenn Hinson, and Wayne E. Oates, 1967, *Glossolalia: Tongue Speaking in Biblical, Historical, and Psychological Perspective.* Nashville and New York: Abingdon Press. 110 pp.

Stark, Rodney and Charles Y. Glock, 1968, *American Piety: the Nature of Religious Commitment, Vol. 1.* Berkeley and Los Angeles: University of California Press. 230 pp.

Stevenson, Ian, 1966, Review of M. T. Kelsey, *Tongue Speaking. Journal of the American Society for Psychical Research* 60.300–303.

Stiles, J. E., no date, *The Gift of the Holy Spirit.* Burbank, Calif.: Privately published and distributed. 156 pp.

Stolee, H. J., 1963, *Speaking in Tongues* (with an Introduction by O. G. Malmin). Minneapolis, Minn.: Augsburg Publishing House. 142 pp. (First published in 1936 as *Pentecostalism, the Problem of the Modern Tongues Movement.*)

Sturtevant, William C., 1968, Categories, percussion and physiology. *Man* (New Series) 3.133–134.

Tambiah, S. J., 1968, The magical power of words. *Man* 3.175–208.

Tellegen, Auke, Nathan L. Gerrard, Louise B. Gerrard, and James N. Butcher, 1969, Personality characteristics of members of a serpent-handling religious cult. In *MMPI: Research Developments and Clin-*

ical Applications, ed. by James Neal Butcher. New York: McGraw-Hill Book Co. Pp. 221–242.

Trinity Whitsuntide. Publication of the Blessed Trinity Society. Van Nuys, Calif. [Begun in 1961, discontinued publication in December, 1965.]

Turner, H. W., 1967, *African Independent Church, Vol. II: The Life and Faith of the Church of the Lord (Aladura)*. Oxford: Clarendon Press. 391 pp.

Van Dusen, Henry P., 1958, Third force in Christianity. *Life* [June 9] 50.113–124.

View ("A quarterly journal interpreting the world-wide charismatic renewal"), 1964–. Los Angeles: Full Gospel Business Men's Fellowship International.

Vivier, Lincoln M. Van Eetveldt, 1960, *Glossolalia*. Unpublished dissertation for Doctor of Medicine in the Department of Psychiatry and Mental Hygiene. Johannesburg: University of Witwatersrand. 439 pp. [In microfilm, University of Chicago Library, Chicago, Illinois.]

Warburton, T. Rennie, 1969, Holiness religion: an anomaly of sectarian typologies. *Journal for the Scientific Study of Religion* 8.130–139.

Warfield, Benjamin B., 1919, *Counterfeit Miracles*. New York: Scribners. [Reprinted as *Miracles: Yesterday and Today, True and False*. Grand Rapids, Mich.: Wm. B. Eerdmans Pub. Co. 327 pp.]

Weber, Max (translated by E. Fischoff), 1963, *Sociology of Religion*. Boston: Beacon Press. (First published in 1922.)

Webster, Douglas, 1964, *Pentecostalism and Speaking with Tongues*. London: Highway Press. 47 pp.

Weller, Philip T. (translator and editor), 1952, *The Roman Ritual, Vol. 2: Christian Burial, Exorcism, Reserved Blessing*. Milwaukee: The Bruce Publishing Co.

Wierwille, Victor P., 1967, *Receiving the Holy Spirit Today*. New Knoxville, Ohio: The Way, Inc. 293 pp.

Willems, Emilio, 1967, Validation of authority in Pentecostal sects of Chile and Brazil. *Journal for the Scientific Study of Religion* 6.254–258.

Wilson, Bryan R., 1959, The Pentecostalist minister: role conflicts and status contradictions. *American Journal of Sociology* 64.494–504.

Withers, Carl (compiler), 1948, *A Rocket in my Pocket: the Rhymes and Chants of Young Americans*. New York: Henry Holt and Co.

Wolff, Hans, 1959, Intelligibility and inter-ethnic attitudes. *Anthropological Linguistics* 1(3).34–41.

Wolfram, Walter A., 1966, *The Sociolinguistics of Glossolalia*. Unpublished M.A. thesis. Hartford, Conn.: The Hartford Seminary Foundation. 115 pp.

Wood, William W., 1965, *Culture and Personality Aspects of the Pentecostal Holiness Religion.* The Hague: Mouton and Co. 125 pp.

Worsley, Peter, 1957, *The Trumpet shall Sound.* London: MacGibbon and Kee. 290 pp.

Young, Pauline, 1967, *The Pilgrims of Russian-Town.* New York: Russell and Russell.

Young, Rosemary, 1968, Words under a bushel. *Practical Anthropology* 15.213–216.

Index

Acts 2:1–14, 15
Acts 8:17, 57
Acts 19:6, 47
Adaptation, 219f
Affect, 89
   in religion, 232
   in speech, 24n, 140n
   see also Emotional meaning
Alakinki, 115, 141
Alienation, 210
Alliteration, 127, 133, 136, 148
Altered state of consciousness:
     see Dissociation
Anointing, 160
Anomalous speech, 12, 17, 36n,
     129ff, 149, 228
   see also Glossolalia
Aquina, Sister Mary, 222, 224
Argots, 139
ASC: *see* Dissociation

Authority, 153, 162, 167, 171,
     172, 224
   competition for, 217
   of speaker, 166
   validated by glossolalia, 217
Automatic writing, 135, 187
Automatism, glossolalia as, 22–26
Ayer, A. J., 165

Babbling, 42
Baby talk, 42, 139f
Baptism in the Holy Spirit, 25, 45,
     178, 232
   benefits of, 3f, 204, 225, 234
   condition of, 49
   definition of, 2
   effects of, 65–68, 198n
   session, 58–60
   with laying on of hands, 57n

Bartleman, F., 8, 54
Basic English, 125
Be-bop jazz, 143–144, 145–146
Belief
    changes in, 110
    reinforcement of, 67f
Berger, P. L., 164
Bias, 175n, 215n, 229
Blakney, C. P., 222
Bloch-Hoell, N., 8
Boas, F., 145
Bourguignon, E., 175
Breath-groups in glossolalia, 78,
    80f
Brown, L., 48, 152
Bwiti cult, glossolalia in, 222

Calley, M. J. C., 117, 214f, 218,
    219
Catholic Apostolic Church: see
    Irvingites
Catholic Pentecostals, 10, 13f, 41,
    194, 219f
Charismatic movement, 4, 8, 214
Child language, 38f, 41f, 69
Chipunha cult, 200
Christenson, L., 10, 52, 161, 206
Church of the Apostles, 224
Church of the Lord, 159, 217
Clergymen: see Authority
Coe, G. A., 22
Cohn, W., 21, 75n
Colossians 3:16, 179
Communication, spiritual, 155
Consciousness: see Dissociation
Consonant variation, 82
Conversion, 138, 198, 205
1 Corinthians 12–14, 6, 15, 50,
    75, 108, 151, 160, 171,
    181, 192f, 209, 221, 235
Cryptomnesia, 63f, 90, 115
Crystal, D., 177

Cutten, G. B., 12n, 19, 22, 24, 36,
    41

Damboriena, P., 199
Delusions, 110
Demonic glossolalia, 16, 75, 97
Demons, language of, 117
Deprivation in Pentecostalism, 38f
Devotional tongues, 151f
Diaglossa, 98
Dini Ya Roho sect, 224
Discharge glossolalia, 40
Dissociation, 10, 25, 26–34, 37,
    54n, 178, 189f, 203, 211,
    220, 223, 226
Divine speech, 201
Double-talk, 140f
Drugs and speech, 209n
Drummond, A. L., 12n

Ecstasy, 56, 171, 203ff, 232
Ecstatic speech, 131
Edification, 206
Educated charismatists, 47f, 74,
    110, 151, 192f
Ejaculations, 117, 208
Eliade, M., 131n, 222
Emotional meaning, 92, 94, 122f,
    142
Emotional release, 36f, 40f
Emotionalism, 43, 60, 188, 223
Emotions
    aggressiveness, 178
    anger, 142, 206f
    anxiety, 33, 36, 206
    peace, 201
Enthusiasm, 13, 223
    see also Emotionalism
Ephesians 1:13, 189
d'Esprit, Rev., 70, 71, 77, 79, 80f,
    82, 83, 85, 86, 87, 94, 96,
    99, 122f, 125

Esthetics in glossolalia, 49, 95, 96, 97, 137, 138, 149, 182, 205, 222

Euphoria with glossolalia, 29, 65–67

Evangelical, definition of, 8n

Evidential tongues, 10, 74, 199

Exorcism, 31, 57, 97, 156f

Exotic
glossolalia, 178, 221
languages, 222
sounds, 208
spelling, 182f
speech, 138

Expectancy, 39, 55–58, 189, 200

Experience: see Baptism

Experiments, 79, 81, 96, 101f, 104, 105, 228

Expressive language, 165

Expressive meaning, 90f

Expressive use of glossolalia, 155, 205–210

Fantasy, 203

Female exorcists, 158

Female glossolalists, 223

Feminism, 223f

Fernandez, J. W., 222

FGBMFI: see Full Gospel Business Men's Fellowship International

Filling with the Holy Spirit: see Baptism

Flournoy, T., 135

Folk linguistics, 52, 109

Folk religion, 158

Free-prayers, 93

Freud, S., 40, 90

Frodsham, S. H., 8n

Frost, R. C., 152

Full Gospel, glossolalia in the, 6

Full Gospel Business Men's Fellowship International, 6f, 11, 58

Functions of glossolalia
change in, 218
psychological, 197–211
social, 212–226
see also Prayer, Messages

Fundamentalist attitudes, 40f

Gee, D., 50, 156, 160, 161, 166, 172, 218, 221

Genres of discourse, 182

Gerlach, L., 5, 21, 33f, 194, 198

Gerrard, N. L., 43

Gestures, Pentecostal, 9, 28, 177f

Gibberish, 11f, 127

Gift of tongues, 151, 160, 167

Gifts, charismatic, 4, 75, 219, 224

Gilmore, S. K., 21

Glock, C. Y., 196

Glossa, definition of, 44

Glossographia, 185f

Glossolalia
abortive, 64, 74
appropriateness, 162, 168, 225
authentification of, 12, 13, 67, 74, 95
benefits of, 4, 31f, 154, 233
causes of, 211, 212, 228, 235
compared to language, 66, 78, 104–106, 121–128, 225
control over, 70–72, 95, 156, 217
conversation in, 190f, 218
cultural basis for, 46f, 166, 222, 228
definitions of, 2, 17, 28n, 120, 131n, 211, 222, 227
delayed, 60f
disuse of, 70, 193f
duration, 152, 205

facility in, 62, 67, 68, 70f, 93, 202
false, 11, 37f, 75f, 113, 159, 190f, 213, 222
fluidity, 125f
grammar, 73, 106
incipient, 51, 52, 61, 69, 70
inducement of, 50, 53, 60, 204
juvenile, 223
loudness of, 175, 178
mistakes in, 71
non-Pentecostal, 77n, 89, 101f, 222, 130, 134f
samples of, 25, 77f, 90, 92, 93, 99, 100, 115, 118, 124, 181f, 228
in sleep, 22, 61
spontaneous, 22, 51
syntax of, 107
use of, 114, 159, 212, 225
varieties of, 93, 102
Goffman, I., 165, 216
Goodman, F., 33
Greek, 89, 118
Green, H., 103
Greenberg, J., 107
Groan-hypothesis, 208
"Groanings of the Spirit," 207
Guilt, 200, 208

Haas, M., 114
Halliday, M. A. K., 98
Hallucinations, 30f
Hayes, D. A., 8, 179
Healing, 45f, 57, 156
Helplessness, 201
Heresy, Pentecostal, 156
Hine, V. H., 5, 21, 33f, 40, 43, 49, 51, 61, 76, 194, 198
History of glossolalia, 222
Hocus pocus, 117
Holiness movement, 9, 153, 154f

Holy Spirit
inspired by, 160
led by, 176
praying through, 155
quenching, 192
Holy words, 159
Horton, H., 82, 161, 163, 172
Horton, W. H., 9, 11n
Hostility: see Pentecostalism
Hypnosis: see Dissociation
Hysteria, 39

Imitation, 76, 98
Improvision, 64, 82, 88, 99, 216
Inspiration with glossolalia, 157, 160
Interjections, 208
Interpretation of messages, 75, 161, 162, 177, 193, 218
Intonation, 34, 92, 94, 109, 177
Irvingites, 12, 111, 186

Jakobson, R., 130n, 208
James, William, 23, 24, 199
1 John 4:1, 75
Jung, Carl G., 39

Kelsey, M. T., 39, 51, 53, 96, 152, 198
Khlysti, 130
Kiev, A., 76
Knox, Ronald A., 13, 188
Krueger, J. R., 98

La Barre, W., 175n
Labov, W., 87
Laird, C. G., 79, 143
Laffal, J., 35, 40, 96
Language
arbitrariness in, 119f
beliefs about, 221
contrast in, 11f

definition of, 120, 234
facade of, 128
features of, 119f
play, 140
pre-grammatical, 42
private, 137
in religion, 183, 229f, 233
social functions of, 225
structure in, 119
types, 108
Languages
  artificial, 103
  disguised, 139
  of glossolalia, 123 (*see also* Xenoglossia)
  mixing, 115f
  pretend, 142
  in science fiction, 98, 156, 236
Lapsley, J. N., 78
Laski, M., 204
Laying on of hands, 57, 157
Leadership
  see Authority
Learning glossolalia, 23, 98, 100
Le Baron, A., 24, 89f, 137f, 164
Lee, R. B., 220
Leslau, W., 139
Lewis, C. S., 205
Linguistic meaning, 129
Linton, R., 175
Literature, Pentecostal, 49, 148f
Lombard, E., 12n, 19, 24n, 26, 41, 107, 163, 175, 194
Ludwig, A. M., 26

Magical, language, 133f
  use of glossolalia, 159
Main-line: *see* Neo-Pentecostal
Mantra, 117
Matthew 12:34, 65
Matthew 15:30–31, 65
May, L. C., 131

Maximizing sounds, 83
Mackie, A., 8
McDonnell, K., 13, 41, 74, 153, 183n, 220
McPherson, Aimee Semple, 223
Meaning, 78, 81, 88–93, 107, 120, 127, 136
  definition of, 122
  emotional, 164
  in religion, 183, 230
  social, 231
  situational, 165
  of glossolalic text, 78
  see also Interpretation, Nonsense
Meaninglessness
  definition of, 18n, 183
  in prayers, 157
Means of grace, 159
Meetings, Pentecostal, 60
  see also Setting
Messages in glossolalia, 22, 93, 97, 152, 159–162, 165, 177, 205
Metrics, *see* Poetry
Miracles, 49, 65f, 109, 112, 154, 156, 200, 232, 234, 235
Molokans, 130f, 184, 186f, 190, 193, 225
Mongoloid speech, 35n
Monotony in glossolalia, 78f, 105
Mood, 176, 204
Mormons, 53, 164n, 218
Motley, M., 36, 80, 83, 85, 93, 94, 98, 168
Mumbo-jumbo, 133
Mystery of glossolalia, 222, 227, 232f
Mysticism, 32, 66f

Names for God, 184n
Neologizing, 64

Neo-Pentecostalism, 2, 5–9, 49, 50, 56, 153, 154, 178, 188, 194, 213, 220, 223, 224
Nettl, B., 145
Nichol, J. T., 8
Nickel, T. R., 184
Noncasual speech, 182
Nonsense, 35, 43, 51, 63, 116f, 133f, 143, 144f, 148f, 234, 235, 236
Nursery rhymes, 133f

Oates, W. E., 38, 41
Obeah men, 159
Obedience to Bible, 46f
Old Testament, glossolalia in, 16
Oman, J. B., 39, 41, 200
Opie, Iona and Peter, 134
Optimism, 156
Oracles with glossolalia, 167
Oriental glossolalia, 94, 108f

Paralinguistics, 183
Parsons, A., 6, 207
Patterning in language, 119
Pattison, E. M., 19n, 36
Peak experience, 92, 195
Pentecost, Day of, 110
Pentecostal Assemblies of Canada, 10
Pentecostal Fellowship of North America, 10
Pentecostalism
  in Africa, 224
  changes in, 44f
  cultural baggage of, 31, 220
  doctrine of, 5, 10, 45, 49, 57, 151
  hostility in, 40f, 161, 167, 214
  in India, 199
  intellectualism in, 201, 234
  recruitment in, 45–50

size of, 2
traditional, 9–10, 32, 37, 38, 57n, 60, 153, 178
  see also Catholic Pentecostals, Neo-Pentecostalism
Personalism, 195
Personality factors, 19–22
Pet names, 140
Peyote cult, 145
Pfister, O., 90f
Phatic communion, 165, 176
Phonetic transcription, 58n
Phonetic variations, 85
Physical states, 28, 54, 61
  see also Dissociation
Pidgins, 139, 213n
Play with language, 127, 143
  chants, 147
  charms, 133f
  game-songs, 146f
  musical refrains, 145
  nursery rhymes, 133f
  rhyming talk, 148f
  see also Poetry
Pleasure with glossolalia, 67, 192, 202–205
  see also Esthetics
Plog, S. C., 5, 224
Pocomania, 11, 215, 224, 230
Poetry, 148f, 181f
  see also Alliteration, Rhyme
Pope John XXIII, 14
Possession, 11, 12, 13, 132, 199, 200, 201, 224
  see also Dissociation
Power, 156, 158, 175f, 178, 192
Practiced glossolalists, 23, 61, 120
Practicing glossolalia, 63, 68–70
Praise, 61, 153f, 219
Prayers, 30, 59, 77, 78, 93, 95, 97, 104, 105, 123, 152–159, 160, 167, 168, 169, 176,

181, 192f, 205, 206, 207, 209, 219, 231f
Prejudice, 42f, 229
Pretend-language, 142
Preternatural pseudolanguages, 130–138
Private language, 137, 140, 165
Prophecy, 160, 184, 217, 219
Pseudolanguage, 25, 35, 130–138, 142
Psychic phenomena, 112
Psychopathology, 17, 34–42, 149, 175n
Psychological benefits of glosso-lalia, 154
Psychological function of glosso-lalia, 89
Psychological states in glosso-lalia, 40, 55–58

Ranaghan, Kevin and Dorothy, 14
Randomness, 79, 88, 119, 124, 127
Recruitment in Pentecostalism, 45–50, 224f
Redundancy, 105f, 125; see also Repetition
Regression, 41, 86
Regulation among glossolalists, 160–162, 165f, 167, 171, 172, 192
Relaxation, 135
Release, emotional, 40f
Religion
  glossolalia in, 46, 114, 216f, 225
  language in, 183, 230, 233
Religious experience, 183, 232
Repetition, 53, 68f, 82, 85, 91f, 94, 132, 136, 148
Repression, 34–36, 38, 40, 195
Reversion, linguistic, 149

Rhetoric, 28f, 32, 36, 56, 62, 65, 154, 159, 201, 204, 214
Rhyme, 89, 127, 133f, 146
Rhyming talk, 148f
Rhythm
  glossolalia induced by, 25f
  of glossolalia, 79
Roberts, Oral, 55, 69, 152, 155, 158, 161, 162, 166, 167, 168, 172, 200, 206, 209
Romance languages, 108
Romans 8:26–27, 155, 208
Russian Pentecostals: see Molokans

Sacred language, 183, 203, 231
St. Paul, 14f, 47, 161
I Samuel 10:5–7, 16
Sangree, W. H., 131n, 224
Santera cult, 131–133
Saxman, J. H., 35n
Scanning, musical, 144f
Schizophrenics, 34f
Self-assertiveness, 201f, 215n
  see also Pentecostalism, hos-tility in
Self-deception, 164
Semantics: see Meaning
Setting
  for acquiring glossolalia, 58–61
  harmony with, 162, 165
  influence of, 191f, 221
  for prayers, 152
Shakers, 88f, 185
Shamanism, 222, 230
Shamanistic
  glossolalists, 158
  speech, 131
Sharing, 210, 214
Sherrill, J. L., 26, 48, 121n, 166
Shor, R. E., 27
"Simon," 164, 186

Simpson, A. B., 111
Simpson, J. H., 78
Simplified speech, 51, 101, 139, 149
Slips of the tongue, 71
Smith, Helen, 109, 135f, 148, 187
Snake-handling cultists, 43, 99, 175n, 215
Social meaning, 121, 123, 164, 165, 190
Song, 32, 63, 179–181, 192
Sounds, glossolalic, 42, 97, 124–126, 127, 137, 165
   see also Esthetics
Spanish, 88, 109, 116
Speak in tongues: *see* Glossolalia
Spirit language, 51, 222
Spiritism, 33, 109, 131, 135f
Spiritual songs: *see* Song
Spoerl, H., 142
Spontaneity in Pentecostalism, 215
Stark, R., 196
Stevenson, I., 112n
Stiles, J. E., 48, 50, 54
Styles in speech, 34, 78, 88, 101, 167, 168, 175–178, 221, 230f
Switching languages, 92f, 191
Syllables, 79–82, 109, 137, 141, 144f
Symbolic meaning, 39, 197–202, 213, 225, 231

Tambiah, S. J., 117
Tarrying service, 37, 56, 60, 188–190
   see also Baptism
Testimonials, 3f, 27–28, 29, 31, 32, 48, 49f, 66f, 69
Theology
   of communication, 155
   heretical, 156

Thought
   breakdown, 24
   during glossolalia, 89, 155, 203, 208–209
   and language, 155
Tiriki, 224
Tongues: *see* Glossolalia
Trance, 16, 51, 135, 138, 174f
   see also Dissociation
Turner, H. W., 159
Twin-language, 140

Use of glossolalia
   instruction about, 59
   oracular, 167
   private, 60f, 151, 192f
   public, 188–192
   summary of, 225
   symbolic, 197–202
   see also Functions, Meaning

Visions, 30, 51, 66, 223
Vivier, L. M. Van Eetveldt, 20, 21, 24f, 26, 40

Warburton, T. R., 10, 38
Warfield, B. B., 12n
Weber, Max, 13n
Whispered prayer, 176
Wierwille, V. P., 53
Willems, E., 219
Wilson, B. R., 172
Withers, C., 147
Wolfram, W. A., 83, 104, 224
Wood, W. W., 6, 20, 38n, 158
Words
   in glossolalia, 80–82, 85, 86, 89–91, 98, 99, 100, 106, 120
   inspired, 167
   of songs, 179
Worsley, P., 38, 41

Written glossolalia, 182f

Xenoglossia, 15, 65, 74, 106, 109–115, 227

Yieldedness, 50, 64, 74, 138, 200f

Zar cult, 200
Zulu Zionists, 12

DATE DUE

New Books *Jan 30 1974*			
MAY 22 1974			
MAR 02 1983			